TALES OF THE EMERGENCY SANDWICH
Punk Rock Tour Diaries: Volume 3

T V SMITH

Published 2012 by arima publishing

www.arimapublishing.com

ISBN 978 1 84549 552 7

© T V Smith 2012

All rights reserved

This book is copyright. Subject to statutory exception and to provisions of relevant collective licensing agreements, no part of this publication may be reproduced, stored in a retrieval system, or transmitted in any form or by any means, without the prior written permission of the author.

Printed and bound in the United Kingdom

This book is sold subject to the conditions that it shall not, by way of trade or otherwise, be lent, re-sold, hired out, or otherwise circulated without the publisher's prior consent in any form of binding or cover other than that which it is published and without a similar condition including this condition being imposed on the subsequent purchaser.

arima publishing
ASK House, Northgate Avenue
Bury St Edmunds, Suffolk IP32 6BB
t: (+44) 01284 700321

www.arimapublishing.com

CONTENTS:

1. THE LONG COLD ROAD TO SUCCESS (2006)
2. MAÑANA, MARIA, MAÑANA… (2006)
3. THE EMERGENCY PEANUTS FROM CHEMNITZ (2006)
4. WASTED WITH THE GANG (2006)
5. BRING HIM BACK SAFELY (2006)
6. SMALL WORLD (2007)
7. TROUSERS' END (2007)
8. NO TIME TO BE 51 (2007)
9. BACK TO THE FUTURE USED TO BE BETTER (2007)
10. TALES OF THE EMERGENCY SANDWICH (2007)
11. A COLD SNAP (2008)
12. STICK TO THE ITINERARY (2008)
13. HOW IT ALL GOES HORRIBLY WRONG (2008)
14. SLUTSIGNAL! (2008)
15. PANK'S NOT DEAD (2008)

1. THE LONG COLD ROAD TO SUCCESS (2006)

<u>16th January</u>
I'm just about to release a new record and I've come to Germany for a twenty date tour to promote it. It's coming out on *Goldene Zeiten,* the small label run by former *Die Toten Hosen* drummer Wölli, and I'm staying at his house just outside Dusseldorf before the tour so I can do some radio and press interviews. There aren't many new releases at this time of year so it's just possible we could squeeze into the charts. What a kick in the teeth for the corporate music business that would be!

Today the big push starts and Wölli drives me into Dusseldorf for three interviews. The first is in a tiny studio for a radio station with, I suspect, a tiny audience. It's not likely to help sell many records but I play a few songs live and chat with the DJ for an hour or so. While I'm in there, Wölli receives news that the second interview, with major station *Eins Live*, has been postponed until tomorrow. We wait around for a while to meet the guy who's supposed to do the third interview but it turns out he's forgotten about it.

<u>17th January</u>
I'm waiting in the rain outside Dusseldorf art museum where I'm going to meet a journalist for the respected newspaper *Frankfurter Allgemeine*. He wants to interview me while we look around the Matisse exhibition, fine by me as I wanted to see it anyway. Through the crowds of people milling around I spot someone waving at me and push my way towards him. We head for the gallery but the attendants won't let the journalist in because of his coat and umbrella, which they say he'll have to leave in the cloakroom. He can keep his bag with the recording equipment for the interview, but only if he wears it on his front, not his back or side. '*Germany!*' he snorts. Instead of joining the long queue, he props up his umbrella behind the far end of the counter and throws his coat over a chair. He sneers at the attendants as we go past with a look that says, *satisfied?* He's more punk than me. We wander through the packed galleries glancing at the paintings as we talk and I find myself unable to concentrate on either the interview or the art. When we come back out, the chair with the journalist's coat has been moved out of reach but he hooks the umbrella handle round it and pulls it back.

TV SMITH

I'm now late for the planned rehearsal with Garden Gang, my friends from Bavaria who will be playing the support slot on the tour and backing me up for some songs at the end of my set. They have a new line-up since last time we met so we'd planned to run through the songs together, but by the time I hurry in to the rehearsal room everything is already sounding good and I don't have much to do. By early evening I'm back at Wölli's place in good time for the *Eins Live* interview, only to find it's been postponed again.

18th January
Garden Gang singer PamP is driving as usual, and I'm crammed into the front seat between him and Andi, with drummer Lotte, guitarist Steff and bassist Jaromir in the seats behind us. The rest of the van is piled from floor to roof with musical equipment and boxes of CDs. We've had to remove a row of seats and leave them along with two speaker cabinets in Wölli's garage because we couldn't fit everything in.

We reach Bremen by late afternoon and when I walk into the club, the *Schlachthof* (Slaughterhouse), it seems familiar. Then I remember: ten years ago I played here with Attila The Stockbroker on the club's opening night when the walls were still being painted and the stage still being built. Tonight the gig goes well, there's a good crowd in, singing along for my solo set and dancing energetically when Garden Gang get onstage to back me up at the end. How different from last time, when thirty people who'd never heard of me sat indifferently on benches while I played, impatient for Attila to start.

We have decided to make the trip over to Hamburg for tomorrow's gig straight after the concert tonight because we have a comfortable sleeping place there at PamP's uncle's house and it will be good to get the journey over and have a lie-in tomorrow. The weather is cold as we load up the van and when we reach Hamburg at three in the morning snow is lying thick on the ground.

PamP has a key to the flat, but when we quietly let ourselves in we find Uncle Hans is still up and waiting for us. Auntie Agnes emerges briefly from the bedroom to greet us but is suffering with a heavy cold and goes straight back to bed. Soon the beers are opened and Uncle Hans is regaling us with stories. Waving his cigar expansively, he tells us that in six weeks he will be retiring, and jokes that then he's going straight into the old people's home. When I go to bed at six in the morning, he is debating about whether to sleep for the ninety minutes before work starts or just stay up.

TALES OF THE EMERGENCY SANDWICH

<u>19th January</u>
Snow is swirling down and there's thick ice underfoot as we crunch our way to the van early afternoon. Garden Gang drive me to radio station NDR and wait while I record an interview and live song, then we head off to the Knust club for soundcheck. The Knust was once a slaughterhouse – that's two in two days, good going for a vegetarian.

After soundcheck I have another interview, this time in the club. As the guy packs away his equipment I mention that I'm not sure if we'll get many people at the gig because my mate Vom's band Spittin' Vicars are also playing in Hamburg tonight. The interviewer says he doesn't think it will make much difference. At that moment I spot Zasso, the promoter of one of the gigs I'm playing next week, heading towards me.

'I had to come and say hello,' he says, 'but actually, er…I'm going to the Spittin' Vicars…'

Through the course of the evening Vom and I exchange text messages:
Only about forty people in…
We've only got thirty…!

It would have been good to meet up after the show but by the time we've packed the van it's well past two and we have an icy journey through Hamburg to negotiate.

Surprisingly, Uncle Hans isn't around when we creep into the flat, but then the bedroom door opens and he pokes his head round, a twinkle in his eye. 'Ah, you're earlier than expected, I set the alarm for three!'

He puts on his dressing gown and brings out a crate of beer.

<u>20th January</u>
When I get up soon after eleven the only other person awake is Uncle Hans, who is in the kitchen peeling and slicing potatoes into two huge pans, ready to cook breakfast for us all. It's a couple of hours before everyone's up, then we spend a couple more around the table, eating the *Bratkartoffeln* and constructing the toys from the *Kinder* eggs Auntie Agnes has placed beside every plate. Steff gets an angry musician who waves his arms up and down, and I get the king.

Ironically, today – the release date for my album – is a day off because the planned gig in Kiel got cancelled when the club failed its fire safety inspection. Tomorrow we'll play in Berlin, but Siberian weather is forecast to move in from the East overnight so we decide to set off this afternoon and avoid it. Just before we leave a report on the radio says there were sixty-five road accidents in our region last night because of the ice.

It's late afternoon and already getting dark by the time we wave goodbye to Uncle Hans. 'I feel ten years younger after a visit from you lot,' he beams as we cram into the van. Coincidentally, after a visit to Uncle Hans many of us are feeling ten years older.

After long hours powering down the motorway, the heater on maximum but barely managing to take the chill off, we finally pull up at a service station to take a break. As we huddle around a table, shivering, drinking coffee and watching the heavy snow swirl down outside, I say to the band, 'So, are you enjoying my album release party?'

21st January
Too cold for sightseeing, so we hang around our friend Viola's flat for the day. I have quite a bit of radio and press reaction to the new record to read through, emailed over by the promo company. Gratifyingly, most of it is favourable, though there are a few stinkers. One radio station gives a three word reaction to *Es Stört Mich Nicht,* my first-ever song with German lyrics: *'Nicht Deutsch singen!'* (Don't sing in German!)

We head off to the Wild At Heart club late afternoon. It's too noisy at soundcheck to do the scheduled interview with Blend TV, a local alternative music channel, so I take them over to the nearby Tikki Bar. Unfortunately the spotlight they've bought with them has blown, and after the half hour interview the camerawoman tells me that on the monitor it's 'candlelight atmosphere,' which presumably translates as 'unusable.'

The Wild At Heart is not only one of my favourite clubs, but also one of the hottest. When I get offstage and the cold air hits me in the dressing room I suddenly start to steam.

Club owners Lea and Uli bring a celebratory round of tequila and we decide to abandon plans to drive the van and equipment back tonight and instead leave it all at the club until tomorrow.

22nd January
Viola drives the band over to pick up the van and they are away for some time. Finally I get a phone call to explain what's happening: it's minus fifteen out there and the van wouldn't start so they have been driving round garages to try and find a jump cable. Everywhere has sold out, and there are broken down cars all over the city. PamP called the rescue service and they estimated they could turn up 'either tomorrow or the next day.' Not much good for our gig tonight in Torgau. Eventually Jaromir was able to get hold of a friend of his who had a cable, they got the van started and now they're on the way back.

TALES OF THE EMERGENCY SANDWICH

Things are looking up at the *Brückenkopf* club, situated on the outskirts of Torgau: the last couple of times I've played here there was no toilet and everyone had to relieve themselves in the fields, but now they have a brand new indoor loo. A good thing, considering it's minus twenty outside. Inside, the wood-fired stoves are struggling to raise the temperature to bearable and I'm looking forward to getting on stage just to warm up.

It's a good gig, fiercely hot under the lights. When I get backstage, I quickly stake a place next to the stove and once again I am soon enveloped in a cloud of steam.

After a couple of drinks with the people running the club, we drive into Torgau. Garden Gang will stay at the promoter's house, but I'm shown to a guest house owned by his mother. I'm delighted to get a room to myself, rather less pleased to find the radiator is switched off so I have to go to bed with all my clothes on.

23rd January

Garden Gang come over to the guest house for breakfast then we head off to the van. It won't start.

We wait around until the promoter's brother arrives with some jump cables, but they don't work either so we get behind and push. Pushing a van isn't that easy when your feet are skidding out from under you on the snow. Once we're over the brow of the hill I realise I've left my bag and guitar sitting in the street so run back to guard them. The van carries on down the slope, the engine still refusing to catch. After ten minutes the promoter turns up again and lets me into his brother's flat. He tells me the van is now stuck at the bottom of the hill and causing a big traffic jam. The breakdown service won't be able to get to it for four hours. Our only chance for getting to tonight's gig in Hanover is that he thinks he knows someone in a local garage who might be able to take a look at it.

It turns out to be a simple problem: the diesel has frozen. Some additive in the fuel tank and we're up and running again. We drive back to the club in a rush, load up the gear and head off.

It's unfortunate that we're running late as tonight we'll be playing a gig with the Spittin' Vicars and they are going to be borrowing our backline. As we pull up at the club the first of the audience are already being let in and we have to push past them carrying the gear.

It's too late too eat, even though we're all hungry. Garden Gang have to get straight out of their winter clothes, into their stage gear and start. There's a

Monday night feel to the gig, not many people in and we have to work hard to warm them up. After all the effort to get here it seems a bit of an anti-climax.

Next to the club there's a small apartment for the musicians, with three bedrooms and a kitchen and bathroom. I put my bags in the smallest bedroom while the bands take the two larger ones, each fitted out with bunk beds. Not that there's going to be much sleeping going on: there's some warmed-over food in the kitchen and a plentiful supply of booze, and the Vicars are celebrating the last night of their tour. Garden Gang and I still have a week to go, however, and at around four I call it a night. The party down the corridor sounds like it could go on for quite a while yet.

24<u>th</u> January
The Vicars had to leave early to take one of the band to the airport and have already gone by the time Garden Gang and I get up. Clearly they had to load their van in a hurry because when we come to load ours we soon realise that they accidentally took quite a bit of our stuff too, including Steff's spare Gibson guitar and PamP's microphones and stands. I phone Vom up but they're miles away stuck in traffic and in danger of missing the flight so there's not much they can do about it. Looking on the bright side, the less gear we have, the more room there is in the van.

On to Braunschweig and a venue I've never been to before, a small café bar with a room for live music beside it. The music room is chilly, so we hang around in the café, where the oven is on and some good vegetarian food is being cooked.

Around sixty people turn up for the gig, not bad for a cold Tuesday night in Braunschweig. Afterwards records are played and a lot of alcohol consumed. I wonder where I'll be sleeping tonight? Garden Gang have played here before and know someone who'll put them up. I'm supposed to be in a nearby flat where there's a spare bed. It's owned by the guy who cooked the meal earlier, and who is now singing along loudly with the music.

A short walk through the freezing streets, then the band and I split up and arrange to meet back at the venue for breakfast. I stay up for a while with the cook, finishing off an already-open bottle of red wine and listening to a couple of his punk CDs. When I enquire about sleeping arrangements, he points out a bed for me in the adjacent room and says he'll be sleeping here on the couch. I mention that there's no door between the rooms. Don't worry, he says, nothing disturbs me once I'm asleep.

Er, well, I was thinking more about *me*.

TALES OF THE EMERGENCY SANDWICH

<u>25th January</u>
Back at the café next to the club breakfast is ready, though it's somewhat less bountiful than last night's meal: some bags of sliced bread and packets of processed cheese. The only other thing on offer is a cucumber, which has frozen solid overnight.

During breakfast I get a phone call from Wölli to report on sales. Although the CD is high in the Amazon charts, unfortunately there's no sign of it in the all-important 'trend charts,' which the industry uses to predict what will appear in the top 100 at the end of the week.

Outside, snowflakes swirl around us as we load the gear into the van. We make good time to Chemnitz despite the weather but once we reach the city we get hopelessly lost trying to find the club. It's late afternoon, already dark, the streets icy, and to make it worse the mobile phone reception is so bad that we can't even get hold of the promoter to get directions.

Over an hour later we finally arrive at the venue. It's called The Bunker, and that's exactly what it is: an underground wartime shelter, thick steel doors across the entrance. PamP reverses the van down the steep ice-slick slope but when we've unloaded and he tries to drive back up, the wheels spin ineffectually and we have to get behind and push. There's no way it would make it fully loaded so it looks like we'll have to carry the equipment up the slope after the gig. There's something to look forward to.

We drive over to the nearby Subway To Peter club to eat. The manager there, Mario, is also promoting tonight's gig. When I ask him about sleeping arrangements for tonight, he tells me that I can either stay in a large room with Garden Gang or get a room on my own in a nearby flat. I go for the latter.

Back at The Bunker quite a large crowd has turned up. I'm introduced to the two people who own the flat where I'll be sleeping. They have already had a few drinks and are very talkative. It turns out that they don't have a spare room so I'll be sharing with one of them. Maybe I made the wrong decision about where to sleep.

The gig turns out great, and we even get a few volunteers to help carry the gear up to the van afterwards. Then it's back to Subway To Peter for a goodnight drink. We leave the van near to where Garden Gang are spending the night but can't park right outside because the road is cordoned off and there's a sign saying the building next door will be demolished tomorrow morning. Maybe I made the right decision about where to sleep after all.

Much later when I get back to where I'm staying, the guy I'm sharing the room with is already out for the count. Trying not to disturb him, I creep quietly onto the folding bed and it collapses under me with a great crash.

26th January
My roommate is still fast asleep when I wake up and there's no sound from the other room either. I'm the only one up except for a slightly surprised cat. Two guys sharing a flat, but the bathroom is sparkling clean – now that is unusual. There's even hot water.

Garden Gang come to pick me up, then it's on to Kassel, a four hour drive. We've played the venue, the Barracuda Bar, before and find our way straight to it right on time, but the sound man isn't ready for us so we go upstairs to the dressing room and drink coffee and eat toasted cheese sandwiches. The heating isn't working so we sit around in our coats.

Eventually everything appears to be ready for soundcheck. While I'm plugging in my guitar on stage the sound man stands next to me and says, 'I'll just find the frequencies that are going to feed back in the monitors.' He speaks into the microphone until the feedback starts, then runs back to the mixing desk while the volume increases. I stand there helplessly with my guitar, my fingers in my ears trying to block out the noise. Finally it stops.

'Okay, ready now!' comes a voice through the monitor in front of me. I move up to the microphone. 'Oh, just a minute…the 60,000 Herz!'

The sound man dashes back to the stage and tries to cover the mirror behind the drum kit with a small piece of cloth. I sit down again. Maybe I should drink a beer. I unplug the guitar, get off stage and go over to the bar.

'Ready now!'

I put the bottle down and climb back onto the stage.

'Oh, just a minute…'

This goes on for some time.

Surprisingly, the Garden Gang soundcheck goes relatively quickly and suddenly we're all done and the bar is open and people are coming in. The gig is good and, even better, I know that afterwards I'll be able to sleep at my friend Steffen's place – the prospect of a quiet glass or three of wine and finally a warm bed in a room of my own is something to look forward to.

27th January
No hurry to get up, its only a short drive to tonight's gig. Steffen takes me back to the Barracuda Bar mid-afternoon, just in time to miss loading the van, and we set off, pulling up outside the youth centre in Marsberg less than an hour later.

TALES OF THE EMERGENCY SANDWICH

Zasso has been trying to get me and Garden Gang to play this tiny youth club for a few years and everyone here seems to be looking forward to it. The kids are falling over each other to help unload the van and carry the equipment in. The stage is so small that by the time everything is set up there's hardly room for us.

Soon the place is packed and has become a sweat box. Every time the front door opens to let someone in, great gusts of steam barrel out. Expectation is high as Garden Gang take the stage for their set, but – disaster! – the P.A. is malfunctioning and the vocals are almost inaudible. PamP carries on singing, waiting in vain for someone to figure out what's wrong, and when nothing improves he switches over to Andi's microphone, which promptly stops working too. I look over to the mixing desk, where the sound man is holding his arms aloft in an *I have NO idea what is going on* gesture, then I make my way downstairs to the dressing room to worry.

When I get on stage for my set the sound man tells me he has figured out what is wrong. He points at an amp by the side of the stage. 'The fan's broken so every time it overheats it cuts out. You should be alright for the solo part, but it's probably going to do it again when the band come back on…'

The solo set sounds fine. There's a great atmosphere with the people crammed in front of the low stage at eye level with me, but it's almost unbearably hot. When Garden Gang join me it gets even hotter and while we play I notice the sound man crouched over by the side of the stage switching off the malfunctioning amp between every song to let it cool down.

Then we're back down in the dressing room, toweling off and getting into dry clothes ready for the load out in the arctic temperatures. Many of the audience come by to say thanks for the gig. One of them asks me how old I am, and when I tell him he says, 'Wow, old enough to be my dad and still doing this! I have just one thing to say to you, privately…' He leans in close and whispers, '*Danke, Papa.*'

Upstairs Zasso is celebrating a successful evening with a beer. He confides in me that he was so worried about the gig that he couldn't sleep last night. When the sound went wrong at the beginning he was almost in tears.

It would be nice if we could hang around with him for a while but we're heading out to a village a few kilometres away, to a large comfortable house owned by the mother of a friend of ours where we'll each get a room. Tomorrow will be a big gig in Dusseldorf so it will be good to get some quality sleep.

All the same, our friend Simse is great company, there's a fine selection of wine, and we stay up until nearly six.

28th January

Back at Wölli's again, we load in the equipment we had to leave behind at the start of the tour and fix the van seats back in place. Over a coffee he tells me about the progress of the CD one week after its release. Even though we didn't get into the chart, we managed decent sales. Things are still looking promising, with many of the interviews and reviews yet to appear. Who knows, maybe we could do it yet.

Tonight we're playing at the *Ratinger Hof*, Dusseldorf's original punk venue. While we're setting up, Thomas from the Spittin' Vicars arrives just in time with our missing guitar and microphones. After soundcheck I do an interview with a fanzine for half an hour, then find out that the promised radio interview for *Eins Live* has been put off again until next week in Cologne, so my promo work for tonight is done and I'm free to concentrate on the gig.

One hundred and fifty tickets sold in advance, and people streaming in as soon as the doors open: looks like it's going to be packed tonight. By the time I get on stage there's not a spare inch of space in the club and a big cheer goes up when I start. It's a great feeling, seeing all those happy faces in the audience.

Tomorrow I fly home to London – five days break then I'll be back for part two.

3rd February

I wander around Frankfurt airport for quite a while wondering why I can't find the entrance to the train station until I realise I'm in a new terminal building, not the one I usually arrive at. It's identical to the old one except it doesn't have a train station.

Silke, who's promoting tonight's show, meets me in the city and drives me over to the *Elfer* club. Even though it's early and Garden Gang haven't arrived yet I get on with my soundcheck because I have to leave for a lengthy interview. Sometimes I wonder if all these interviews are worth it: they're exhausting and I don't know if they even help sell any records. This week's chart was announced today, but I haven't heard anything from Wölli so I'm sure we haven't made it in.

The club is fairly full and the gig goes well. Afterwards it's noisier in the backstage than it was onstage. It lies directly under the large *Batschlapp* club and the whole room shudders and vibrates from the volume of the records being played up there. It doesn't seem to disturb one guy who is laid flat out along one of the benches, snoring. Nobody knows who he is.

TALES OF THE EMERGENCY SANDWICH

Garden Gang will be staying at Silke's flat tonight, while I drive back with my friends Roland and Christine to their place about half an hour out of Frankfurt. Once there, we settle into the kitchen. Rudi, the pet parrot, recognises me and we do our little dance: I bob up and down in front of the cage and he bobs up and down on his perch. Roland opens a bottle of wine, and Christine covers up the cage. Normally this would send Rudi to sleep, but instead he goes berserk, crashing around and squawking, furious at being left out. As soon as the blanket comes off he immediately calms down again, fixing us with a beady eye, listening intently and occasionally adding a *peep* or repeating what we say.

Soon, though, there are a number of empty bottles on the table and it's time to put a blanket over my cage.

4th February
Roland and Christine apologise for the noise, and I say, 'What noise?'

Apparently, the postman rang the doorbell at 8:30, then the siren in the village was sounded repeatedly for a fire alarm test. Lucky I had in my red wine earplugs.

I eat breakfast with Roland and Christine and their two young daughters and as I load slices of red pepper and tomato and cucumber and various types of cheese onto my seeded wholegrain bread roll I point out that it's a big improvement on breakfast In Braunschweig, and explain about the frozen cucumber, which gets a laugh.

Roland drives me over to the nearest motorway service area to meet up with Garden Gang, and we pull into the fuel bay directly behind them. We're making a reasonably early start to Munich because we've heard that there will be a big anti-globalisation demonstration there this afternoon. Reports on the radio are warning motorists not to come into the city because of the inevitable chaos. Luckily everyone else does the sensible thing and stays away, which means that we drive straight through without a problem, only seeing the first lines of police forming just ahead of us as we park up right in front of the club.

Unusually, this club has its stage is in the middle of the floor so people will be able to stand around us and behind us as we play. If we get to play, that is – at the moment half the P.A. isn't working. We troop down to the backstage room in the basement to wait, and Garden Gang seem surprised at how smart it is. There's been a bit of renovation done, apparently. Steff tells me that last time they played here he came down the stairs and when he switched the light on he saw a mass of cockroaches scuttle off under the furniture.

The P.A. is finally working so we soundcheck, then I do an interview with someone from a radio station. The gig starts early but there is already a good crowd in the club when Garden Gang go on. Satisfying to see that despite the bad weather, the police presence, and all the warnings about riots, people still turned up.

5th February
Must be getting tired: after the load-in at the Mikado club in Karlsruhe I get a strange pre-migraine which sends a luminescent 'C' floating around in the corner of my vision. I sit down on the floor hoping it will pass, but then promoter Gerhard sits beside me and starts to question me about some of my lyrics. I try and explain them while the colours roll and shimmer in the air around me. It's like having a job interview on acid.

Soundcheck is good, and even though it's a Sunday and we're some way out of the centre of town the place is soon packed. The gig is hot and sweaty and exciting. Afterwards someone collars me and says, 'You know TV, the word *authentisch* isn't a real German word – they brought it into the language to describe you.'

6th February
It's a long cold drive to Grünberg. There's a narrow uneven stone staircase down to the club and it's a miracle no one gets injured carrying the gear down in this icy weather. As we get near to stage time 120 people are in, near capacity, which is impressive for a snowy Monday night. Roland arrives and hands me a present Christine and the kids have made 'to make up for breakfast In Braunschweig.' It's a chocolate cake, little sugar hearts sprinkled on the icing. Very thoughtful, although I can't quite see what it has to do with Braunschweig until I ask Roland and find out that they thought I'd been given a frozen cake (*Kuchen*) for breakfast, not a frozen cucumber (*Gurke*.) Must work on my accent.

The gig is great, and afterwards a fan comes up and says to me, 'TV, for me you are like Stonehenge – a symbol of England…somehow mystical…'

And very, very old.

7th February
On to Siegen, where the planned gig in a nice club called Myers got cancelled recently. Instead, some people from a nearby youth centre have persuaded us to play there. They usually come to my gigs at Myers but say a lot of the local

punks won't go there because it's 'too commercial.' I'm a bit concerned about what the non-commercial punk club will be like, so when we pull up outside I'm pleased to see a building painted a cheerful yellow instead of covered with the expected graffiti. The café room above the venue is very pleasant, decked out with wooden tables and chairs and a small stage in the corner, ideal for a gig. The promoter is extremely welcoming, makes coffee, tea and snacks for us and says just let him know if we want anything.

Well, an audience would be nice. Downstairs in the brutally bare venue where we are actually playing, only twenty-five people turn up.

While Garden Gang play I start worrying about the lighting. The main rig isn't working and there are just two spotlights – a dim green one that's pointing centre-stage and making PamP look like a zombie, and another brighter, flesh-coloured one pointing at the wall. I ask the promoter if it would be possible to move the brighter spotlight to point at the stage so people can see what's going on up there and he tells me it shouldn't be a problem, just ask the sound guy. The sound guy tells me it shouldn't be a problem, just ask the promoter. The promoter is now nowhere to be found. When Garden Gang finish I manhandle a large pair of stepladders from the backstage into the venue, climb up them and set about aiming the spotlight at the stage, not easy as all the bolts are broken. Steff feeds me up some strips of tape and we get it more or less aimed right. This is probably enough entertainment from me for the sparse crowd but I play the gig anyway and afterwards everyone apologises that so few people came. Someone points out that although Myers is too commercial for punks, this venue is too punk for anyone else. A regular to the venue tells me it used to be much better here, but then the town council started harassing them. For instance, they told them that they'd close the place down if they didn't paint over the graffiti outside – that's why it's now this horrible yellow.

I am very happy that I am going to be getting out of here and sleeping at my friend Sebastian's flat in Cologne tonight. Garden Gang had been promised somewhere to sleep by the promoters, but as I hurriedly make my exit it's becoming clear that they face the prospect of having to spend the night in the backstage room.

8th February
The Sonic Ballroom in Cologne has changed a lot since the last time I was here, when I played on the floor in a corner. It's now got a stage, good P.A. and lighting, and – to Garden Gang's relief – three rooms upstairs with beds. Lotte tells me that last night he ended up sleeping on the stage next to his drum kit.

After soundcheck I finally get to do the big interview with the guy from *Eins Live*. It seems unlikely to make much difference: disappointingly there's no sign of my record in this week's trend charts again despite all the promo work over the last three weeks.

At least people are coming to the gigs though – downstairs it's packed, and we have another great show.

Afterwards I'm standing around chatting with some people when I feel something thump into my back. A young Mohawk-haired punkette is standing there, preparing to swing her handbag at me again.

'Arschloch...!'

Er..what?

'You didn't play Useless,' she says. 'I've been feeling useless at work for weeks and came tonight to hear you play it...and you didn't play it!'

Then she hits me with her bag again. Quite hard.

Then I go back to Sebastian's flat and have a nice glass of red wine.

9th February

The last time we played the Bistro 108, a small music club in a village called Niederbrechen, they had the first snowfall of the winter and almost no one turned up, so it's with a sense of resignation that we watch the blizzard beating against the windscreen as we make our way towards it. The place is run by old school rock fans, decked out with all sorts of rock'n'roll memorabilia and fitted with a powerful sound system. The DJ plays some records before the gig and it's so loud I can feel my insides moving around. Despite the weather, by the time we play there is a small crowd in and compared to last time this feels like a real gig, even though we're in somewhere that can't be found on a map.

These out of the way places are often the most friendly: we hang around for a while at the bar afterwards accepting offers of free drinks, and discretely taking the piss out of the clichéd rock music being played. I end up in a conversation with the two barmaids about the best type of lip salve.

10th February

Two days to go and we must be getting into the swing of it because we get to the venue in Viersen early. Very early. The couple running it are embarrassed because they pride themselves on being good hosts and had been planning an extravagant catering buffet for our arrival but haven't even started preparing it yet.

TALES OF THE EMERGENCY SANDWICH

Viersen is not that much more of a metropolis than Niederbrechen but it's in the catchment area of Dusseldorf and Cologne so we are confident of a good turnout tonight. Meantime, there's a lot of waiting around. You know you're in a town where not much happens when everyone gathers round and watches you change your guitar strings before soundcheck.

11th February
The last gig of the tour, and I have the feeling building up inside me already: this is going to be something special.

All the signs are good. A nice club, big enough to pack a couple of hundred people in but laid out so that it will still feel intimate. A backstage room upstairs where I can escape if I need to. Lots of friends and people I recognise pouring in as soon as the doors open. Garden Gang going down well. Applause as I get on stage for my solo set. Requests being shouted out. A new song, roars of appreciation. Garden Gang backing me up and the excitement building. People dancing. Vom down there in front of the stage, holding up a bottle, cheers! Encores and more encores until we've played everything we know. People thanking me at the bar, asking me, 'how do you do it?' and, 'how long will you keep doing it?' A beer with my friend and website manager Klaus, and reminiscences over my last gig here in Mullheim, ten years ago, when almost no one came. 'When I saw the show tonight,' says Klaus, 'it reminded me why I will *never* give up doing this website.'

Upstairs the dressing room is crammed with people. Wölli puts a CD into the player and 'Good Times Are Back,' the first tune on my new, not-in-the-charts album comes blasting out of the speakers…in moments the whole room is up dancing and singing along, waving their arms in the air, smiles on their faces…

If this isn't success, what is?

2. MAÑANA, MARIA, MAÑANA… (2006)

PART ONE: MAÑANA

<u>4th March</u>
Yesterday I wrote an email to Jonathan asking if he was going to meet me at the airport or if I should take the train into Barcelona. He wrote back: 'We'll pick you up at the airport with a HUGE CAR, ULTRA MODERN, exactly what you deserve!' It turns out to be an old Mini, owned by Claudio, the new guitarist in the band. It's only just possible to fit the three of us and my guitar and luggage in, but thankfully it's not far to where we will be rehearsing this afternoon. Jonathan jokes that we will be doing the whole tour in the Mini. At least, I hope he's joking.

The band is actually most of Suzy & Los Quattro, but are calling themselves the Bored Teenagers for this tour and will be backing me up on a set of Adverts songs. They've been rehearsing without me over the last few weeks, and when we get to the rehearsal room I'm relieved to hear that everything sounds great and a couple of run-throughs is all we need today. Claudio buys me a beer from the vending machine as we pack away. It seems fitting – Jonathan told me earlier that he is 'the beer man.' He checked Claudio's description of himself on the internet before he auditioned for the band, and it said: 'I am Claudio. I like beer. All kinds of beer, warm or cold, draught or bottled…' He was in.

<u>5th March</u>
Another rehearsal, and everything sounds tight. We're all really looking forward to the gigs now; it's just a shame that there will be two days off before the first of them.

<u>6th March</u>
Jonathan has arranged for the two of us to spend the time before the tour starts at his parents' beachfront holiday apartment in nearby Calafell. We'll head out there this evening when he gets back from his job at Wild Punk records, where he has just recently been taken on. Wild Punk are also, coincidentally, releasing my new album in Spain

Jonathan arrives back from work with the disappointing news that the vinyl copies of the album that were supposed to have been shipped last week from Germany on a two day delivery promise still haven't arrived. Maybe *mañana*.

We walk over to Sants station and arrive in Calafell fifty minutes later. There's a fierce wind whipping down the narrow streets of the town, which will be bustling with tourists in a couple of months but is deserted this early in the year. To our disappointment there is no wine in the apartment. Jonathan says, 'I don't think there's been a single evening since I met you when we haven't shared *at least* one bottle of red wine.'

We settle into a nearby bar with the intention of having a drink there then buying a bottle to take back with us. At the back of the room, someone is standing on a chair removing the television from the wall. He places it on one of the tables and covers it with a sheet, then he leaves for a moment and comes back with a bucket and some brushes and starts painting the ceiling pink. You have to walk under the stepladders to get to the loo. At one point he falls off and knocks over a bottle of beer with a crash. The barman is playing chess with the only other customer.

We buy the bottle of wine and make our way back, stopping for a few moments to watch a wheelie bin on fire, great orange flames flapping in the buffeting wind. Sirens in the distance.

Back in the flat, Jonathan opens a tin of olives and starts cooking up some pasta. 'These are very good olives,' I say.

Jonathan glances at the tin and his oven glove catches fire. 'Oh –ah – TV, can you forgive me,' he says as he shakes out the flames, 'these olives have anchovies in them!'

I've had a UFM (Unexpected Fish Moment) and I didn't even realise it, which is strange as anchovy isn't the most delicate of flavours. I read the label and see 6% anchovy listed. Jonathan and I go back to the bowl of olives and start dissecting them with a knife. Only the occasional one is stuffed, so it looks like I must have had a couple from the lucky 94%.

7th March
Jonathan goes off to work in Barcelona and I spend the day by the sea. Things could be worse. However, there's still a chill wind blowing and I soon beat a hasty retreat from my walk along the beach, head to the shops to buy some food and a bottle of red wine, then go back to the apartment and cook a meal for the evening. Jonathan phones around ten to say he's on his way, and when he arrives I serve up the food and say, 'Hard day at the office, dear?'

Actually, it was a pretty hard day, and the records still didn't arrive. The delivery company have promised they will be there *mañana*... Seems like the Germans do *mañana* better than the Spanish.

Bored Teenagers - the official publicity shot...

...and just after.
Barcelona 2006

<u>8th March</u>
At breakfast Jonathan tells me he had a dream where he got into work and found the vinyls had arrived – a huge cardboard box full of them, towering over his head…he tried to reach up and open it but couldn't cut through the tape…

But a couple of hours later he emails me from work to say they still haven't come.

Here in Calafell the weather has improved and there's almost a spring-like feel to the warm sunshine. I don my shorts for a walk up the beach and at one point even dip my toes in the water. After only a few minutes the feeling comes back into my feet and I can move on. Then the wind starts to blow stronger again and a mini sandstorm peppers my exposed legs, driving me off the beach and back to the apartment where I do the washing up.

In the evening I meet Jonathan at a bar for a beer. He has got a haircut for the tour and is feeling self-conscious because it turned out rather shorter than he expected. Later, back at the flat with a bottle of red wine, we break into song to the tune of 'No Time To Be 21':

Hair's short
They made a mess of it
To the end of the ears
Should be the length of it…

9th March

Jonathan texts me to say he'll get to Calafell with the rest of the band in the van at six to pick me up – oh, and, the vinyls haven't arrived. That's a shame, particularly as one English guy, an extreme vinyl fan called Rancid Tom, is flying over for the gig and had especially hoped to pick up a copy.

I gather my belongings together - time to say goodbye to my beachfront apartment, we'll be going back to Barcelona after the gig. It's less than an hour's drive to Tarragona, where we cause a bit of a traffic jam in the narrow street at the back of the Zero club and have to dump all the equipment hurriedly by the side of the road so Claudio can drive off to find a parking space and let the other cars pass.

It's the third time I've been to the Zero and I still find it strange to play on a solid concrete stage, no give under the feet at all. Bit of an ankle-breaker if I should start stomping around. Soundcheck is fine and anticipation is building for the gig – soon we're going to see if all this planning was worthwhile.

First though, as is the tradition here, the promoters take us out for a meal. While band and club staff devour all kinds of exotic Spanish chorizo and chicken dishes, the English vegetarian gets omelette and chips, and a strange look from the waiter.

As stage time approaches, and after a brief panicky moment when I manage to lock myself in the restaurant's toilet, we head back to the club. Rancid Tom arrives soon after and I have to explain that the vinyls haven't arrived. He's not too bothered: mainly he's just happy to be here because in Barcelona he got on a train going the wrong way and it took him quite a while to realise what was happening and find a way back.

By 11:30 the club has filled out nicely, my best turnout yet here and it's great to finally get on stage with the band and play. A lot of people thank me after the show, a few even ask for autographs. I sign one guy's CD and then he unexpectedly signs me: a thick scrawling signature going down most of my arm, ending with an A for Anarchy sign. With my *permanent* marker pen. There'll be some serious scrubbing in the shower tomorrow.

10th March

After only three hours sleep I wake up because my chest is so congested I can hardly breathe. I pace up and down the silent flat for a while then head back to the bedroom and spend the rest of the night worrying about tonight's gig. When I hear movement in the rest of the house I shuffle out to the living room.

'I have a slight problem,' I wheeze to Jonathan. We go back to my bedroom and he spots the dimples of cat paw marks all over the duvet and deduces that the cleaning lady must have left the door open while we were in Calafell. His cat has been making a bed of my bed and stirring up my allergy. Jonathan's mum says she'll get the sheets washed and leave the window open and we'll hope for the best.

I go for a long walk to try and clear my lungs, and end up on Montjuic hill, where I spend a couple of hours at the Miro museum. Outside the gallery a five minute walk takes me to a funicular railway which delivers me almost directly to the door of the Apolo Club, tonight's venue. It's a beautiful old ballroom, and now the tightness in my chest is easing I feel myself starting to look forward to the gig. As I head out of the venue in search of a coffee I bump straight into Alan and his son Chris, two of the British TUTS (TV United Tour Supporters), the fan club which formed on my website a few years ago. We all go into a café across the street, then spot two more TUTS, Mr and Mrs Fleagle (not their real names), apparently looking for the venue. They head into the Apolo Theatre, a few doors down from the club, which currently has a stage production of The Mikado. Let's hope they don't buy tickets. When they come back out we call them over, but just as they arrive I get a call from Jonathan to say that I'm needed back at the venue to do an interview. I rush back there leaving the TUTS to find their own way later and – it occurs to me shortly afterwards – also leaving them to pay for my coffee.

TV SMITH

The television crew set me down on the fire escape steps outside the back of the venue, attach a microphone to my lapel then switch on the camera and ask me a few questions. I can't help feeling the seriousness of my answers is undermined by the sound of toilets flushing down the pipes beside me.

Back in the venue, the doors are now open and people are slowly arriving. We had never hoped to fill this large venue, but by the time we take the stage there are about a hundred people in, not too bad. During the first song I look down to see Rancid Tom carefully setting beers on stage in front of each musician. How am I going to tell him the vinyls still haven't arrived?

When the Apolo closes it's all up to the Barbara Ann, where until recently Jonathan worked behind the bar. The place is packed with people from our gig so it feels like an official after-show party. At one point I notice Jonathan lying on the pavement outside, but when I go to check on him he reassures me that he's quite okay, just finally releasing the stress of the day. The rest of the band don't seem too worried – they are more concerned with getting a photo taken while they pretend to piss on him.

The party continues, and soon Jonathan revives and is back indoors with a beer in his hand. When the bar starts closing we take a cab to his place and sit up for another half hour, relaxing and talking about the day, Jonathan happy that he doesn't have to stay behind and clean up the bar now he doesn't work there any more. Outside the wind is howling, and is so strong that the plastic furniture is moving around on the patio. At one point the wooden shutters are ripped from one of the windows and blown to the ground with a great crash. Which reminds me – the window in my bedroom is still open. Should be thoroughly aired by now.

11th March

We all meet up at the café just around the corner from Jonathan's flat. I go there so often when I'm in Barcelona that I have started calling it my local. We have a coffee, then there's a three hour drive before we finally get breakfast at a petrol station in Castellon.

Good news greets us at the Ricomoar club – the gig has already sold out in advance! Admittedly it's so small it will only hold about fifty people but we're all well pleased, and it's a fitting end to the first leg of the tour.

Tomorrow I fly back to the UK for a couple of days, then I'll be back for part two...

TALES OF THE EMERGENCY SANDWICH

Bring the cow down. Spain 2006

PART TWO: MARIA

<u>15th March</u>
The plane is a little delayed leaving Heathrow because, as the captain informs us, 'perishable fish are being loaded into the cargo hold.' Obviously you can't hurry that.

I take the bus into Barcelona and meet Jonathan at my local. He has some good news: the vinyls have arrived! Unfortunately Rancid Tom is now back in Britain. Drummer Tommy meets us and we all go to Suzy's flat for a few hours. Walking back to the bus stop later, Tommy spots a piece of brand new carpet on the side of the pavement and grabs it to replace the worn-out one he puts under his drums on stage. The buses have stopped running so we get a cab back to Jonathan's place, the roll of carpet between us down the middle of the car.

16th March

The band's regular driver Uri is coming along on this leg of the trip. He and Claudio and Hank, who's doing the merchandising, arrive at midday and we load up the van and set off for Madrid in the dependable hands of Maria, the name assigned to the voice on Jonathan's new GPS navigation system. But not even Maria can alleviate the mind-numbing boredom of a six hour car journey to Madrid over the barren high plains of Spain. 'Have you ever been to the moon before?' says Claudio at one point, casting his eyes across the desolate landscape. He tells me about his day job as a broker for a private plane hire firm used by celebrities and other rich people who pay obscene amounts of money so they can fly when and where they want without having to brush up against the common herd. He's thinking of a change of job to something a bit more music-related, and was recently interviewed by the Gore company for a position marketing a more durable type of guitar string they have developed. We consider some ideas for potential sponsorship if he gets the job – calling the band 'Gored Teenagers,' for example. Or perhaps a few changes to some of the song titles:

One Gore Wonders
The Gore Times Are Back
The Good Times Are Gore
Gorey Gilmore's Eyes
My String Won't Snap

Or, considering the price of the strings:

It's Expensive Being Gore

Yes, it's a very long journey.

Maria sleeps for most of the time but she wakes up as we get into the outskirts of Madrid and Uri is soon arguing with her about how to get to the hotel, which turns out to be a one star *Hostal*. We have just half an hour there before we have to leave for the venue. Maria tries to take us the quickest route, but the Madrid traffic police have other ideas.

I've played the *Gruta 77* club once before on a weekend and there was a reasonably large crowd in. This time it's a Thursday, not such a good day, but I see the club has made my new album 'CD of the Month' in their magazine, so that should help.

TALES OF THE EMERGENCY SANDWICH

After soundcheck we walk over to a tapas bar where the only vegetarian food on offer is a cheese sandwich. Back at the club I'm disappointed to see that there are only twenty people in and we delay the start of the show. Over the next half hour the place slowly fills up. There are around a hundred in when we hit the stage, and the gig goes well.

When the club closes we walk to a nearby rock bar. Jonathan and Uri are a bit delayed because they needed to find somewhere to park the van, and Maria was under the impression that you can fit a 2 metre high van in a 1.9 metre high underground car park.

It's always good to know where the hotel key is.
Madrid 2006

17th March

We meet in a restaurant next to the hotel where there are so many dead animals' legs hanging overhead that it looks like a herd of cows has just fallen through the ceiling. I have the only vegetarian thing on offer – an omelette on bread, admittedly a change from the usual cheese on bread. Claudio points out that I am sitting under a sign that says *Prohibido Cantar* (No Singing).

Jonathan and Uri go to collect the van, and the rest of us wait in a nearby Vermouth bar. It's an atmospheric place, decked out with dark wooden wall panels and a set of brilliantly grotesque Goya prints. I order a coffee, then notice Claudia with a glass of vermouth and say, 'I thought you were The Beer Man?'

He says, 'I am flexible.'

It's another long boring drive North, through the ring of mountains that have helped preserve the Basque Country from being invaded through the centuries, and on into Andoin. We pull up to a very unpromising looking club, a characterless building backing onto a railway line with trains roaring past every few minutes. The sound of a sax player rehearsing drifts down from an upstairs window. He's playing 'The First Noel.'

We walk into the club to find a chilly room with concrete floors. I stand under the stage lights to try and get warm while the band set up their gear. Soon afterwards local punk legends NCC (*Nuevo Cataclismo Catolico*) arrive from San Sebastian. They've agreed to play support for us tonight and tomorrow, even though they're very popular around here and would normally be headlining.

People arrive at the venue late, but by the time NCC start it's filling up nicely and the atmosphere, as well as the temperature, is finally starting to warm up. Everyone is very friendly, the staff are making sure we're happy and keeping us supplied with beer, and when we get on stage the room is nearly full and we play a killer gig, the best of the tour so far. A few hours ago I wouldn't have believed it possible.

At around two in the morning we say our goodbyes and head off for Durango, an hour's drive away, so we will be there ready for tomorrow's gig. When we get to the outskirts and start looking for our hotel Maria leads us up a blind alley into a housing estate. Uri lets off a string of invectives which I don't understand but includes the word '*puta.*'

Jonathan starts singing:

Mar-ia
Let Uri ste-er
You've fucked up he-re...

The idea of getting anything to eat or drink at this hour of the night seems remote, so after we've all said our goodnights and headed to our rooms it's a nice surprise when there's a knock on the door and I find Jonathan there with a bag of crisps and a bottle of beer, a feast, the perfect nightcap.

TALES OF THE EMERGENCY SANDWICH

<u>18th March</u>

The great thing about driving here last night is that we get to sleep late and don't have to meet until one in the afternoon. Maria must still be tired because we have to drive round the first roundabout three times until she wakes up and takes us to the venue.

It's a great-looking place: inside there's a huge stage with steps down to a high-ceilinged auditorium which is currently being used as an upmarket restaurant. When we've loaded the gear in we take seats at a table and have a leisurely afternoon breakfast. There's even an excellent vegetarian dish – stuffed tomatoes in a vegetable puree – and of course some good red wine.

We leave the van at the venue and walk back through the picturesque old town to the hotel to rest for a couple of hours. From my room I can hear the sound of fireworks exploding in the town square, and when we return to the club at six we find ourselves in the middle of celebrations for Basque Independence Day: banners are being waved, drums beaten and horns tooted; people are chanting, cheering and shouting. We feel a bit incongruous as we push our way through the crowds, struggling with our guitar cases and bags. I'm having a good look around and soaking up the atmosphere as we make our way through the square and am quite startled when one of the groups of young musicians we pass breaks off from playing the Basque anthem, points at me and starts singing 'Bored Teenagers.'

The venue is in the process of being transformed from restaurant to club; tables and chairs are being taken away, a P.A. has been set up, a tall pair of stepladders has appeared in the middle of the stage and the lights are being adjusted. My only worry is that the club is large, Durango is quite small, and I've never played here before.

Back in the dressing room there's a fridge full of beer and we're getting ourselves in the mood for the show. Claudio is not too happy though.

'Heineken, that's terrible beer,' he says. 'You drink it, and all that happens is your piss turns green.'

The gig itself is very good, the 200 people in the audience are considerably more restrained than last night, but we play well and the sound is superb.

Soon after we finish, the venue undergoes its third transformation of the day. The stage is cleared to become a dance floor and a disco begins. There are now over a thousand people in the club. I bump into the guy who sang 'Bored Teenagers' at me this afternoon. It was on the first record he ever owned, he tells me, a punk compilation, and he was really excited when he heard I was coming to play here. He could hardly believe it when he saw me walking past.

The band and me all end up on the balcony looking down at the heaving crowds below, being handed beers by the crew, cheering every time a half-decent record gets played, then we stagger back through the deserted old town to our hotel at around five.

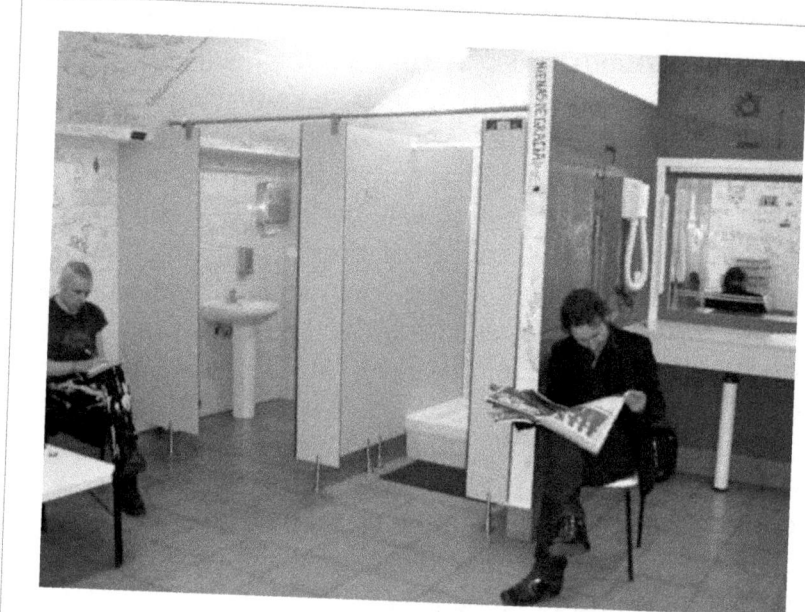

Hank, this dressing room is a toilet.
Durango 2006

19th March
Looking on the bright side, at least I didn't actually get in the shower before finding out there was no hot water. Claudio did.

The band now have a day's drive to Barcelona, and on the way they're going to drop me off in Bilbao. I've got a cheap flight from there back to Stansted this evening so I'll be able to spend a couple of days back at home before the final gigs. That gives me the whole afternoon free in Bilbao, a perfect opportunity to visit the Guggenheim. Maria drops me off right outside, I say goodbye to everyone, then head to the museum café for breakfast and coffee. There is a lot of meaty-looking stuff and a couple of small sandwiches, one with a sign saying 'Vegetarian Sandwich' so I ask for one of those. The woman behind the counter says, 'Do you want that with chicken or without?'

TALES OF THE EMERGENCY SANDWICH

Stoked up on coffee and my hunger slightly quelled by the overpriced mini-sandwich which seemed to be mainly mayonnaise, I go to the ticket desk. Entry is half-price because most of the permanent exhibition is closed, but there's still enough to spend a couple of hours on, and the building itself is extraordinary, a titanium spaceship set in the middle of this pocket-sized city in a hollow in the hills.

Outside, mid-afternoon, the temperature is over 20 degrees and I'm very tempted to just laze around in the sun before my flight goes, but my stomach is reminding me that the mini-sandwich just wasn't enough. At first sight nothing vegetarian seems possible but I finally find a restaurant in a shopping mall that has a menu that I can more or less understand. My limited Spanish is finally paying off: I recognise a vegetarian dish – artichokes, cheese, pasta – sounds good. I take a seat and, getting confident with the language now, allow the waitress to persuade me to have the dish below the one I'd chosen, as she tells me it is really good and also vegetarian. But a little Spanish is a dangerous thing: when the plate arrives I dig in and find that lurking beneath the tagliatelle is an unmistakable chunk of fish.

The waitress passes by and seems surprised I'm not eating.

'Don't you like it?'

'It's got fish in it.'

'No, there's no meat in it'

'Not meat, fish. I don't eat fish.'

'It's just vegetables!'

She seems a bit put out by my gagging noises as she takes my plate away but I catch her muttering the word *trucha* ('trout') to herself.

Ah, the humble trout: that well-known swimming vegetable found in so many of our rivers and streams.

There are still a couple of hours to go before I need to catch the bus out to the airport so I sit on a park bench in the warm sunshine, near the spilled remains of someone's shopping bag which is attracting a lot of interest from the local wildlife, and am able to clear up a question that has often bothered me: yes, sparrows *do* eat dried spaghetti.

At Stansted, it's one degree above freezing, cold enough to see your breath.

20th March
Jonathan emails to say that the journey back to Barcelona was not too bad, but they 'passed a fresh HUGE accident on the road involving a truck and seven cars, and there was DEAD people on the fucking highway.'

21st March
I post off a copy of the vinyl to Rancid Tom.

22nd March
Claudio emails to say, 'Good news! After TV Smith and the Bored Teenagers' gigs in the Basque Country…Eta declares permanent ceasefire.'

23rd March
Pack the bags again, then back to Spain *mañana* for part three…

PART THREE: MAÑANA

24th March
Gatwick to Murcia, that makes six different airports in the last three weeks.

The band pick me up in the van and it appears they have discovered a soundtrack for the tour: a Jonathan Richman Spanish-language song called '*Vampiresada*' (Vampire Girl) is blasting out of the speakers and everyone sings along as we drive the half hour to tonight's gig in Cartagena. The venue is called The Underground and has adopted the London Underground logo, but with the wrong colours. On the opposite side of the road is a café I should probably avoid, *Cafeteria Belchi*.

After soundcheck we go to check in to the hotel. The place is undergoing extensive renovation and looks like a building in a war zone, the outside walls pockmarked with holes, but I'm relieved to find that the room is fine. There's just time to dump my bags and sort out what I need for tonight before we all meet up again in the lobby.

The owner of the club takes us out to a pizza restaurant but even though the pizzas look great I don't eat because there's only an hour to go before stage time. Dessert is the speciality of the house, chocolate pizza: chunks of chocolate lavishly sprinkled over a bread base then put in the oven for a few minutes. I don't eat any of that because chocolate pizza is *wrong*.

The promoter is very pleased to have an authentic '77 punk rocker playing in his venue. During the meal he says to me, 'TV, you must have played with the Sex Pistols, the Clash, all of those…?'

'Oh yes,' I say.

'Must have been great days,' he says, a dreamy look in his eyes. He asks me if it's my first time in Spain and I tell him I've been here quite a few times now, and it's been getting better every time, the audiences slowly building. Then Jonathan tells him about my first solo gig in Barcelona, in a pub where the guy running the gig turned up to soundcheck carrying the entire P.A. in two plastic shopping bags.

'I bet that never happened to Johnny Rotten,' I say.

Back at the venue, the promoter tells me how difficult it is to get people out to gigs in Cartagena, and says he's trying to encourage them by letting them in for free tonight. Still not many come. Those that are there when we finally start are pretty enthusiastic and the few days off has done the band no harm – we play our best yet. Shame most of Cartagena missed it.

After the show Jonathan and Tommy take over the record decks as 'The Quattro DJs' and there's a party atmosphere. Loosened up by drink, quite a few people forget the language barrier and try to tell me how much they enjoyed the gig. One guy comes up and says enthusiastically, 'TV – you are the WORST!'

We only have a short journey tomorrow and won't have to leave the hotel until midday, so we're in no rush to break up the party, and I finally get to my room at 4:30.

25th March
At 8:30 I'm woken by a thunderous hammering. Even though I'm up on the third floor it sounds like the noise is coming from somewhere very close. I fumble around for my earplugs and put them in, but they don't help. After half an hour I can't take it any more so I haul myself out of bed and take a peek out of the window. I find myself staring straight at at a huge hydraulic platform, three men on it knocking a hole into my wall.

I storm down to Reception, where the staff apologise profusely and give me the key to another room but by the time I've got back up the stairs and dragged my bags and guitar over to it I'm too angry to sleep.

At midday I meet with the band. From their rooms on the other side of the hotel they didn't hear a thing.

The view from my window...

...and how they got there. Cartagena 2006

We're supposed to be getting a meal when we get to the next club in Pedreguer but I've been awake a long time and can't wait, so while the others load up the van I pop across the road to *Caféteria Belchi* where I manage to find enough Spanish words to successfully get a spinach and cheese *empañada*. No UMM, no UFM – also no *belchi*.

TALES OF THE EMERGENCY SANDWICH

It's a beautiful sunny day, the town shimmering in 21 degree heat. We set off for Pedreguer and a couple of minutes later Maria brings us right back to the front door of The Underground. We forgot to change her settings.

But then we set off for Pedreguer, and less than an hour later we are pulling up at the club. The promoter, Paco, is waiting for us outside, and takes us up the road to a restaurant where there is a table booked. Most of the conversation is now in Catalan or Spanish and I'm soon completely unable to follow what is going on, but it seems that efforts are being made to get me something vegetarian. At least, I assume that's why the waitress is looking at me like I am an alien. A fine-looking salad arrives for us all to share, a heap of fresh peppers, tomatoes, lettuce, asparagus, sweetcorn, tuna – ah…

'Perhaps you could eat around it?' suggests Claudio.

When the main course comes, there's an embarrassment of vegetarian stuff for me. While the others tuck into the dishes they have ordered from the menu I get served a bowl of spaghetti with pesto, followed shortly after by some mushroom and shredded courgette with eggs, then just when I can take no more, a huge plate of grilled aubergine, artichoke and more courgette. I have to leave half of it. They really must think us vegetarians are hard to please.

Paco takes us down to the venue and I settle down on one of the sofas along the side wall while the band sets up their gear. Soundcheck goes really well and it seems there's every chance we'll have a great gig later. The only problem is, it will be much later: there's another band playing first and we're not scheduled to start until one in the morning.

We drive back to the hotel for a siesta. No sooner have I got in to my room than a fireworks display starts nearby over the old bullring so I go out to my balcony to watch. After the display finishes, many of the crowd make their way noisily down the road and gather in the hotel restaurant below my window to carry on the festivities.

When I meet up with the band at the van an hour later, Claudio says, 'TV, you are a noise attracter. If *you* don't want to sleep, please think of the rest of us.'

Back at the venue, we're invited out to an evening meal with everyone who works there. There are around thirty people at a table that runs the length of the room. Dish after dish is brought out, meat and seafood of course, and an identical selection of grilled vegetables to what I had at lunchtime, even though it's a different restaurant. I feel like I couldn't eat another thing but pick at the food all the same, sip some wine and enjoy the atmosphere as everyone chats around me.

Back at the club not many have turned up yet even though it's already getting near to midnight. Despite the language barrier I finally manage to exchange a few stilted words with Paco. It seems he's almost the same age as me, and apart from being a music fan and running this club he tends a nearby piece of land, growing only organic produce because he knows the value of good food. He is proud of the club, wants all the bands to feel happy here, and tells me that it was 'worth a million' to him when he saw me walk in and relax on the sofa.

By the time the support band have played it's past two in the morning when we get on stage. To make it worse, the clocks go forward today, so it's really past three. There are now over a hundred people in the club and the gig is wild and great. In true rock'n'roll style Jonathan crashes into the drum kit on the last note and then the gig is well and truly over.

They sure know how to enjoy themselves in these small towns, and we do our bit too. At six in the morning, though, it's time to leave. Some of the people walking home at this late hour are startled to find a van full of musicians pulling up beside them, the windows wide open, raucously singing along to a gentle latin swing beat:

Toma el vino, toma mescal
Hace sacrificio ritual
Vampiresada, vampiresa mujer…

The only one not singing along is Maria.

Finishing off the last of the beers in the hotel at seven in the morning we all agree that this has been a most enjoyable tour, and we are convinced that given the opportunity, *mañana* we could go on any stage in the world and rip the place apart.

But *mañana* the tour is over.

3. THE EMERGENCY PEANUTS FROM CHEMNITZ (2006)

<u>22nd June.</u>
Petr, my promoter in the Czech Republic, has found me a flight with advantages and disadvantages: on the plus side, it's cheap and it goes from Heathrow, my nearest airport; on the minus, it's a day earlier than necessary and involves changing in Amsterdam, an ideal opportunity for my baggage to get lost. To avoid the chances of that happening I'm just taking a small carry-on bag containing a few clothes and an emergency cheese sandwich. Of course, I still have to persuade the staff at the KLM check-in desk to let me take my guitar on board, but after some discussion they say I can take it as far as the gate, where the crew on the plane will decide.

The crew don't give the guitar a second glance, and seem only too happy to put it in the first class wardrobe, which makes a refreshing change from me having to push other people's luggage out of the way in the overhead bins to make room for it. Actually, I wouldn't have minded a place in the first class wardrobe myself, as the flight is full and I've been allocated a middle seat wedged next to someone with the build of a sumo wrestler who immediately falls asleep and slumps against me.

The onboard snack is quite a good cheese sandwich. Looks like my emergency cheese sandwich will live to be eaten another day.

There's an hour and a half stopover in Amsterdam, then comes the second leg of the flight, operated by Czech company CSA who pretend there is no first class wardrobe. I manoeuvre the guitar into the overhead bins, then settle into a window seat – relief! – where I am served the onboard snack, a very small and tasteless cheese roll with a piece of lettuce in it that is going brown.

I'm surprised to find myself in a shiny new terminal in Prague that hadn't even been built last time I was here. Petr is surprised too – after half an hour he calls to ask where I am. When he eventually finds me we walk over to where the car is parked and set off, air-conditioning on full, the temperature outside still punishingly hot even though it's mid-evening. The carpets are damp because Petr went to a car wash this afternoon and forgot to wind the window all the way up.

After a four hour drive we arrive in Valašské Meziříčí in Moravia. The stage for tomorrow is already set up on one side of a pretty courtyard with fountains and trimmed hedges, tables and benches around it. The courtyard is bounded on three sides by a beautifully restored Renaissance mansion housing a cultural centre, theatre, restaurant, and bar. Petr takes me up to the office where one of the organisers is still at work, looking rather tired – it's now nearly two in the morning. We collect our passes for tomorrow then drive over to our hotel, a few kilometres away in a typical no frills ex-communist block. At two-thirty I'm settling into my room with a can of beer from the petrol station and a stirring of hunger. It seems a shame to eat the emergency sandwich before I've even played a gig, particularly as I've already had two over the course of the day, but it occurs to me that in this stifling heat it's not going to be edible much longer so there's no point in saving it.

23rd June
Petr told me in an email that I'll be playing early, at around seven in the evening, but we'll have time during the day to 'go in small trip one scansen.' I had no idea what he meant, but Scansen turns out to be a folkloric 'living museum' village of wooden houses, the oldest dating back to 1551. There are also some tourist stalls selling local delicacies – I buy a metre-long plait of smoked cheese to take home – and others demonstrating local crafts. One artisan is keen to show me a Russian doll-style knife set he has made: it consists of a penknife as big as a forearm whose wooden handle he opens to reveal a slightly smaller knife, which in turn contains a still smaller one, and so on down, until he opens the handle of the penultimate one with a flourish and throws out a sprinkle of thumbnail sized knives onto the table. I hate to think what airport security would have to say about that. After this, Petr drives me up a mountain to a ski resort to see some elaborate wooden buildings designed by a Bratislavan architect. No snow around at the moment of course, the weather muggy and in the high 20s, but the ski lift is still operating and there's a queue of schoolchildren getting on and swinging down into the swirling grey clouds below towards Ostrava.

There is virtually no one at the festival when we arrive late afternoon, just a few staff milling around and a band from Bratislava doing a soundcheck. I'm shown up to one of the dressing rooms on the first floor, plush and mirror-lined and big enough for about fifty people. I leave my bag and guitar there, then head back down to the courtyard. The band starts and is pretty good, but the handful of people drinking beer at the tables don't even stand up. I'm the only one who seems to be paying any attention. At one point a couple of punk rockers come up to me and ask for my autograph and a photo, which is slightly embarrassing as more people are now looking at me than at the band. Even the band are looking at me.

TALES OF THE EMERGENCY SANDWICH

I'm relieved that when I start my show an hour later a small enthusiastic crowd has gathered on the grass in front of the stage. It feels good to play so early in the evening and out in the open air instead of in a stuffy club, and it unexpectedly turns into a very nice gig. When I finish there are a bunch of people waiting beside the stage to talk to me, including a wiry grey-bearded elderly chap who talks animatedly at me in Czech even though I point out that I can't understand a word he is saying. The normal fans can't get a word in. When one of them, an American living here in the area, manages to interject, Greybeard starts gesticulating and shouting. I ask what he's saying and the American guy explains, 'He is warning you that when I have finished talking to you I am going to take you somewhere and kill you.'

When Greybeard finally wobbles off I end up sitting at one of the tables with the fans and they start getting rounds of vodka in. Up on the stage a soft rock band with a girl singer wearing a large white cowboy hat starts to play, to general indifference. Soon my new friends are looking a little glazed and have to head for home, leaving me with a backlog of shot glasses in front of me that I promise I will drink later even though I know I won't, and soon Petr arrives to drive us back to the hotel.

The crowd went wild.
Valašské Meziříčí 2006

24th June

A good long sleep and down to breakfast at 10:30. The remnants of the communist system are still present in the breakfast menu: everything on it is itemised according to weight: Coffee – 2 grams, sugar – 1 gram, butter – 3 grams. I order the vegetarian option, bread and cheese, and am surprised to be presented with a plate of ham.

Only a sixty kilometre drive through the sweltering heat to today's gig, another open air festival, in Studénka, near the Polish border. Before we go to the site we check in to our motel. It's situated next to a motorway, which is convenient as we have to leave at five in the morning tomorrow for my flight from Prague. The rooms aren't ready when we arrive so we take a short trip up the road to Příbor, Freud's birthplace. He only lived here for a few years before moving to Vienna but it's all Příbor has and they're making the most of it, particularly this year, the 150th anniversary of his birth. Quite what Freud would have made of a Freud Rock festival with a lot of useless bands, or the tacky Freud puppets in the shops, or the life-sized Freud mannequin I don't know. Still, it has to be done: I wander down to the house where he was born and get my photo taken on the bronze couch outside. On a strip of polished brass running below the couch is the phrase, 'Sit down and meditate – stand up and act.'

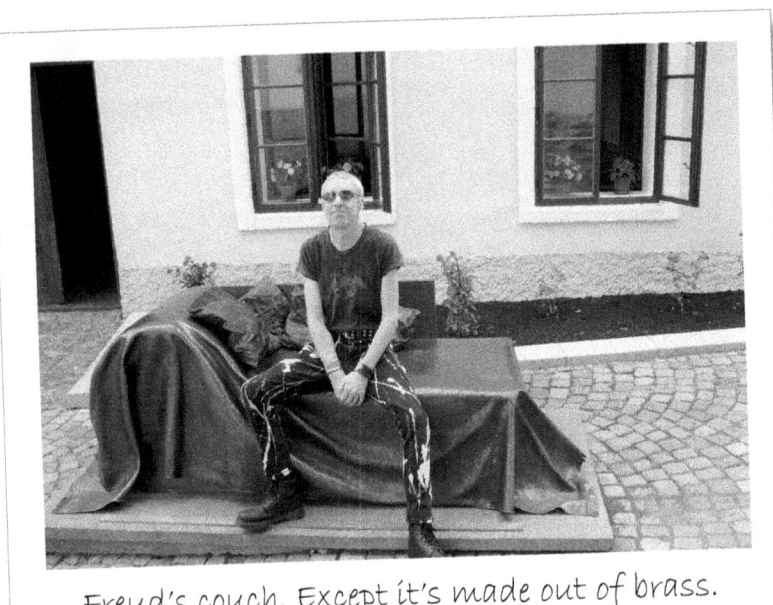

Freud's couch. Except it's made out of brass. And outside. Příbor 2006

I was lucky enough to snatch a photo of the great man himself. Příbor 2006

Another forest, another festival. Studénka 2006

TV SMITH

The festival site is way out in the countryside, surrounded by trees with a small muddy stream trickling along beside it, and there aren't many more people here than yesterday. In fact I get a sense of *déjà vu* when I see the same band from Bratislava as yesterday soundchecking. There are some technical problems with the P.A. system, which is emitting loud interference, and while the band battle with that I walk round to the area behind the stage and am surprised to see that Petr has got a rod and line from somewhere and is happily fishing in the stream.

*Typical backstage behaviour.
Studénka 2006*

By the time I play, a few punks have started to appear and are even standing in front of the stage, dancing a bit and calling out for a few requests. The Bratislavan band is there too, and their singer shouts out for 'Lion And The Lamb,' which I play. Someone else shouts for 'Gary Gilmore's Eyes,' then gets up on stage and sings along very badly, which gets a laugh.

When I come off stage, a group of people who traveled here from Poland invite me over to their table and soon a bottle of vodka appears. Before things get too dangerous I slip away to pack up my gear, then I go and stand at the back of the site with the Bratislavan band. They tell me they saw me watching their set yesterday and wondered if I was TV Smith. Then when the punks came up to me and took a photo they exchanged a glance amongst themselves on stage – yep, that's him.

TALES OF THE EMERGENCY SANDWICH

I'm a minor celebrity in Moravia!

The site is now filling up for the real celebrities of the day, a well-known local folk-rock band who have been around for ten years but only started pulling a crowd recently when a film was made about them which did well in Czech cinemas. Suddenly their album sales soared, and tonight there are hundreds of people in front of the stage cheering them on. That gives us minor celebrities licence to take the piss out of them, particularly when the drummer launches into a lengthy solo. The Bratislavan band's singer says, 'This sounds like…like… sack potatoes' then mimes them being emptied onto the ground.

The Poles stagger past on their way home, promising to try and fix me up my first gig in Poland sometime. The band is still playing but Petr and I have to think about the early start tomorrow and can't stay much longer. We say our goodbyes and make a dash for the car as the band get into their final encore. Just in time – suddenly there are floods of people heading for the exit and a stream of cars clogging up the dirt paths leading to the nearest road.

The special vegetarian food the organisers of the festival promised to arrange turned out to be a meat goulash so I haven't eaten anything since breakfast. Back in my room I set the alarm for 4:40 and fantasise about the emergency sandwich I wish I now had. I do have a metre long plait of smoked cheese, but without any bread it wouldn't make much of a snack. Then I remember that when I played a gig in Germany last week I grabbed a packet of peanuts from the bar as I left and they are still in my bag.

Oh, emergency peanuts from Chemnitz: your hour has come.

25th June

At five in the morning a red blob of a sun is just dragging itself above the misty fields and Petr and I are getting in the car for the lengthy trip to Prague. Two hours later we're still on schedule and have time to stop for a quick coffee and something to eat at a rest station which has a few goats penned up outside it. There's always time to stroke a goat. Breakfast is a cheese sandwich.

I'm at the airport in good time but come across a particularly surly Czech airlines check-in operative, who before he even says hello eyes up my guitar and says that unless I have paid for an extra seat I can't take it on board with me. 'There's no way it will fit in the overhead bins,' he says, 'the flight is overbooked and it's a Fokker.'

You're a Fokker, I'm tempted to reply, but what I actually say is, 'Just because you woke up in a bad mood this morning there's no need to take it out on me.'

Eventually I persuade him to tag the guitar and let me take it down to the gate, where it will DEFINITELY BE TAKEN AWAY FROM ME AND PUT IN THE HOLD, although when I get there I find it's a KLM operated 737, not a Fokker and the delightful Dutch staff immediately offer to stow the guitar in the first class wardrobe. 'It vill be much easier zan putting it overhead,' the purser says with a big smile. 'Also maybe you vill forget it at ze end of ze flight. I have always vanted a nize guitar!'

The onboard snack is a cheese sandwich. The flight attendant is quite a number, trying to persuade everyone to have a drink with the snacks as he passes them round, 'Go on, have some wine. We also have whisky. It is after ten o'clock, after all. It's only normal...'

I'm in an aisle seat, and the young woman next to me must have spotted that I'm reading a German book because she haltingly says *'Entschuldigung'* and *'Danke schon'* when I let her pass to use the loo. When she comes back I tell her I'm English and she asks me what I do. I tell her I'm a musician and she says, 'Actually, I pretty much guessed that from the way you look. You can't always tell what someone does from the way they look though. I bet you would never have guessed I'm in the sex toys business, would you? It's not like I'm wearing a dildo on my head.'

I check, and she isn't. She and her boyfriend, who is snoozing in the window seat, have just been drumming up some business in Prague, a new market for them. The plane makes a little bump and she blanches. 'I really hate that,' she says. 'Doesn't that sort of thing bother you?'

I tell her that I fly so much that I don't care any more – in fact I find the bumps quite relaxing and often doze off during take-off and landing. I say, 'I think of it as mother's hand rocking the cradle, only mother is a bit drunk.' This seems to calm her down a little.

The purser is wheeling the trolley up the aisle, calling out 'Tax Free goods!' as he goes, but no one is buying anything. 'Oh, ve are a *great* success!' he chuckles as he sweeps past.

Dildo lady is telling me a bit more about her business. She's been living in Amsterdam for a while, and no one there cares about her job, but back home in Chicago people tend to get upset about it so she just tells them she sells toys, 'ordinary toys, like Toys R Us.'

Sex Toys R Us?

The plane suddenly lurches. 'Oh my God,' she gasps. 'Mommy's on crack.'

I change planes in Amsterdam and see on the boarding pass that the bastard at the Prague check-in has booked me into a middle seat for the second leg of the flight. I wait at the gate with sinking heart as fifty noisy South African adolescent schoolchildren, all carrying large rucksacks and wearing tracksuits emblazoned with 'Cricket Tour of England and Wales 2006' gather noisily, bouncing footballs against the windows, shouting amongst themselves and pushing ahead of the queue. On board I am surrounded by them, and they immediately start throwing sweets at each other then hiding behind their seats. The only other person nearby who isn't one of the school group is in the seat behind me, fast asleep. The stewardess comes by handing out the snacks, pointing at the seat behind me and asking each of the school kids, 'Do you know who that is? He told me he has had ten hit records…'

No one knows. I sneak a look and I don't know either.

The snack is a cheese sandwich.

4. WASTED WITH THE GANG (2006)

<u>9th August</u>
I try and do something different every year for the annual Wasted punk festival in Blackpool and as this is being billed as the last one ever I want it to be special, so I'm planning a solo performance of the entire 'Crossing The Red Sea With The Adverts' album on the acoustic stage, and a band show on the main stage with Garden Gang. I'm also going to play a couple of warm-up gigs with them, and the first is tonight in a little real ale pub in Shoreham-by-Sea, a few miles down the coast from Brighton.

The band have been driving over from Germany for the last couple of days in two minibuses packed with all their equipment. I'm going to come down from London by train and meet them in Shoreham.

From the station I make my way over to the pub and say hello to Roy, a friend of mine who has recently become landlord here. He's done a great job on the place but it's even smaller than I had expected, with a stage that's barely big enough for a drum kit, never mind a whole band.

Roy shows me upstairs, where his irresistible new puppy is relieving itself on the floor. The puppy development might be something Garden Gang won't be too happy about, as this is the room they're supposed to spend the night in, but Roy points out that if they prefer they can sleep downstairs in the bar. Puppy pee in your sleeping bag, or free beer on tap all night: that'll be a tricky one.

Soundcheck time comes and goes and there's still no sign of the band. I phone up PamP and am surprised when Jenny, the singer from the Midnight Creeps answers his phone: she flew out from Boston to Munich a couple of days ago and is coming along for the ride. She tells me that they have been lost in Shoreham for the last hour. Shoreham is so small I didn't think it was possible to get lost in it for an hour.

Meanwhile, two TUTS, Mr and Mrs Fleagle, arrive from London. Another TUT from Brighton called Step arrives, slightly shaken by the sight of the massed chavs hanging around outside Somerfield.

Eventually the two vans arrive. So now the Gang's all here, but so are most of the audience so we have to load the gear in past them, and try and figure out a way to fit everything in, eventually setting up the drum kit on the floor and dividing the amps and microphones between floor and stage. Things are running very late and there is now no possibility for a soundcheck. I'm worried because I have to catch the last train back to London tonight so I switch the order of the sets around so that Garden Gang will play together with me first, then their own set afterwards.

Having been part of the will-they-won't-they-arrive drama earlier, the audience are right on our side and it's a thrill playing for the first time with Garden Gang here in this little pub on the coast. It's just a shame that moments after I get off stage, still dripping with sweat, I have to dash for the train and miss the Garden Gang show.

Before I leave I ask at the bar for a beer to take with me as I haven't actually had time to drink all evening. From the large selection available I choose the Bavarian *Weizen*, not just because Garden Gang are here, but also because the bottle has a flip top and I don't have an opener with me. The ex-manager of The Evening Star, a little real ale pub I occasionally play in Brighton, offers me a lift to the station so I pack up my things, gather up the Fleagles – who are also taking the last train back – and off we go, arriving on to the platform just before Step, who's heading home too. There are a few minutes to spare before the train arrives so I take the opportunity to use the platform as my dressing room and change into a dry T-shirt.

We grab a few empty seats so we can sit together, and comment on how ridiculous it is to have a first class section at the front of the carriage – it's exactly the same as the area where we are sitting, but separated from us by a glass door. No one in it, of course. I crack open the bottle and finally get the chance to enjoy a beer. Step leaves at Brighton, and the Fleagles and I chat away until Croydon an hour later, where they get off to take a bus home. Then things start to get frustrating. The train seems reluctant to make it the rest of the way to London, slowing down and stopping with increasing frequency, and I realise that I am not going to make my connection to the last tube at Kings Cross. No announcements are made as to what is causing the delay or when we are expected to arrive in London.

There's also a problem of a more pressing nature: the beer has started to work its way through, and a quick search up and down the train has revealed that all the toilets on board are locked and marked 'not in use.' Tell that to my bladder. As we stand, marooned again, at signals somewhere in South London this problem becomes rather urgent and I find myself eyeing up the deserted first class compartment and the empty flip top beer bottle.

Eventually the train pulls into Blackfriars and stops there for twenty minutes, still with no announcement or explanation, even though we are over an hour late now. I consider getting out and trying to find a taxi from here, but I can see down to the Embankment below and there is no traffic around. By the open doorway there is a huddle of three railway staff on the platform who don't seem in much of hurry, and I can catch a little of what they're discussing: 'If it works,' says one, 'buzz through to me and let me know, then hop off.'

Eventually we are on the move again, and there is finally an announcement: with an apologetic tone, the driver informs us, 'Sorry for the delay, everyone. There was a security issue with the last carriage that had to be resolved before we could move off.'

So that explains everything, and is also the reason I had to pay a twenty-five quid cab fare to get home, and why there's a bottle of piss in a *Weizen* bottle in the first class compartment.

10th August
I get to the Bull and Gate late, but find Garden Gang have only just arrived. They're not looking happy. They tell me they parked outside while they came in to introduce themselves, then went back two minutes later to find the window of one of the vans smashed and some items stolen, including drummer Uli's expensive digital camera. Now the police are outside taking down the details and the band are stuck with a van with a broken window, impossible to keep their equipment in securely.

Welcome to London!

Soundcheck is difficult because someone has to stand by the van the whole time to stop anything else being taken. Meanwhile Jennie is attempting to mediate with the insurance company as the band's English isn't good enough to deal with something complicated like this, and as I'm the only one with an English mobile phone she arranges with the insurers to call me when they have some idea of when they can get the window fixed. Sure enough, ten minutes later they ring and tell me that the windscreen repair company will call me in two hours with news of when they can replace the glass. I tell them I'll be on stage by then and won't be able to answer the phone, and I try and impress on them the urgency of the problem. Tomorrow night we'll be playing in Blackpool, and the window has to be repaired tonight because the band have already booked a hotel for halfway up the motorway.

I arrange with the pub landlord to let us move the vans into the narrow alleyway that runs around the back of the pub and is guarded by a locked barrier, then I ring the windscreen place to let them know where we've moved them. They inform me that they've just found out they don't have the right glass and can't get it until Monday. All they can offer is an appointment at their workshop in Hendon at two in the morning to put in a temporary perspex replacement.

It's all distracting me from the gig, but suddenly it's time for Garden Gang to start. Looking around, I suddenly realise that after all the work that has gone into this – my first gig with my regular German band in my home town, and with support from iDou, comprising members of ex-chart toppers Carter The Unstoppable Sex Machine – there are just 37 paying customers in.

Despite the low turnout we all play our hearts out and the gig is good, but we end up with £130 to share between three bands. It's now nearly midnight and time I took the last tube home, but as Garden Gang pore over the London A-Z and try to work out how to get to Hendon it soon becomes clear that they're never going to make it on their own. I'm reluctant to go in the van with them and navigate because I'd intended to set off early tomorrow for the drive to Blackpool but there's no alternative.

As we pull into a deserted industrial estate in Hendon at 1:45 and see the sign for the windscreen replacement firm, Jennie gets quite excited. 'YAYYY!' she squeals from beside me on the front seat, pointing at the lights of the garage where a couple of mechanics are standing, 'They're waiting for us! They're...ROLLING UP THE DOORS!!'

We drive the van right into the workshop and while the mechanics run around measuring up and cutting Perspex, I ask one of the guys in the office to call me a cab. Then I stand outside for a while, anxiously checking the time and eyeing up the traffic until with some relief I see a car pulling up. I run up to it, dragging along my roller bag and guitar, then beat a hasty retreat when I see that it is actually a police car. But then the cab arrives and I'm finally home at three, the plan to leave early for Blackpool fast fading from my mind.

11th August

It's not long after midday when Gaye and I finally get on the road, and things run pretty well until we hit the first batch of road works which slows us down to a crawl. Then after I pull off into a service station for fuel I accidentally take the wrong slip road back onto the motorway and end up in the southbound lane which means we have to crawl through the road works twice more before getting back to the service station again twenty minutes later. I'm not in the best of moods by now, and it may well have been me muttering 'never again,' as I often end up doing on the annual drive up to Blackpool – but this is supposed to be the last-ever Wasted so this time it may actually be true.

At around four Jennie phones to say that she and Garden Gang have arrived in Blackpool and are going to look for a hotel. Gaye and I have a hotel already booked, but we're still at least a couple of hours away and stuck in heavy traffic. Further North the road clears a little and I'm able to put on some speed and arrive with still enough time to find the hotel before I'm due on stage. I've just picked up the keys to the room when Garden Gang walk in to Reception. They hunted around for a cheap late deal and out of hundreds of hotels in Blackpool ended up at the same place as us.

Half an hour before we are due to go on stage in the huge Empress Ballroom we gather in the dressing room, a buzz of excitement in the air. As soon as we start playing the place erupts. There are a couple of thousand people in the ballroom and on the sprung dance floor the whole crowd is jumping up and down whether they want to or not. We come off stage elated.

Despite my best intentions, I don't actually get to see any other bands after that, instead spending the time bumping into old friends, having a few drinks and a laugh until security sweep me and Gaye out of the dressing room – oops, we're the last ones there – at two in the morning.

12th August
I don't have a gig to play today, but Gaye and I drop into the festival anyway. A lot of people tell me that they're looking forward to my solo set tomorrow, which is pleasing and terrifying in equal parts as I'll be attempting quite a few songs that I haven't played for thirty years.

I bump into Dave, a friend who promotes gigs for me in Derby, and he has some news about the '3 Men & Black' tour that I'm hoping to be playing support for later in the year. 3 Men & Black are an occasional band comprising Pauline Black and Nick Welsh from The Selector, Roddy Radiation from The Specials and Jake Burns from Stiff Little Fingers. Dave spoke to Jake on the phone a couple of days ago, and Jake told him he's really keen that I join the tour. That's encouraging news. I met Pauline and Nick at a gig recently and got on very well with them. Now if only I could believe the booking agency was as committed as the musicians: so far they've only provisionally offered me three dates, and have said that I definitely can't do the Scottish ones because it would be too expensive to get me up there.

I intend to turn in early tonight to make sure I'm fit for my performance tomorrow, but mid-evening some friends of mine from Berlin in a band called Church Of Confidence arrive. Their drummer couldn't make it, so at the last minute they drafted in Vom. Having him around puts paid to my plans and we stay until the beer runs out.

TV SMITH

13th August

We're at the venue early to catch Garden Gang playing their first ever set at Wasted. They've been given the opening spot on the Olympia stage, and have a good few people in even though the doors have only just opened. I'm proud to see them putting everything into it and the audience obviously enjoy their performance. At one point PamP waves his arm over his head and at the same moment a pigeon flies past as if attached by string, then lands on the lighting rig, where it watches the rest of the set.

Wandering around the Winter Gardens afterwards I bump into Jon and Sophie from Florida, who have brought me a bottle of my favourite Spanish wine. There's a bit of a trend developing here: when I saw them in New York last year they smuggled a bottle past the security men at CBGBs; this year they've smuggled one into the biggest punk festival in Europe.

By the time I'm due to play my show on the acoustic stage the room is packed. I say a few words about my plan to play the entire Red Sea album, then get straight into it without saying anything else between songs until it's over, around 40 minutes later. I get a big round of applause, and am happy with my performance – and above all relieved that I pulled it off.

Backstage, Pauline Black and Nick Welsh arrive for their 3 Men & Black set and we have time for a quick chat about the tour, then Gaye and I head over to see The Damned playing at another venue. We watch the first couple of numbers of the set, but I have to leave to pick up my merchandising, which I've left at various stalls throughout the complex. When I have everything gathered together I dump it next to my guitar in the dressing room of the acoustic stage and notice an interesting thing: while nearly all the other dressing rooms in the Winter Gardens have run out of alcohol, there's still plenty left here. So that's where Gaye and I spend the rest of the evening, disposing of the remaining free beer and getting involved in conversations with two punk girls about the best types of veggie bacon, and a Blackpool fanzine writer about the time he saved the life of a moorhen.

14th August

Back home by early evening, I check my emails to find a message from Liam, the manager of Dead Men Walking, saying they want me to play support on a three week tour in October. This is a similar format to 3 Men & Black, but with Mike Peters from The Alarm, Captain Sensible, Kirk Brandon from Spear Of Destiny and Slim Jim Phantom from Stray Cats. It wouldn't really be possible for me to do both. Typical, you wait ages to play a tour with a punk supergroup and then two come along at once.

15th August
I phone up the agent for 3 Men & Black and explain the situation and he agrees that the other tour is a better prospect for me. Then I have to go about moving the other gigs I already have in October. The main problem is that my friend Max in Vienna has asked Kerni, the drummer in a band called Skeptic Eleptic, to organise a tour of Austria around then. I don't know how advanced the booking has got, and when I email Max I get an automated response that he is on holiday in Croatia for two weeks.

I don't have contact details for Kerni, but leave a message for him on the Skeptic Eleptic MySpace site and have to just hope he reads it. Liam needs to know if I can do the Dead Men tour by the day after tomorrow.

16th August
Still no word from Kerni, and I have just a few hours left at home before I need to head for Birmingham for the final gig with Garden Gang.

The last train I can take on a cheap ticket leaves just after two in the afternoon, but I have a stack of emails and phone calls to get through before then. Max calls from Croatia – he's picked up my message and gives me Kerni's phone number, but when I try ringing, the call won't go through.

I send a message to Nick Welsh through MySpace apologising for the fact that it looks like I'm going to pull out of the 3 Men & Black gigs. He writes back: Three week tour? Go for it!

By now I've missed the last cheap train by a good two hours so I make the decision to drive to Birmingham and home again after the gig. So it's back up the M40, and I arrive at the venue soon after six. The Market Tavern is a pub with a small upstairs music room and Garden Gang are already there setting up their equipment.

The gig is good, very hot and sweaty even with all the fire exit doors open, the little room packed with people. The PA system can hardly cope. During the set someone comes up to the front of the stage and shouts to me, 'We can't hear your vocals over the band!'

Just like the old days!

After the show I say my goodbyes to Garden Gang – who will head North tomorrow for a show that I arranged for them with Danny, the crusty from Hull – and I power back down the motorway, getting home just after three.

17th August

Still no word from Kerni, and time's up to make a decision on the Dead Men Walking tour, which will start in just six weeks time.

I phone up Liam and tell him I'm in.

5. BRING HIM BACK SAFELY (2006)

<u>4th October</u>
Dead Men Walking is my first major tour in the U.K. since supporting Tom Robinson ten years ago. It's a great chance to play in front of some reasonably large audiences, and it's going to be a relief to travel in a tour bus and sleep in hotels for a change.

But first I have to get up to the opening date in Liverpool on the train, as the band are coming from Wales where they've been in a recording studio out in the countryside for the past couple of weeks. Tonight's venue is right next to Lime Street station, easy to carry my guitar and bags over by foot, and I walk in to find Kirk Brandon and Slim Jim both on their mobile phones. They tell me there was no signal at the studio – the only way they could make a call was to walk up the hill and stand on a bench.

I'm introduced to road manager Liam, and soon Captain Sensible and Mike Peters arrive. We all squeeze into the tiny dressing room and chat for a bit while Vince and Craig, who are looking after the equipment and stage, set things up for soundcheck.

The band are looking tired from their weeks in the studio, where they've been up late most nights trying to get the record finished in time for the tour, and the mood isn't helped by problems at soundcheck. Jim comes backstage looking exasperated as the noise from Public Enemy soundchecking in the larger venue upstairs drowns them out, and Kirk's monitor isn't working at all. The local engineer promises everything will be okay by showtime, and the band abandon soundcheck because they want to dash back to their hotel and get a shower – the studio was 'a bit hippy.'

I knew before I started this tour that there would be times when it was hard to get people into the venue early but this is even worse than I expected: when I walk onto the stage half an hour after the doors open there is absolutely no one in front of it, not one single person, although luckily about thirty or forty are in the bar off to one side and when I play a few chords and ask them to come into the room, nearly all of them do. After a few songs the room starts to fill a bit more, about as many as at one of my solo gigs, but the room is bigger so it looks emptier. The response is fairly muted, but I am saved by a girl I recognise from my German dates, who dances the whole way through, and one of my regulars from Liverpool who is happy to stand at the front and shout for songs, which breaks the ice for everyone else. I play Gary Gilmore's Eyes at the end and get a big round of applause – I can almost hear them saying, '*Gary Gilmore's Eyes?*... Oh, it's *that* guy!'

I didn't feel I totally won over the audience, so it's good to go and hang around by the merchandising stand and find everyone saying how much they enjoyed it. One guy tells me that Flava Flav from Public Enemy was standing at the back, complete with bling jewellery and his trademark giant gold clock on a chain round his neck, tapping his foot and getting into the songs.

The fact that this is an audience here specifically for Dead Men Walking is clear from the moment they get on stage; the place has filled up and there's warm applause from the word go. They put in a great performance playing a selection of hits from their individual bands, although Kirk's monitor is still not working and he has to spend most of the evening hunched over his amp with his back to the crowd, not the ideal start to a tour.

After that it's back to the hotel – luxury! Some things never change though: we didn't get round to eating all day apart from a sandwich from the backstage fridge, so Captain and me and the road crew head out to a Chinese restaurant. I am Captain's veggie ally on this tour and together we can happily ignore the cries of 'rabbit food' from the carnivores as we order. I understand what he's been up against when Liam says to me 'I've nothing against being a vegetarian, mate, but I don't know how you could live without Kentucky Fried Chicken. That's just not possible.'

Not many vegetarian dishes on the menu, though, and the waiter comes back shortly after we've ordered to tell us we can't have the meal we asked for because they don't have any bean curd left. We order some vegetable spring rolls instead, and the waiter turns up again a few minutes later to ask us if we want chicken in them. Chinese restaurants are a potential U.M.M minefield. A P.U.M.M.M.

5th October

It's a dreary seven and a half hour crawl through terrible traffic down the M6 and M5 in heavy rain to Bristol. We're in a smallish van, all the gear packed in behind a partition at the back, and although the airline-style seats are comfy enough, we're all looking forward to getting out and stretching our legs. When we finally arrive in Bristol we find that the town centre is being dug up to build a new shopping centre – oh boy, another shopping centre! – and it takes us another half hour of traffic hell to get to the venue.

I last played the Fleece about 20 years ago with Cheap and it's improved a lot in the meantime, better laid out with a higher, bigger stage, and a new dressing room on the other side of the building in a small upstairs garret. Not particularly comfortable, but it used to be right behind the stage, separated from it by only a curtain so there was no escape from the noise. And another thing that's different from the old days: up in the dressing room there are sandwiches in the fridge and a wireless internet signal.

I'm surprised to find that even though it's early when I get on stage there are quite a few people in the venue. It's hard to make headway though, I find myself putting everything into it but consistently getting just a smattering of applause after each song until I play Gilmore at the end. But it's a repeat of last night: when I go out and chat with people at the end of the evening I get loads of positive feedback. Quite a few people tell me they have never heard of me before but really enjoyed it, others say they only realised who I was when I played 'that song' at the end. It occurs to me that for this tour I should play 'that song' at the beginning.

6th October
We meet early in the hotel lobby because the band have to do an interview for BBC Radio Bristol. Captain and Slim Jim have both gone down with a cold and are dosing themselves with Day Nurse. We run straight into traffic again, then there's a sudden downpour just as we arrive at the studios and we get drenched as we dash across the car park. Even the cardboard box I put over my head isn't enough to keep me dry. As we shake ourselves off in Reception, the rain fizzles out as fast as it started. Slim Jim eyes up the dark skies overhead and says, 'Funny how it had to happen *right at that exact moment...*'

It turns out that the DJ is doing the show from a different studio, but we're supposed to pretend we're all in the same room. Before the interview starts, Captain does his best Jimmy Saville and Alan Freeman impersonations and pretends to fiddle with the faders, which has us all falling about with laughter. We're still laughing when the DJ comes online and says, 'Welcome to BBC Bristol, great to see you all here this morning, you're all looking very well!' Considering he can't see us at all, two of us are ill and we actually look like drowned rats, this leads to another outbreak of the giggles which probably baffles the listeners back home.

We're in the outskirts of West London by mid-afternoon to drop Mike off for a meeting before driving on round the North Circular to tonight's venue in Edmonton. When Mike gets out to look for a taxi to take him on into town so the van doesn't have to get bogged down in traffic it occurs to me that I'm a ten minute walk from home so I get out too. It's a strange feeling, being back mid-tour on the street where I do my shopping, keeping an eye out for a cab while Mike tells me how he was diagnosed with leukaemia last year and about his subsequent treatment and recovery.

Back home for a couple of hours, time to load the washing machine, then I set off for Edmonton in the car, the idea of a quick getaway after the gig in mind. It starts to rain, traffic slows down to a crawl, and I arrive with about ten minutes to go before doors open, just time to get a quick soundcheck.

The venue is an all-seated theatre, very smart, very un-rock'n'roll, and opens at seven with a curfew at ten-thirty. I'm on early, and I get the feeling that this is not an audience I am going to be able to whip up into a frenzy, but this time I start off with Gary Gilmore's Eyes and it's my best-received set of the tour so far. Unfortunately, when I chat to people in the lobby during the interval some of them tell me they missed my set because they didn't know I was on the bill.

After the show I'm in the car by 11:15 and heading home, but two lanes of the North Circular have been closed and within minutes I'm stuck in a traffic jam, the signs showing roadworks in 800 yards. It takes me an hour and a half to crawl the 800 yards and over two hours to get home.

7th October

Tonight is the real London show, at the Islington Academy. This is a proper rock venue so I feel at home up there on the stage and the gig is a real stormer. At the end of the Dead Men Walking set I join them on stage for their version of Joy Division's 'Transmission.' Over the past few days we've been puzzling over what song we could play together at the end of the show. 'One Chord Wonders' was the favourite, but the band still haven't got around to learning it. Watching them play 'Transmission' last night I realised that not only is it a great song, but it also only has two chords in it, whereas 'One Chord Wonders' has six, so it seems the obvious solution. While we're playing it, Captain wanders over and nonchalantly, deliberately, steps on my foot, pinning me in position while he swings his guitar around wildly at my side, blatantly upstaging me. At the end of the song he innocently removes his foot and releases me as if nothing had happened

There are a few friends and a couple of crates of lager in the subterranean dressing room after the show. Gaye reminds Kirk that they were both at the same art college for a few months and he is genuinely baffled and apologetic that he can't remember it. Captain gets a packet of Hobknobs out of the dressing room and tells me to pass them round. Yes, it's a rock'n'roll aftershow party – with biscuits.

8th October

I take the tube into Kings Cross to meet up with the band at their hotel, then we set off through heavy traffic to Norwich. A diversion leads to more delays and we're running too late to stop for the coffee we're all craving. We finally pull into a petrol station to put some fuel in the van about ten miles from our destination.

It's warm and sunny, ridiculously summer-like for this time of year. We hang around the van while Vince tops up with air and water, then Captain grabs the water hose curiously. 'Look at this Teev…' he says. I bend over to investigate and he switches it on, soaking me, then runs away, shouting 'AAAH – SORRY TEEV!'

Although mellower than in 1977, it's the same old Captain Sensible – he just can't help himself. Some sort of response seems to be required so while I dry myself off I announce that my revenge will come at a time of my own choosing. Back in the van, Captain looks contrite and offers me half his Eccles cake.

I've never been to Norwich before. It looks a bit posh, not exactly punk rock central, but has lots of old houses and churches and quaint street names, which brightens up the walk from the hotel to the venue, which I find just at the bottom of the appropriately-named Music House Lane. They're still having a few technical problems in the soundcheck, but there's wireless internet in the dressing room so I can catch up on my emails while I'm waiting.

I recognise quite a few faces in the crowd when the doors open. Someone offers to buy me a beer, and suggests the organic ale from a local brewery. It's delicious, and when I get on stage I recommend it to the crowd. Not one of my best ideas: by the time I get off stage again it's sold out and I have to go back to the ordinary stuff.

9th October

A long haul across the country to Hereford, on the Welsh borders. It's another beautiful historic town, the venue a smart all-seated theatre. While Vince and Craig set up the stage I sit outside in the waning sunshine for a while, chatting to Kirk. 'You know, T, it's amazing,' he says. 'If anyone had asked me before if I knew Gaye Advert, I would have said no…' He shakes his head in wonder.

Kirk and Vince have both started calling me 'T'.

I get a text from Darren Russell, the promoter of the Wasted punk festival, to tell me he lives nearby so how about meeting up in the bar. I join him there and he tells me that a mate of ours called Chris has made the front page of The Guardian today. He pulls the paper out of his bag and shows me the article. Chris – who we know better as Stretch, punk rock photographer and occasional manager of Max Splodge – has won the world conker fighting championships.

I'm starting to like these theatre gigs. You know it's never really going to go crazy out there, but it gives me the chance to vary the pace of the set a little, talk more, play different songs, and when the audience listens respectfully and applaud warmly like tonight, you know you've done your job.

Backstage, Kirk is of a different opinion. 'T, why are you so angry? Why don't you just relax and chill a bit up there? I bet you've got loads of songs that aren't so ANGRY, why don't you do some of them?'

Another bonus with theatre gigs – they finish early, so it's back to the hotel with a couple of beers. Tomorrow is a day off – the band will be heading in the van down to the South Coast, I've got a cheap advance train ticket back to London for a day at home.

10th October
Day off.

11th October
The coach from London to Portsmouth is not the most luxurious way to travel – very little legroom, and the smell of the onboard toilet wafting up the aisle – but I got a ticket for one pound so I can't complain. I hadn't quite realised how far the venue was from the bus station though. I head off confidently, carrying my guitar and wheeling my bag through the streets, one eye on the map expecting to get there in about ten minutes but it takes me four times that. You really notice how many streets are cobbled when you've got a wheely bag.

The Wedgewood Rooms is a venue I last played on the tour with Tom Robinson. Back then it was red décor, carpets, tables and chairs – now it's another 'black box' rock club, carpets and furnishings gone, a large security barrier in front of the stage. After soundcheck we're told that a meal has been cooked for us, a traditional roast dinner which the crew waste no time in laying in to with enthusiasm. The chef tells me there's a veggie version for me which he will leave on a plate in the kitchen for later – it's getting too near stage time to eat now.

There's a decent crowd by the time I start and they keep on trickling in while I play. I get a good reaction and am happy with the gig.

'Very angry, T,' says Kirk.

While the Dead Men play I grab a beer from the backstage fridge and notice that there is also a tray of dessert jellies covered with whipped cream on the top shelf. It briefly crosses my mind that I could exert a jelly revenge on the Captain for the water-spraying last week, but then I realise the lunacy of it: no one could beat Captain Sensible in a jelly fight.

Afterwards I go out to chat with some friends and quite a few people come over and ask me to sign their tickets, which I notice are printed with the words, *No Support.* One girl asks me to sign her belly. 'I'll never shower again!' she says, then waves her camera at the person next to her. 'Excuse me mate, could you take a photo?' She shows him how to hold it and what button to press. I don't have the heart to tell her she's asked my mate Ray Stevenson, one of the most famous rock photographers in the world, who has photographed Hendrix, Bowie, and the Sex Pistols among others. He gamely takes the snap and hands the camera back to her without letting on.

When everyone has dispersed and the van is being loaded I root around in the kitchen to look for the meal. It has congealed into one solid, fatty lump. They say that revenge is a dish best served cold; but roast potatoes, brussel sprouts and vegetable lasagne is a dish best served warm.

12th October
Today we're playing in Bilsden, a few miles from Wolverhampton, in a rock club that Captain tells me is a favourite with the Damned. Dead Men Walking also had a great gig here last year. We stop off at Birmingham on the way so the band can do an interview with *Kerrang!* Radio. We park in a backstreet, and while the band are in the radio station I hang around outside in the sun. Suddenly a couple of chav-looking lads come running up and for a moment I think I am about to be mugged. One hangs back a little way, while the other leans right up close and says, 'Excuse me, can you sign my duck.'

I'm waiting for the catch, the moment when the other guy moves in – but no, he really does just want me to sign a small rubber duck he's holding out. 'It's for charity,' he says. The thing is covered with smeared scribbles, impossible to make out. The other guy thrusts a duck forward too.

'Can you sign mine as well?'

'Why don't you just write on a load of names yourself?' I ask.

'Oh no, they'd soon catch on to that...'

We're driving into Bilsden, Vince and Craig keeping an eye out for the restaurant they ate at last time. There are a lot of places offering cheap buffets and meal deals but they look pretty grim. 'Look at that,' shouts Craig, pointing at a board outside an Indian takeaway, '50 samosas for five quid!' He says he's tempted to pop back later, but then realises: what the hell would you do with 50 samosas?

We stop by the hotel to check in. Worryingly, it's called The Quality Inn. I never trust hotels with the word 'quality' in the name – I always suspect they're overcompensating. There is a gym, sauna and pool somewhere in the building. 'I expect to see you all in the pool in the morning,' says Liam with a straight face.

I won't be needing the gym: it's a ten minute walk from Reception to my room, which is large but depressing in a way I can't put my finger on. There are some interesting scorch marks on the carpet where the heater has at some point fallen off the wall, strategically covered by a table which is stacked with ranks of leaflets advertising the over-priced services the hotel has to offer. When I get back down to Reception to leave for the gig, Captain is coming back from the bar, complaining loudly, 'Six quid for a salad baguette!'

The rest of the band will stay in the hotel until they get picked up for showtime so it's just me and the crew in the van for the couple of miles drive to the venue, the Robin 2, which turns out to be a surprisingly well-appointed rock club for such an out-of-the-way location. As I get out of the van someone approaches and asks for an autograph. Rather surprised to have been recognised I say okay, and he gets a Stray Cats CD out of his bag.

This may have been a good gig for the rest of the band in the past but it's my first time here and I don't really feel I'm getting the audience on my side. Even my anti-Xmas song, 'Xmas Bloody Xmas,' which I've noticed has been a high point of the set on most of the dates so far seems to fall a bit flat. Luckily the German girl who danced all the way through the set in Liverpool is here again tonight, and as I walk off stage at the end of the set to fast-dwindling applause, she gives a big cheer and shouts, '*ZUGABE!*'

Hooray for the Germans.

Dead Men Walking get a great reception. It's a strange feeling to stand by the side of the stage watching them go down so well when I was having to struggle.

I'm musing on this with the Captain in the upstairs dressing room later, while eating the baked potato and ratatouille that's been warmed up for us for after the show. A girl comes in uninvited and heads straight for Captain. 'You were brilliant,' she tells him. 'You could just say any old rubbish out there and they loved it!'

I'm not sure that was quite the compliment she intended. Then she turns to me. 'And, wow, what a surprise that you were playing tonight! I've got the original single version of Gary Gilmore's Eyes at home. Do you have any idea how much it's worth?'

'Probably quite a bit,' I say.

'Great!' she says. 'I'm going to put it on eBay. I need new curtains.'

13th October

I wait a while with the taps turned on full and eventually some water does come sputtering through. There are sounds of hammering and drilling from somewhere overhead.

On the way to Accrington we stop off in Stoke to get lunch, and while the rest of us settle into an Italian restaurant Captain goes off to get a haircut and comes back half an hour later deeply distressed because the cut makes him look like Paul Weller.

Accrington is even more down-at-heel than last time I was here about ten years ago. Even the Pound Shops are boarded up. The venue is a huge old Victorian municipal building with a pillared portico, the stone festooned with carvings of symbols of strength and prosperity: lions, grapevines and heads of sweetcorn. The lift is broken, which means lugging all the gear up the grand central staircase to the upper floor. We ask the doorman if they have internet access here and he shakes his head. 'Nay lads, that's never come this far.'

You get a friendly welcome here in Lancashire, though, and soon the tea is brewing and a selection of biscuits on a tray is brought out. Captain – who seems to be biscuit monitor on this tour – passes the tray round, then leaves. A moment later he pokes his head back round the door.

'I bloody hate biscuits. They're stuffed full of animal fat. And you know which ones are the worst...*bourbons!*'

Damn! That's the one I chose. It's an Unexpected Meat In A Biscuit Moment. A U.M.I.A.B.M.

Even though there are a few people in by the time I get on stage, they seem marooned in this massive hall. Still, the applause booms and echoes around and it's an enjoyable show. Afterwards I meet up with my mates Carl and Paul, who've come over from Poulton-le-Fylde, near Blackpool, and I arrange to go back there with them so I can stay the night at Paul's place and save myself a hotel bill.

14th October

I dream that one of my back teeth is loose and I fiddle with it and it comes right out. I'm really annoyed because it's going to be difficult to find time to get it fixed back into place on my day off. I'm relieved to wake up and find it was just a dream but then check the tooth and the damn thing actually does come out. Then I realise I'm still dreaming and that when I actually wake up the tooth will be okay. But when I wake up again that turns out to be wishful thinking as I'm holding the tooth in my hand.

Eventually I really wake up, have a shower and brush my teeth very carefully.

Paul drives me down the road to Carl's place and we have breakfast there. A neighbour comes over to tell Carl that there are plans to demolish his house to build a dual carriageway. What a great start to the day!

I take the train into Manchester and arrive at Oxford Road station mid-afternoon, then walk up in the warm sunshine to the venue at the far end of the road. I'm hours early for the gig but am hoping there might be a wireless internet connection in the dressing room. I'm told that there should be, but one of the bands stole the transmitter.

The gig is sensational, best of the tour so far, and I'm in a good mood when I go back with my old friend Mick to stay the night at his place. He even has some pasta back at home ready to microwave, and a couple of bottles of wine.

Unfortunately as soon as my head hits the pillow I feel my sinuses blocking up and I realise it's coming: The Tour Cold.

15th October

It's coming, it's already here, I'm next. Mick drives me, snuffling and sneezing, to the hotel where the band stayed the night, then I set off with them to Nuneaton. We puzzle over one of the street names on the way in: while stopped at the lights we see we are on 'Poanne Pingway.' It takes a few moments before we realise that some wag has changed all the R's into P's and we are actually on 'Roanne Ringway.' If you're going to mess around with lettering on signs, there are better options around Nuneaton, which lies on the River Anker.

We stop off at the hotel, a Travelodge next to a Harvester restaurant on the outskirts of town with an accompanying odour of rancid fat. Captain wrinkles his nose, 'Hmm, reminds me of the smell of the crematorium where I used to work.'

It's too far to walk to the venue, so I get straight back in the van with the crew after I've checked in because I want to make sure I get a soundcheck. By the time we get to the club I am in full cold, aching all over, head blocked up, nose streaming and all I really want to do is get today over with. Luckily tomorrow is a day off and I'll have some recovery time at home. Meanwhile I sit out the couple of hours left before the gig, hoping that I'll be fit enough to play. As bad luck would have it, today is the first time on the tour that there's no backstage, just a little room at the back of the club, which used to be the kitchen but has just had all its fittings ripped out and is now being used as storage space. The sound guy points out a mark on the wall where the dumb waiter used to be.

'Can you believe it – it cost us fifteen grand to get that dumb waiter and when we took it out we couldn't give it away. We even put it on eBay: *Dumb Waiter free to good home,* but no one would take it. It ended up in the skip.'

Liam phones the hotel to warn the band about conditions at the venue and they decide to come at the last minute: Vince will pick them up, they'll come up the back steps from the van and get straight onstage, then leave for the hotel right after the last number.

Stage time, and I play a high power set to try and sweat out the cold. It goes well, there are just a couple of moment when I have to clamp down on a sneeze in mid song, requiring some tortuous facial expressions. The worst one is during my punk rock poem. It's hard to hide a sneeze when you're reciting a poem. My sinuses are so blocked that the sound I'm hearing from the stage monitors is whooshing and distorting as if it's being put through a giant wah wah pedal, one minute almost inaudible, the next tortuously loud. It's a relief when it's all over, but I'm happy with the way it went – now I just have to keep it together until the song I play with the band later. While they're on stage I stand at the back of the club near the old kitchen, so I can dive in there for the odd sneezing bout. It's also right opposite the club toilets, so quite a few of the crowd pass by and say how much they enjoyed my set. The conversation usually starts with a hello and a handshake, which tonight is possibly the most unhygienic greeting ever, as I've just sneezed and they've just come out of the loo.

Then I'm up again for 'Transmission' and it goes fine. I throw even more shapes than usual, mainly because I'm surreptitiously trying to wipe my nose on my sleeve while playing guitar. A couple more songs from the band and it's all over; they're down the back steps and in the van back to the hotel, and I'm hanging around the club talking to a few fans while the equipment gets packed away. The German girl who has been at a few gigs on this tour and is always down the front dancing says hello and tells me that although she lives in Berlin she is actually Dutch. Hooray for the Dutch! Her boyfriend takes a photo of us so I get to see exactly how red my nose is.

One hour and a couple of medicinal beers later we're just about ready to leave so I head down the back stairs and find Mike sitting in his car. He'd been hoping to drive back to his home in North Wales straight after the show but the car's broken down and he's still waiting for the rescue services. 'Bit embarrassing really,' he says. 'I've already arranged to part exchange this car. It's going to look great when the guy comes over with the new one and I say, "Thanks mate, there's yours up on the back of the AA truck."'

After nightfall Nuneaton turns into chav central. There are loads of dangerously drunk people roaming the streets, boy racers screeching round corners on two wheels, and the potential for violence in the air. One of the audience is threatening to have a go at Liam for not letting him meet the band, refusing to believe that they have already left. We're glad to get away.

Back at the hotel I switch on the television for a few minutes of News 24 while I rinse out my handkerchiefs in the sink and hang them out around the room. There's a piece about the last ever gig at CBGBs in New York tonight. Then something about a baker who has made a wedding dress entirely out of profiteroles.

16th October
Day off.

17th October
Like a hurricane of the nose, my cold has blown itself out and I'm on the train to Leeds feeling a bit spaced-out and shaky but otherwise okay. I'm particularly looking forward to tonight's gig because it's in a historic venue, the City Varieties Theatre, which I remember from a television programme in my youth called 'The Good Old Days' – a high camp recreation of music hall with the audience all dressed in Edwardian costume, and a dandy master of ceremonies introducing each of the 'turns' with a string of tongue-twisting adjectives which had the crowd *oohing* and *aahing* at each successive verbal excess.

Television plays tricks: the theatre is much smaller than I expected. It's a beautiful building, all seated, decked out in red velvet with a balcony and royal boxes along the sides of the upper floor, but it's surprisingly petite – a few good strides would take you across the entire stage. I'm a bit worried about the fact that I'm supposed to play at eight this evening, exactly the same time the doors are advertised as opening, and I go down to the ticket desk to check if that's really the schedule. The two ladies there tell me that the doors are actually opening at 7:30, but they'll be locking them at eight. I ask them if they're joking, and they explain that they have to lock the doors before the show starts because they've had gangs of youths come storming into the building and disrupting the performances. Anyone who arrives after eight these days has to ring the bell to be let in.

There's a palpable sense of history to the shabby, cramped dressing rooms backstage. I can only imagine what it was like 150 years ago for troupes of music hall stars doing full costume changes – luckily I only have to change my t-shirt. There are still quite a few empty seats when I start but the bell must be ringing away downstairs because people gradually trickle in. The incongruousness of the venue seems to add to the enjoyment of the evening. There is an intimacy which makes tonight the funniest gig of the tour so far, the audience shouting out so much witty stuff between the songs that even Captain Sensible can hardly get a word in. Tonight's a big one for him – not only is he a fan of the venue, but it's the launch of an alternative political party he's involved in, the Blah! Party. The campaign is being sponsored by a company who make potato crisps. There are quite a few mentions of the brand during the course of the evening and free bags of crisps are thrown out to the crowd. Honestly, the Blah! Party has barely started and already it's embroiled in corruption.

After the show as we walk through the city in the drizzle to find an Indian restaurant, promoter John Keenan tells me that Laurel and Hardy once played at the City Varieties. What I wouldn't pay for a time machine to take me back to see that. In the restaurant Captain realises he has forgotten his glasses so I read out the vegetarian dishes on the menu to him. He offers me a position in his government.

18th October
Up country, across country, a long journey to Glasgow. The audience are enthusiastically on my side right from the start and it turns out to be one of the best gigs of the tour. Then there's a lot of hanging around, the tiny dressing room crammed with people who have had a lot to drink, which seems to makes them larger and louder. I don't know any of them. Eventually the crowd disperses and the band gather out in the back yard in the drizzle by the van, keen to go to the hotel and finally get some peace, but we can't leave yet because Liam is still in the club's office sorting out the business and he has the van key with him. Captain sighs and puts down his bag.

TV SMITH

'It's the first ever known case of the band desperate to get *in* the van.'

19th October

This makes a change: it's a privately run hotel instead of the usual chain. No danger that the rooms will all be identical here – something I get the chance to prove when I find that the extractor fan in my bathroom sounds like a malfunctioning lawnmower. I go to the lobby and get a different room which lies in a far flung corridor where, apparently, chambermaids fear to tread. The extractor fan in this one doesn't work at all. But there is a slightly better class of complimentary biscuit.

At the venue Kirk, Captain and I go on a fruitless hunt for a wireless internet connection which is supposed to be beaming out of a nearby arts centre but is in fact nowhere to be found. Still, some of the residents of dreary Warrington had their afternoons enlivened by the sight of three old punk rockers wandering around the streets with their laptops open in front of them, going: 'Nope, nothing here either…'

One of the places we visit is a restaurant which turns out to be preparing the food to take over to our backstage. Extremely good it turns out to be too: a home-baked ciabatta roll filled with grilled goats cheese and artichokes. Sandwich of the tour!

But oh my, it's another of those massive municipal halls and very little chance of packing it out. Liam puts my stage time back a bit in the hope there will be a few people in later, but by the time I start there are still not many there. Still, relieved of any expectation that this one is going to be a rocker I just get out there and relax and enjoy it, and get a good response. The Dead Men show is a few notches down in excitement levels from usual too but still goes down well and Mike soon has them singing along and forgetting the fact they're standing in a half-empty hall on a Thursday night in Warrington. Bit of a let down after the last couple of nights, but what a great sandwich!

Even better: the bar is open back at the hotel. We settle ourselves in there for a while. Liam's girlfriend is here for the evening, and as there was no one at home to look after their dog Shady, she's bought him with her. All us punk rockers suddenly go all soppy when dogs are around. In the end I only have one glass of wine from the bar but it lasts out remarkably well with the aid of the bottle of wine from the dressing room that somehow ended up in my bag, and in the small hours I stagger back through the lost corridors, up stairs, down ramps, around corners and past the slumbering kitchens to my room.

TALES OF THE EMERGENCY SANDWICH

20<u>th</u> October

By the time I find my way out of the hotel everyone else has already gathered at the van and Craig is packing the bags into the back. Vince has just handed the dog's lead to Captain who is scampering off into the distance with him. Vince shouts after them: 'Make sure you bring him back safely, Shady!'

The hotel in Darwen is a grand old building on a hill above the town, and we are shown to our rooms in a modern extension which is currently being renovated. We edge past the workmen and everyone disappears into their rooms. I look at my key tag, and say to the guy from Reception, 'So that's my room down there, is it, just past the stepladders?'

'Ah, yes, ah ha, if you can just get around them…'

But when I get my bags and guitar around the stepladders I find the door to the room wide open and a trail of plaster dust footprints across the floor, so I go back to the lobby and ask for a different room. The one they give me is in the old building and must be above the kitchen because when I unplug the scent dispenser the room quickly fills with the smell of chicken fat. The toilet has also had one flush less than necessary after the last occupant. Twenty minutes after I get in the room there's a knock on the door and I open it to find two hotel staff who are there to explain how to switch on the radiator as 'the nights get very chilly up here in Lancashire.' Funnily enough I already know how to switch on a radiator. I'm fifty years old and I've been around a bit. Shortly afterwards there's another knock on the door and when I open it one there is someone outside holding a television.

'Just come to give you a new television, sir.' Looks very like the old one, which he carries out. Ten minutes later he comes back with a remote control. I hunt through the thick wallet of hotel information and eventually find a 'Do Not Disturb' sign.

Towards the end of the afternoon we head off to the venue. On the way we pass a large pile of rubble where some old buildings are being pulled down. Kirk's so impressed that when we get to the venue he goes back on foot to take a photo.

The venue is a nice intimate little theatre, another all-seater. I'd been told by the Captain that it's a great room, but so quiet between songs that you can hear a pin drop. I take a pin with me to test this theory, and – what do you know – after explaining to the audience what I'm going to do I let go of the pin and everyone in the place hears it hit the stage. It gets a big round of applause. I play quite a few slower songs, keeping away from the punk stuff, and when I get backstage afterwards Captain says, 'I really enjoyed the set tonight, Teev.

Watched the whole thing, nice choice of songs.'

Kirk says, 'So you decided to follow my advice, eh, T? See – you're not really that angry, are you? It's all a pretence! T, you...you...*SELL OUT!*'

21st October

Somehow all the stuff doesn't fit in the back of the van any more. Craig has one foot up on the bumper and is peering in with a confused expression, muttering: 'Day 207. Craig is losing his mind.'

Driving out through the town we make a quick stop for a group photo in front of the rubble; it's a lovely sunny day, good rubble photo weather. Then it's a long drive up the motorway and on to the A roads for the stretch across the Lake District to Whitehaven, far out to the west on the coast. We stop in sleepy Keswick, a picture postcard town full of shoppers and tourists. There's a market in the high street, with stalls selling local produce and knick-knacks, as well as one with some ultra-powerful binoculars set up in front of it. I have a look through one pair which are focused on a distant chimney. You can see every brick! Captain stops at a record stall and buys a second hand copy of Hawkwind's 'Space Ritual.' Then we all split up to pursue our various dietary needs: some go for a pub lunch, while Captain and I end up in a tea room with a goat's cheese and sun-dried tomato salad and an organic baguette. Later we meet up again with Kirk and have a look at the exhibits outside the mining museum, old pit carts and cutting machinery preserved in good condition but painted so garishly they look like toys. Kirk spots some rubble and Captain takes a photo of him lying in it.

We see the rest of our party walking past and accompany them back to the car park. At that moment the heavens open and we get soaked. 'Why now?' moans Jim, then looks up. 'It's that *same* cloud,' he mutters darkly.

Back at the van, I notice Liam has a cup of Costa's coffee.

'Bloody hell, Liam, you found a Costa's in Keswick?'

'I nearly found a Kentucky Fried Chicken as well, mate. I saw the KFC sign up the street and went to have a look but it turned out to be a computer shop. Very disappointed I was.'

There's no time to visit the Cumberland Pencil Museum, which the brochure boasts is 'the only attraction in the world devoted exclusively to the rich and fascinating history of the pencil' and whose star exhibit is the world's longest coloured pencil – we have a soundcheck to get to.

Sleepy Whitehaven. I notice US resident Jim raise a somewhat cynical eyebrow as we pass the 'Manhattan Diner' on the way in. The venue is a dull municipal hall, large and lacking in atmosphere. There are some depressingly decrepit dressing rooms under the stage, not a nice place to hang around so I wander down to the seafront. I don't see another person as I amble through the streets and there is no one but me on the bleak harbour jutting out into the choppy grey sea. A sign warns me to walk with care because the stone blocks underfoot have been worn uneven by the battering of the elements. Darkness is falling, the waves are surging around below me and the wind is knocking me off balance. I have a bit of a 'French Lieutenant's Woman' moment.

The skies are lowering in a way that suggests the cloud from Bristol will be here soon, so I make my way to shore and take a different route back to the venue to see a bit more of the town. On the way I notice a newsstand with a banner headline from the local paper: 'MAN THREATENS TO CHOP OFF WIFE'S HEAD.' Maybe Whitehaven isn't as sleepy as I thought. I remove the banner and take it back to the venue to warn the rest of the band.

There's a really good reaction to the show considering the size and emptiness of the room, and loads of people come up to say thanks while I'm hanging around at the bar after the set. One guy says he was surprised to see that I was playing today: he saw me getting the train back down to London after the Nuneaton gig. 'Very Woody Guthrie,' he says, 'climbing on to the train with just your guitar and bag.'

I have a chat with Kalle and Annette, who hosted my TUTS fan club gig in their bar in Essen earlier this year, and who've come over from Germany to see this gig tonight and the New York Dolls in London on Sunday. Unfortunately they met Rancid Tom earlier and were still in the pub while I was playing so all three of them missed it.

While I watch the Dead Men's set from the wings I notice a sign saying: *SAFETY CURTAIN MECHANISM. To operate CURTAIN DRENCHER move lever in direction of arrow.* I'm not sure what would happen but it sounds wet. I could have done it, Captain.

And now it's late, and we're going to get in the van and drive down to Birmingham, which will get us halfway towards the South London gig tomorrow, stopping off in Keswick on the way to pick up Mike's bag which he accidentally left hanging on the back of a chair in a restaurant this afternoon. Four, maybe five hours on the road ahead of us before we can get some sleep. The horror.

22nd October
Captain's excited about this one – we're playing in the Ashchurch Theatre, part of the Fairfield Halls complex where he had a job as a toilet cleaner before he

joined the Damned, so it's a trip down memory lane for him. Not only that, he's arranged for his old mate Johnny Moped to come on stage and sing 'Darling Let's Have Another Baby' during the Dead Men's set. I haven't seen Johnny for a few years and when he comes into the dressing room he plainly doesn't recognise me, because he asks me if the Captain is around then says, 'Er, in case you're wondering I'm Johnny Moped and I'm supposed to be doing a guest spot with the group tonight.'

Johnny is with some other ex-members of his band, including Dave Berk, who was the musical mastermind behind the whole thing and seems to be here pretty much as Johnny's minder. We reminisce about the Moped comeback gig in the early eighties at the Marquee, where all the band came on stage in dresses, swapped instruments half way through, and then got Kirsty MacColl up from the audience to duet on 'Darling, Let's Have Another Baby,' which – by the way – contains the heart-warming couplet, *'Darling, if you ever leave me I'll cry a million tears, I'll go to the nearest boozer and drink ten pints of beer.'*

There's just time at soundcheck for Johnny to have a quick run-through of the song, and as he bellows away rather out-of-tune on stage with Captain bravely keeping pace on guitar I notice some bemused looks exchanged between members of the band and crew who obviously have no idea of the punk rock phenomenon that is the one and only Johnny Moped.

Not long until doors open, and I need to figure out the route to East Croydon railway station so I can get home after the gig. Captain is brushing his teeth in the dressing room when he sees me puzzling over the map, and offers to help. 'Actually it's easiest to just show you,' he says, with a mouth full of toothpaste. We walk out through the drizzle into the multi storey car park next to the theatre, Captain pointing out the short cut to the station with his toothbrush and explaining how he used to play here as a kid, him and his mates terrorising the security guard by calling him names and running away.

It's the poshest theatre of the tour so far, and the hardest venue to get anything going; a large room and a very small audience spread out sparsely among the rows of seats. There's a good sound, and I'm happy with the way I play, but there's no atmosphere at all. When I go out to chat to people in the foyer during the interval someone says to me, 'Great set TV, but please NEVER play this place again!'

I get back to the dressing rooms just as the Dead Men are getting on stage. Johnny is already pacing around in full stage gear, which includes an extravagant suede jacket with tassels and studs but curiously no shirt or shoes, thus exposing a bosom many women would kill for and the longest toenails in rock'n'roll. An hour later his time comes, and I watch from the side of the stage as he sings 'Darling' to a hero's welcome – this is his home patch after all, and he is rarely seen on stage because his wife has banned him from playing gigs. I go back to congratulate him afterwards but he's not around. Dave tells me, 'He's just popped outside for a smoke. He may be a while as he doesn't have any cigarettes so he'll be rolling one up from any dog ends he can find.'

Then I'm dashing through the multi-storey car park with my bag and guitar, and onto the station platform in time for the last train into central London and a couple of nights in my own bed.

23rd October
Day off.

24th October
It's hard to get back into the tour rhythm after a free day and we're already late by the time we near the border into Wales towards the end of the afternoon. As we head towards the Severn Bridge, Captain is busy applying antiseptic cream to his finger – he's played guitar so hard over the last few weeks that it's starting to swell up – when he suddenly realises where we are and looks up in a panic. 'Vince! Can't we avoid the bridge? Isn't there another route?' I knew he was afraid of flying, but I didn't know he was worried about bridges. He turns to me and holds out a hand, 'Look at that…!' He is shaking and has broken out in a sweat. We're approaching the bridge now, though, and there's no way to avoid it. 'I'll be all right if I keep me eyes closed. Teev, pass me a beer…'

None of us usually drink during the day, but we have a box full of beers on board, rescued from dressing rooms along the way over the last few weeks. Captain opens the beer I hand him and downs it in two gulps, then slightly calmer explains that he can't stand any high bridges, but the original Severn Bridge is reputed to have been built on the cheap and is a potential death trap. The new one, a few miles down the estuary, lower and built to a better standard, would have been a lot more bearable, he says. Vince turns from the front seat. 'We're not going over the original bridge Cap, we're going over the new one.'

Captain says, *Burrrp!!*

By the time we've checked into the hotel and then got stuck in the Cardiff rush hour traffic on the way to the venue there are barely a couple of hours left before doors open. An attentive lady working for the venue shows me where the dressing room is, explains that it's normally the conference room, tells me about the timings for tonight, then says, 'You are Liam?'

Do I look like a tour manager?

Captain has arranged for ex-Damned and Eddie And The Hot Rods bass player Paul Gray to come up and guest tonight on the Hot Rods song 'Do Anything You Wanna Do,' and they are trying it out in the dressing room, hampered by the fact that Paul hasn't played it for about twenty years, and the Dead Men will be playing it in a different key than he's used to. While they run through it a few times, his young son totters up, points at me and tells his mum delightedly, 'Grandad!'

Do I *look* like…oh, never mind.

I take Mike's advice and say 'Good Evening Cardiff!' in Welsh as soon as I get on stage. It's not the best start to a gig, as clearly no one understands what I've said, but after that things go extremely well and afterwards I can't get back to the dressing room because I'm surrounded by people congratulating me, and I then get diverted to the merchandising stand where I sell loads. Someone who looks vaguely familiar comes up and says, 'Remember me? I used to put on gigs for Cheap at the Yew Tree Inn in the 80's and you all used to sleep on my floor afterwards. I once had a band pull out of a benefit concert at the last minute, so I phoned you up the day before and asked if you could do it – for no money – and you did!'

We did too.

I'm still there at the back of the room signing stuff when the Dead Men take the stage. After a slight altercation between those factions of the audience who want to stand and those who want everyone to sit down, the band plays a great gig, and it's really Mike's night as he has everyone singing along with 'New South Wales' and other Welsh-leaning crowd-pleasers. Paul gets up for 'Do Anything You Wanna Do' and switches all the knobs on Captain's bass guitar and amplifier up to full, which makes it stunningly loud. He was once in UFO, you know.

Afterwards it's all back to the conference room for take-away pizza, then we get in the van and drive back to the hotel, where most of us stay in the lobby to use the free wireless internet access. Liam heads back out to the van with Captain to take him to the nearest hospital to get his finger checked out, but half an hour later they arrive back with the news that there's a four hour wait at the A&E ward so they're going to have to risk leaving it. Just one date to go.

TALES OF THE EMERGENCY SANDWICH

25th October
The venue in Worksop is only a ten minute walk away from the hotel, so the crew suggest I stay there and relax for a couple of hours while they set up the stage. There's a wireless internet connection in the room, so I sort through my emails and find directions to the venue, then there's just time for a change of strings, a coffee and a complimentary biscuit before I head off through the dark rainy streets to the old Regal cinema, where I arrive soaked to the skin. 'At least now I don't need a shower!' I say brightly to the lady behind the ticket desk who regards me with a pitying look as I drip my way through the foyer.

Things are going very slowly at the venue: the stage has been set up, but the local sound man is struggling to get everything working. Mike is backstage working on his laptop, editing up a film about his recovery from leukaemia for the hospital that treated him. We have a chat about the tour and he says what fun it's been and offers me the support slot for an Alarm gig in Edinburgh next month. Liam has just come into the dressing room and points out that if I'm doing that, I could play the Spear Of Destiny gig in Glasgow the next day. Great! Even though the tour's nearly over it looks like at least some of us will be meeting up again soon. These people have become my friends over the last three weeks and I'll miss them.

Tonight is the last gig though, and when the sound problems are finally sorted out, the doors finally opened and people finally in – full house by the look of it – I am the first victim of the traditional last-night-of-tour pranks. Captain wanders on stage between songs and tells me that the crew have requested that I play 'Xmas Bloody Xmas.' Halfway through the song he reappears with a large broom and starts sweeping up around me, then suddenly Vince and Craig dash onstage with a Xmas tree, hurriedly drape some fairy lights over it and plug them in, then stand beside it like choirboys, singing along with the chorus. When it's over we all give the tree a good kicking.

After the show they tell me the reason they suggested I stay in the hotel earlier was so they could drive round to a local DIY superstore to get the tree.

My set went down really well, and as I watch from the wings I see the Dead Men are also having a great show. Everyone in the room is enjoying it and I'm looking forward to getting back up there for 'Transmission.' When the time finally comes, I'm full of energy and ready to jump around on stage and throw some shapes with Captain as usual, but as I plug in the guitar he leans over and whispers, 'Not too much dancing around tonight, Teev, I've just had a curry.'

We're on the extended ending to the song when I notice Jim gesturing at me with one of his drumsticks and I slowly realise he's offering it to me to hit the final beat. I let the guitar ring on, grab the stick and raise it over my head, and me and Jim smash down on the cymbal together. High Five! What a nice way to end the tour.

I spend some time with the audience in the bar after the gig and get a lot of great feedback, many of them saying that tonight was the best gig they've ever been to. It's a good feeling, but by the time I get back to the dressing room, everyone is packing up to go back to the hotel, and Mike has already left for home.

At the hotel, Captain – nursing his increasingly-swollen finger – goes straight to his room, the rest of us sit in the bar for a goodnight and goodbye drink.

26th October
When we gather at Reception at midday, Craig has already left for home on the train – his last day as a roadie over, next he'll be back in his regular post as bass player for the Alarm. We leave Captain at the hotel where he'll be staying another night, ready for a Goth festival in Whitby with the Damned tomorrow. He is just about to head off to hospital to have his finger treated. The rest of us have a long drive back to London, during which Jim spends much of the time on the phone trying to sort out problems with his upcoming Japanese and Australian tours, and Kirk is deep in discussion with Liam about the Spear Of Destiny tour they'll be starting soon. It's strange to feel this group of people I've been with for the last three weeks splintering to follow their own ways.

We pull up outside my place and start unloading all the remaining unsold merchandise. 'Blimey, this isn't very punk rock is it?' says Liam with a grin, eyeing up my flat as he helps carry the boxes inside. 'I was expecting all banners hanging outside with 'CONFLICT' painted on them, and graffiti and Anarchy signs and all of that…'

Kirk says 'You fraud!' and lobs an empty can of Lilt from the van over the gate. I pick it up and neatly drop it into the plastic sack in the alcove. 'Round here, we recycle our cans,' I tell him primly.

We say our goodbyes and promise we'll all meet up again soon. As the van pulls away, Vince leans his head out of the window and calls back, 'Oh, just one other thing…' and at the top of his voice shouts, 'HAPPY FUCKIN' CHRISTMAS!!'

What will the neighbours think?

6. SMALL WORLD (2007)

Part One: Finland

<u>22nd January</u>
I'm playing a short tour in Finland, then flying to the other side of the world for my first ever gigs in Australia. It's going to be an interesting few weeks.

It's been late coming, but winter has finally arrived in Finland: yesterday I checked the weather for Joensuu, one of the places I'll be playing in a few days time, and the forecast was minus 29 degrees.

On the plane, someone has altered the COAT HOOK button on the seat in front of me to read GOAT HOOK. Plane journeys can be boring.

My friend Tommi is there to meet me at the airport and we take the bus into Helsinki. He shows me the local paper which has a photo of me and a piece about the gig in it, which is encouraging: it's been three years since I last came to Finland and tonight is a Monday, so I've been worrying if people will actually come. Tommi points out an article on Brian May on the opposite page and says with some satisfaction, 'There, his photo is slightly smaller and he has terrible hair.' According to the interview, Queen have made a new album. *'We went into the studio without any ideas and came out with a brilliant album,'* Tommi reads. 'He is a very modest man.'

I check into my hotel on the way to the Semifinal club, and notice that next to it there is an 'Aussie Bar.' I wonder if there will be a Finnish Bar when I get to Australia.

The Semifinal used to overlook a large open space, but now the entire area has been filled with a shopping centre. I'm pleased to see that the Semifinal hasn't changed though – it's always been one of my favourite clubs. Tommi and I say hello to the manager Tomi (pay attention at the back) and to the sound engineer, who I'm surprised to find is Mikko, who I toured with in Germany recently when he was mixing the sound for a Finnish band called the Tigerbombs. I have to borrow a guitar cable from him as I realise I've left mine back at the hotel but apart from that soundcheck goes swiftly. After it I trudge back through the snow to fetch the cable, and when I eventually get back to the venue I notice Tommi and his wife Annastina chatting with a few friends in the Ilves bar upstairs.

'Annastina says she just had a look downstairs and there was no one there,' says Tommi. When he sees me looking worried he hurries to reassure me:

'When she says no one there, she means no one we *know* there.'

One of his friends pipes in, 'Yes, the place is full but there is absolutely no one there.'

Ah, Finland.

On the dressing room wall there is still a list of timings for the bands who played yesterday. At 20:30 it was Anal Nosorog. A sticker nearby describes them as a 'bulldozer fuckin' grind core scum band.'

Well, there'll be none of that tonight. The club has filled nicely, there's a cheer as I get on stage and I play for two hours and get loads of encores. The place empties rapidly afterwards because most people have to be at work tomorrow. By midnight – 10:00 pm English time – I'm the only one left so I grab a couple of beers and head back to the hotel for an early night. There is an arctic wind blowing and the temperature has plummeted. I'm fairly insulated by the heat I've worked up on stage, but unfortunately I have lost a glove so the other hand soon goes numb. I hurry past the Aussie Bar – 'Service by descendants of criminals!' boasts the poster – and into the warm haven of my hotel room, where on the T.V. there is a programme with Russian comediennes doing stand-up. I soon switch over to an animated cartoon featuring some Eskimos who are hiding from a herd of reindeer under their canoes.

23rd January

Mid-morning, Jukka phones to invite me around to his place in Tampere tonight to have a sauna and something to eat with him and Harri, the tour agent. 'That way you will get at least one good meal while you are here,' he says. He also promises to meet me at the station to walk me over to my hotel.

Here's a tip. If you go to Finland in the winter and travel by train, don't put your suitcase on the rack above your seat. As it warms up, all the snow caught in the wheels will melt and drip on your head.

When we get to Tampere the train comes to a stop before reaching the station but people start getting off anyway so I throw down my bag and guitar into the snow and jump down after them. After dragging the suitcase past a couple more carriages I reach the platform and am able to start wheeling it again, although it's a bumpy ride over the packed ice and grit. At the far end of the platform I find Jukka. 'Usually the trains stop here,' he says.

As we walk through the town towards the hotel, Jukka tells me about a Finnish promoter who invited a well-known reggae star over for a tour and decided to accompany him on the long drives, even though he could hardly speak any English. The singer wasn't very communicative either, and over the course of the following days the silences became more and more uncomfortable. Eventually, one day as they were passing a porcelain factory called Arabia, known to all Finns for its manufacture of toilet bowls, the promoter decided to lighten the mood. He nudged the reggae star, pointed across the snowy fields towards the factory and shouted, 'Look! Arabia!'

That was the only joke he attempted on the entire tour.

Punk Lurex OK, who I recorded an EP with a few years ago, broke up recently and the two girls in it, Ritta and Tiina went on to form a new band called Tina, which means 'Tin.' Pay attention at the back. At six, I meet with the band for a rehearsal, ready for the gig we will be playing together on Saturday. It's the same studio where we recorded the EP and the sound engineer there is now the guitarist in the new band. We intend to play four songs together at the gig, and after we've tried them a couple of times everything sounds fine, even though Ritta couldn't be there because she lives in Seinäjoke. When I play in Seinäjoke on Friday she will be in Tampere rehearsing with Tina. As we go back into the control room, drummer Manu groans, 'I've been playing for thirty years but this punk stuff is exhausting. I'm too old for this! I'm 47!'

Tiina asks me how old I am now, and I tell her, fifty. 'In Finland when you become fifty,' she tells me, 'they give you a black walking stick with a silver top.'

Maybe I could do with one. On the way out I skid on the packed snow for a few feet and Tiina says, 'Uuups, that was close...'

I tell her my secret fear that I will fall over somewhere over the next few days and arrive in Australia with a broken arm. 'Hello Australia, I'm finally here! I can't play guitar...but I'm here!'

Manu drives me over to Jukka's home, where he is busy in the kitchen, while Harri sits at the table with a beer. Jukka puts the food out and gestures at me to help myself. I spoon some rice into my bowl then realise I have made a mistake when I see that Harri is spooning soup into his. I apologise to Jukka and explain, 'I wasn't sure if it was soup or sauce.'

'Erm, I am not sure either,' says Jukka,

After the meal and a few beers the sauna is ready so we strip off and get in there for a while, which brings on the necessary calm that goes so well with a couple more beers.

In the course of the relaxed conversation that follows, Jukka tells me of the time some years ago when he was attending a festival in Finland and found himself staying in the same hotel as the Ramones. He was a huge fan but promised to himself that if he met them he wouldn't embarrass himself by saying, *I'm a big fan – I have all your records!* After all, they'd have heard it a thousand times before. One day he was in the hotel lobby talking to a rather strange guy who was known for having more musicians' autographs than anyone else in the world. He'd even got in the Guinness Book Of Records for it. Out of curiosity, Jukka asked if he could see a few of the autographs, but was rather surprised when afterwards the guy told him that now he expected to be paid. Jukka reluctantly agreed to give him something and took out his wallet, but the guy suddenly grabbed it out of his hands and started removing money from it. As Jukka tried to get his wallet back one of the prized autographs fell to the floor and the frame broke. Even though it was only a cheap frame, the guy demanded fifty euros for it. After an increasingly bad-tempered discussion Jukka eventually paid just to shut him up. Extremely annoyed now, he swung round to leave and walked right into someone coming the other way, almost knocking him off his feet. To his horror, he saw that it was Johnny Ramone. 'I'm so sorry!' he wailed. 'I'm a big fan! I have all your records…!'

Harri drives me back to the hotel, where I put on the T.V. to find a rather good animated film, and when that's over there's a documentary which features fooootage from a miniature camera going up someone's rectum.

24<u>th</u> January
The hotel throws me out at midday, and I spend a couple of hours in an internet café before getting the train for Turku. Before long we are travelling through a blizzard, white-out conditions with the snow sweeping horizontally over the fields. At Turku I find that my new wheelie-suitcase is impossible to roll through 12 inches of fresh snow and I have to resort to carrying it by the handle. It's heavy.

I wait in the station café until tonight's promoter Janne arrives, then he helps carry my things over to the hotel. There are still a couple of hours before soundcheck so Janne heads back home, where he was in the middle of cooking dinner for his family when he got my text message to say I'd arrived. He offers to take me to a restaurant later, but I say it's not necessary and instead drop into a nearby supermarket and buy a couple of bread rolls, some cheese, salad and fruit. In the hotel I wash the lettuce and tomatoes in the sink then dry them on the bath towel. There's a microwave oven – something I'm not that familiar with – and I pop a bread roll in there for a few seconds to warm it up, but nothing much happens so I set the dial for another minute. When the roll comes out it is like a rock. I don't have a knife, so I attempt to cut it with a plastic spoon, which melts.

TALES OF THE EMERGENCY SANDWICH

At 7:30 Janne knocks on the door. The weather is so bad that he's brought his car, so together we go to pick up the sound man, who is over at the TVO club, where I played the first time I ever came to Turku. It's the same sound man, Tomi. Pay attention at the back

The club I'm playing tonight, The Paivakoti, is chilly inside and Janne goes around the place switching up the radiators. We look out at the snow swirling around outside. 'Normally we would have this much snow over the whole winter, today we've had it all at once,' says Janne. We're both a bit worried that no one will turn up tonight because of it.

Soundcheck is over quickly but I'm not due on stage until eleven so there is a lot of hanging around. At eight the club opens, and three people wander in. 'People so early – that's a good sign,' says Janne, brightening. He suggests that to kill some time we could go into the park opposite and make snow angels.

'Snow angels?' I say. 'In England we call them snowmen.'

'Snow angels are different. You lie down on your back in the snow with your arms outstretched, then stand up and all the snow drops off your arms like wings.'

Maybe another time.

Still two hours to go before I play, and Tomi decides to go home for a while. Shortly afterwards Janne does the same, so I go into the backstage room with a beer and play guitar for a while. By eleven the place is packed and the gig is tremendous. I sit on the stage afterwards and sell some CDs and it seems everyone in the room wants to tell me how much they enjoyed the gig. It's very gratifying. One girl comes over shyly after most of the rest of the people have gone and gives me a charm bracelet, and a fluorescent wristband with wording on it that reads, *Odotettavissa selkenevää*: 'Everything is getting better.'

Janne drives me and Tomi back to our respective sleeping places after the gig. It's stopped snowing now, but the snow ploughs are out in force, trundling out of every side street and chugging along the main roads, often in tandem. So many snow ploughs. I never knew there were so many snow ploughs.

Back at the hotel I switch on the television. There is nothing on.

25th January

A crystal clear sunny day, the snow sparkling pristine on the streets. I'm at the station by eleven for today's eight hour journey to Joensuu, far out to the east near the Russian border.

Perhaps a snack to while away the time? In the buffet car I'm tempted by the '*Jättilihapiirakka* – Giant meat pie' (but what does giant meat taste like?)

and the '*Half pipe* – warm sandwich,' but settle for a cheese and salad rye bread roll. Which reminds me – back in the fridge at the hotel in Turku there is a bag of washed lettuce.

Much later I am standing in the snow outside Joensuu station. Night has fallen. The promoter, Miko, is not there to meet me and hasn't answered the SMS I sent him asking how to find the gig. There are no taxis.

I start to trudge my way towards the lights of the town I can see in the distance over a long bridge crossing a pitch black river, and along the way notice a town map on a bus shelter. I have the address of the venue on the tour schedule that Harri has given me and locate the street, which turns out to be just over the other side of the bridge. It's still a struggle to get there though. About halfway across the bridge, the grit underfoot starts to become scarce, my shoes can't get any purchase on the packed snow, the bag starts to slide rather than roll, and as I drag it along behind me I find I am pulling myself backwards almost as fast as I am pulling the bag forwards. That Isaac Newton: he knew what he was on about.

By the time I reach the club, my hands are burning with the cold even though I'm wearing gloves. The sound man sees me walk in, introduces himself as Antte, and we go downstairs to the venue, which is a horrible disco. I'm playing at the far end of the dance floor, no stage, just a small area cleared of tables and chairs with a chest-high barrier around it. 'We have to have that there because all the drunk people break things and fight,' he explains. 'By the way, we were expecting you at 17:00…'

'My train didn't even get in until 17:45,' I say.

'This always happens. Miko never tells us anything. What time will you play tonight?'

I show him the print-out of my schedule: Arrive 17:45. Get In: 18:00. Soundcheck 18:00 – 19:00. Dinner 19:00. Showtime 22:30 – 23:30.

Antte sighs. 'You won't be playing at 22:30. This is Finland. The club doesn't even open until 22:30.'

After a quick soundcheck I notice someone I recognise back by the mixing desk. It's Ronski, the drummer from Nollaseiska, who I toured with in Finland a few years ago. He tells me he is now playing in another band and training to be a lighting engineer. Then he gets on the phone to find out what's going on and establishes that I am due to go on stage at half past midnight.

Hmm. I have to get up at seven in the morning tomorrow for the train to Seinäjoke.

Still no sign of Miko. Ronski and Antte sit with me in the bar upstairs for a while and when Miko still doesn't turn up, Ronski asks around and finds out that I am sleeping in a hotel just around the corner, and that I am supposed to have dinner in a Mexican restaurant upstairs. He walks me to the hotel entrance and helps me check in, then I go to the restaurant, where I order the only vegetarian thing on the menu: quesadilla, which is basically a variant on the bread, cheese and salad I've been eating for the last couple of days. But it is a damn sight better than a rock-hard roll.

Talking of rock – and roll – while I'm eating, '2-4-6-8 Motorway' by the Tom Robinson band comes over the sound system. I send Tom a text to tell him I have just heard his hit in Joensuu, and he replies 'Hurrah – fame at last!'

Twelve days ago we were playing a gig together in Antwerp. It feels like twelve years.

I go back down to the bar but there's still no sign of Miko. There is however a free internet terminal, so I while away a couple of hours going through my emails. When I head down to the venue at midnight the place is filled with dry ice and swirling lights, and disco music is blaring out through the P.A. system. Two people are being dealt cards at a green baize blackjack table near the entrance stairs, and another three are sitting at tables around the dance floor. I go back up to the bar and buy a beer. A large one.

Half an hour later I go back downstairs. Things don't look much better. Antte arrives and gives me a sympathetic look. 'Perhaps we should go into the backstage and get away from this shit music.'

'There's a backstage?'

Antte frowns. 'Miko always does this...'

He takes me to a side room off the dance floor, where a sliding door shuts out most of the sound, and shows me a crate full of beer. 'Usually there is a crate of beer for the whole band. Of course that is quite a lot of beer for one guy.'

Yes, but I've been paying for beer upstairs because MIKO HASN'T SHOWN UP.

Ronski arrives. 'I have about twenty friends coming who really want to see you, TV. Please play a good show!'

I peek out into the club. It looks a bit more promising: there are thirty or forty people in and a few more just arriving, so even though it's half past midnight now, I decide to leave it another twenty minutes before I start.

'If only that DJ could play something a bit more suitable,' I say, 'some Clash or something like that.'

Antte says that all the bands say the same thing but it's no good – one of the conditions of the DJ's job is that he plays records from a playlist of popular middle-of-the-road dance records.

A playlist! In a live club! I am losing the will to live.

I get my guitar on at around one. I'm not really in the mood to play, but at least it will stop the god-awful music for a while, and before I start I chat with some of the people who are up the front leaning on the barrier and am encouraged to hear that they feel the same as I do. It's a horrible club, but it's the only club in town.

The gig is okay, better than I thought it was going to be. I play a bit shorter than usual, people applaud and some even dance. As soon as I'm off, the disco music starts again and everyone leaves.

Still no sign of Miko.

26th January
A speedy top up with muesli, yoghurt, a red berry mix and half a kiwi fruit at the hotel breakfast bar, then I slither over the bridge back to the station where I catch the train for an eight hour and ten minute journey to Seinäjoke. As I settle into my seat a text message comes through from Tommi to tell me that there is likely to be a British Airways strike on Tuesday, and he hopes that it won't affect my trip to Australia. Normally this would be a cause for panic, but I am able to text back triumphantly 'I'm flying Qantas!'

The only other interest on the painfully long journey comes in Tikarilla, where I change trains. I find the right platform for my connection but the train is delayed. There's a blizzard whipping through the station and I spend one of the coldest half hours of my life watching the boards as the expected arrival time is put back ten minutes, then another ten, then another, while the wind batters into me, the snow builds up on my luggage and my hands go numb.

I have a feeling of *déjà vu* at Seinäjoke station when Ville, the promoter, isn't there to meet me, but as I wait in the lobby he comes rushing in from the platform where he missed me walk past.

What a difference to yesterday! The club is a nice intimate room, well lit and laid out, tables and chairs arranged around a low stage. Ville introduces me to the sound man, Antte, and the barman, Miko – pay attention at the back – and the owner of the club comes in to say hello. He tells me he's taken a lot of trouble to make this club a nice place to spend time in and that as far as he's concerned the customer always comes first. It shows.

Upstairs to the kebab restaurant for some falafel and salad, then I settle down with my guitar in the dressing room for a four and a half hour wait until showtime. By then, the place is full and when I hit the stage the sound is crisp and loud and I feel confident. By halfway through my two hour set many of the audience are up out of their seats and dancing.

By now it's nearly three, and Ville wants to drive me to the place I'm staying – the band room in a large venue a couple of kilometres out of town. I'd like to hang around in the bar a bit longer, but instead find myself in a tomb-like narrow room, no windows, just three bunk beds and a shower, lots of empty beer bottles (but no full ones), old food cartons, and everywhere the drone of the air conditioning unit. I put in the earplugs and call it a night.

27th January
I'm surprised to hear the peeping of my alarm clock in the distance through my earplugs. It feels like the middle of the night, but actually it's eleven already. I get up and shave tentatively in the cleaner of the two sinks, trying to avoid the dried-up toothpaste and hairs of dubious origin, then have a shower and attempt to get my socks on afterwards without actually having to tread on the grubby floor.

When Ville picks me up to take me to the station, he says, 'Some bands complain that sleeping in there is like sleeping in a submarine.'

Mmm. I decide not to complain because I have come to a momentous decision: I will never sleep in a 'band room' again. If I wanted to sleep in a band room I would join a band.

Back in Tampere I make my way over to the Iltätahti, the place I stayed the first time I came to Finland. It's a hostel, small clean rooms with shower and toilet – not exactly luxury, but much better than last night.

I meet up with Tina in the studio at six. With Ritta and Tiina in the room it's just like the good old Punk Lurex OK days. Tiina tells me that an English friend who works in Tampere university has become quite well known since I last saw him for some papers he has written about ageing. I say, 'If he finds out anything important, can you let me know? Urgently.'

We take a taxi over to the venue, which is just outside of town in a place called Pispala. It's a nice looking small club with a rock'n'roll vibe that suggests the gig will be exciting. There are already a few people in, and when the band and I run through a couple of the songs during soundcheck one guy gets up and starts dancing and shouting out requests. Afterwards someone else comes over and introduces his friend. 'He has the same name as you,' he says. 'Tim Smith, meet Timo Seppä.'

The band and me head down the road to the Pulteri bar, where I once spent a memorable evening with Punk Lurex when we were recording the EP, and I hear a familiar voice at the table next to me: it's Rancid Tom, over from England for the gig.

Tina play, then I'm on stage at midnight. I've played a lot in Tampere over the years, and quite a few people who saw Monday's gig in Helsinki have made the trip up for tonight, so there's a lot of singing along right from the start. After about an hour on stage I try and work my way towards a natural ending to the solo set so I can introduce Tina as my surprise backing band for the last few songs, but so many requests are getting shouted that I can't get around to winding it up. Then I look round and see the band are all on the stage behind me. I give a questioning look to Tiina, 'They have to stop the music at 1:30,' she whispers.

So we're straight into the band set, people dancing away enthusiastically, while the house lights flash on to signal that the bar is closing. Then it's suddenly all over, we're in a taxi to Tampere to have one last beer at the Telakka, we say our goodbyes, and I'm in my room at 3:30 in a strange mood – leaving all my friends in beautiful, snowy Finland behind, one day at home to come, then the trip to Australia ahead of me.

28th January
What I think must be the alarm clock is actually a text message coming through from Roger, who is putting together the Australian tour: *BA strike Tuesday. All BA passengers now coming on Qantas so will be full. Triple confirm your seat and get there early to avoid being bumped.*

Oh God.

Part Two: Australia

29th January
Packing shouldn't be too much of a problem. Out with the heavy waterproof coat, pullovers, thick t-shirts, scarf, hat, gloves – in with the short sleeve t-shirts, suncream, sunglasses, swimming trunks, weird-looking plug adaptors, Australia guide books…

Last thing at night the BA strike is called off. Things are looking up. I set the alarm to half an hour later than it was.

TALES OF THE EMERGENCY SANDWICH

<u>30th January</u>
It seemed sensible to give myself two and a half hours at the airport, but I get through check-in and security fast and am left with two hours to hang around. Despite being so early, someone next to me at the check-in desk was told that there were no aisle seats left, so I'm extremely glad mine was pre-booked: 23 hours trapped between other people is not my idea of fun.

The plane is completely full, not one spare seat. My strategy to read a German book on the plane so other people won't talk to me is a bit of a non-starter when I find I'm sitting next to an Austrian and two Germans.

<u>31st January</u>
Twelve and a half sleepless hours later we land in Singapore for a two hour stopover. I'm very keen to stretch my legs, and we're told we can go and look round the terminal if we want to, but as I get out of the plane, one of the Qantas staff is saying we have to be back in half an hour. I take the moving walkway and find an electric socket where I charge my laptop battery for twenty minutes and get it up to 24%. My legs remain unstretched.

The onward flight to Sydney is another seven and a half hours. I don't know if it's the melatonin, which I took for the first time on this flight, but I feel pretty fit by the time we land in Sydney. It is a bit of a disappointment, though, to see that it's raining.

Roger rings me just as the Immigration official is looking through my documents and asks me if everything's alright. At that exact moment my passport gets stamped. 'It is now,' I say.

After I've picked up my guitar and luggage I get pulled out of the line waiting for customs clearance. The guy looks through my papers and says, 'So what band do you play for, Tim?'

I say, 'I play solo these days.'

In a tone of voice that suggests he thinks I'm being evasive he says, 'Well, what band *did* you play for?'

'I was once in a band called The Adverts.'

'Oh, The Adverts – I know them.' He tells me about all the musicians he's had through the airport lately. 'That Johnny Lyndon, or Johnny Lydon – whatever he calls himself now – he was here the other week. I had a chat with him – ' (I bet he did) ' – and he seemed like a perfectly nice chap.'

His favourite bands ever are Led Zeppelin – 'I had that Robert Plant through here once…' – and the Beatles – 'I got to shake George Harrison's hand…'

He shakes my hand, then I join the queue for the customs X-ray, where I get pulled out of the line again and told I can go straight through. I have clearly passed some kind of test.

The Chinese taxi driver plays a Charles Aznavour CD while we head into the city, and sings along in French. Roger texts me a few times during the journey to ask how things are going, and is waiting in the lobby of his apartment building to meet me as the cab pulls up. Roger was bass player for original '77 Oz-punks the Thought Criminals, then went on to work in music publishing and band management and has been trying to find a good excuse to get me over to play in Australia for ages. Last year the band reformed for a successful comeback show, and have decided to play another one this year, so here I am to support them and play a few gigs on my own. We'll also play a few Adverts songs together.

The Thought Criminals have been rehearsing today and are now in a Chinese restaurant just around the corner so I drop my bags at Roger's place and we head straight round there. He promises the best salt and pepper tofu in the world. On the way I tell him about the bloke at Customs and complain, 'He obviously only picked me out so he could tell all his friends he's met me.'

Roger says, 'Of course. *We've* only got you over so we can tell all our friends we've met you too. Get with the programme! That's why you're *here*.'

I am introduced to the band, then a Chinese lady takes a photo of me and them together, which half an hour later is delivered to the table mounted on a souvenir key ring. I have been awake for over thirty hours, but this really did happen.

Over the next hour or so I try out Roger's 'white wine method' solution to jet lag, which seems pretty effective as when we eventually get back to his apartment I go out like a light.

1st February
I sleep eight hours straight through and wake up feeling great. Roger and I do a quick phone interview for a radio station and the DJ tells me that not only is he an Adverts fan but also absolutely loves my new album 'Misinformation Overload.' Then I pick up a few more emails from people in Sydney offering to show me round the city. Unfortunately it doesn't look as if there'll be much time to look around as we're going straight to rehearsal, but it's nice being made to feel so welcome.

It's not far to the rehearsal room, but we take a taxi as we're carrying instruments and bags. We chat outside for a minute before we start, and singer Bruce – real name – says that he had to wait fifty-five minutes in the station this morning for a train that was delayed. While he was waiting, Ravel's 'Bolero' was played over the public address system, a pleasant way to help the time pass. When it finished, the piece started up again from the beginning, which was just about acceptable, but after the third time it was beginning to get tedious so Bruce went to the information desk to ask if they had anything else. They told him, 'We don't do requests.'

While I rehearse my songs with the band, Bruce gets busy in a side room stenciling and paint-splattering some stage shirts for the gig. They look authentically punk and when I tell him that he could probably sell them for a good price in London he tells me that he used to have a shop in Paddington selling punk stuff in the seventies and back then lived in Shepherds Bush. I ask him where exactly and it turns out he was less than half a mile from where I live now. It's a small world but you wouldn't want to have to paint-splatter it.

The rehearsal is quite hard work as the band have ambitiously gone for learning six Adverts songs as well as their own lengthy set, and when we run through them there are still quite a few bits that need ironing out. After a couple of hours we stop to have a break and then while the band carry on with their own set I head up the road to look for a coffee.

I walk for about ten minutes back towards Roger's place through some rather uninteresting suburban streets until I reach the monumental shiny new Exhibition Centre, and opposite that I find a bar called The Glasgow Arms, where I order a cappuccino. The woman serving it is very friendly and helps me out with the money after I've done that thing of minutely examining each coin, instantly marking me out as a tourist. One cappuccino's not enough. I go back to order a second and when I proffer a handful of change, the same woman smiles and says, 'Oh, that's alright darling,' and waves me to put my money away. I sit outside at a table and a very light, warm rain starts to fall. At another table a guy belches and explains to his mate how all his chest hair came to get burned off. It involved a stripper, shaving cream and a cigarette lighter.

Back at the rehearsal room, the Thought Criminals are just finishing their set, and then tell me they've thought it over and have decided to just attempt three songs with me. I agree with them that it's much better to have three good ones than six shaky ones, and when we run through the three they are soon sounding excellent. Then I have a go at singing backing vocals on three of their songs and we leave the room feeling confident about tomorrow.

While we wait for a cab, I tell Bruce about the bar and ask if it's normal in Australia to get your second coffee free. He looks surprised and says, 'No, they normally charge you more…'

When we get back to the apartment, sleep seems very far away even though it's past midnight. I go out on the balcony to look out at the city and notice, just up a rise on the other side of the Exhibition centre, the familiar lights of the Glasgow Arms. That's how much I've seen of Sydney since I arrived – about 15 minutes walk in a straight line from the place where I'm staying. I am, however, thrilled beyond all reason when a fruit bat with a metre wide wingspan glides gracefully past and circles over the park across the street. You don't see that in Shepherds Bush.

Austalia smiles. 2007

2nd February

I decide to walk to the venue and see a little of Sydney. It doesn't involve passing any major sights but at least I get a feel for the place and it's great to spend a leisurely couple of hours in the warm weather wandering around new neighbourhoods while cockatoos screech overhead.

I'm at the Annandale Hotel right on time at four, and the band are just arriving with the equipment. Bruce – real name – Griffiths is also there. He once introduced himself to me at one of my gigs in London and said he was a friend of Roger. I didn't know at the time that he was also an established stand-up comic, and it turns out that Roger has persuaded him to open the show tonight. The place is looking slow to fill up, and I say to Bruce it must be hard to do comedy with only about fifty people in but he replies that he's rather hoping not many people will be there as he's a bit nervous about performing in front of a punk crowd. 'About 50 ears would be fine,' he says. 'No, hang on, that's only 25 people. 100 ears.'

Bruce's lack of self-confidence is misplaced. He performs a hilarious set of one-liners and goes down a storm.

The room is fairly full by the time I get on stage and my first-ever gig in Australia doesn't disappoint. Roger introduces me, I get a big cheer before I've even started, and I almost get mobbed when I finish by people wanting to talk to me. I finally manage to get away to the dressing room upstairs and find the Thought Criminals there in their crisply-ironed splatter shirts ready for the stage. Drummer Ken looks at my sweat-drenched bleach-streaked jeans and t-shirt and says, 'You look like a real punk. We look like King's Road punks.'

Despite a few mistakes – it's a year since they last played a gig and about twenty-five since the one before that – the band play well and the audience crowds down to the front of the stage and are singing along and dancing. When I get up for the three Adverts songs at the end the place erupts. Then I stay there to sing the three Thought Criminals songs we rehearsed, even though I have to surreptitiously refer to some cheat sheets I've placed by the monitors as I haven't had time to learn the lyrics.

I hang around chatting to people after the show and am really encouraged by the enthusiastic feedback I get. There are two brothers from Brisbane who have flown down specially for the gig and say they will see me again when I play their home town next week. Another guy asks me to sign his arm, and says he is going to have it tattooed tomorrow. I decide that I love Australia.

It's got late by the time all the gear is packed away, and plans for us all to get something to eat together are shelved. We split off our separate ways, and Roger and his partner Lucia and I end up back at the Chinese place with the best salt and pepper tofu in the world. It's the weekend, so there's quite a queue of Chinese people dressed in their Saturday night best waiting for a late dinner, and when we finally get in we're given a table which is right under the air conditioning so a chilly breeze is streaming down over us. Lucia puts one of the spare punk shirts over her shoulders and when she sees me shivering passes me one too. Roger still has his on from the gig, so in this restaurant full of smartly dressed Chinese diners there appears to be one table seating three King's Road punks. While we're eating and chatting away I notice something hard in my mouth and remove it to find a metal spring clip, presumably used to hold the orders in the kitchens. It's a UMOM – an Unexpected Metal Object Moment.

3rd February

At eight o'clock the sound of a masonry drill wakes me up. I struggle with trying to go back to sleep for a while then submit to the inevitable and get out of bed. The noise is filling the whole apartment. Roger is up too and explains that at eight he went down to the lobby in his dressing gown and complained. He was told that they are building a new shopping centre next door. 'It's Sunday! Can't they start later?'

'How about nine?' they suggested.

'How about noon?'

Today's gig is in Melbourne, an hour's flight away. In the taxi to the airport Roger tells me about a band he knows whose PA truck broke down on the way to Melbourne so they had to try and flag down passing vehicles to help them get the gear to the venue. Eventually a big truck stopped and said, 'Melbourne mate? No problem – I've got an empty truck here – load it in.' When they got to the gig and unloaded the PA they found out it was a refrigerated truck and the equipment didn't work any more. 'A PA system is a bit like a soufflé,' says Roger. 'You can't really re-heat it.'

Band and girlfriends, Bruce Griffiths, and Marshall the sound man all gather at the airport. The equipment and band merchandising is already on the way by road. Once we land it's a twenty minute cab ride to the hotel then I take a stroll with Roger and Bruce to the venue. It's a beautiful warm day, the sun shining.

The Tote is a small bar, about a half hour walk from our hotel in the centre of town. When we arrive there is a band already playing on a rather cramped floor area and I assume that that's where we'll play too, but when they end their set we are shown through to a larger room in the back with a proper stage and sound system, a little outdoor courtyard off to one side. Promoter Bruce Milne soon arrives and Roger does the introductions: Bruce, this is Bruce…

We talk about how hot it's going to be on stage tonight, and Bruce (pay attention at the back) says that in the past it's been so bad that he's had bands run off stage and throw up in the courtyard.

Not many people have arrived by the time Bruce does his routine but those who are there soon warm to him and there's a lot of laughter. By the time I start my set the room is about half full and once again I really get the feeling that the people are getting into it. Towards the end I get a request for 'Cast Of Thousands,' which surprises me as I hadn't expected anyone here to know the second Adverts album. When I get off stage the guy who shouted for it tells me that he saw me in a punk festival in Newcastle a few years ago, and

TALES OF THE EMERGENCY SANDWICH

also at an Explorers gig in London back in 1981. To prove it, he then quotes the slogan that Ralph Steadman painted on the T-shirt I was wearing that day: *Gonzo Brain cannot be bought so we do not advertise.*

'Amazing!' I say. 'That's word perfect!'

'Oh yes, I remember it all,' he says proudly. 'I've got the original vinyl of your first album Crossing The Red River, and there's that song I asked for tonight, er…' He turns to his girlfriend. 'What was it again?'

Well, we've all had a few beers. I sit in the courtyard cooling off a bit with a guy from Belfast who can't understand why I haven't played there since 1977, reckons I would go down a storm and says he thinks he could organise something. So now I am booking my U.K. gigs from Melbourne.

After that it's the same routine as yesterday. The place has filled up by the time the Thought Criminals come on and they play even better now the first gig is out of the way and they are all more relaxed. Unfortunately it's also their last gig, as they will be disbanding again after this. I get a cheer when I get back on stage, shuffle my cheat sheets into position for later and launch into the three Adverts songs which go brilliantly. Then I move off to the side microphone to do backing vocals on the Thought Criminals songs and am a bit disturbed to see that the cheat sheets have already been taken by front row souvenir hunters. Luckily I more or less have the lyrics in my head now and manage to bluff my way through, although for a few of the lines I just sing 'Aaaaaah, mmmm, uuuuuuuh…'

I'm surrounded by people again after the gig. I'll be playing here again tomorrow, and one guy tells me that he has something special for me that he'll bring then, but won't tell me what it is. A woman asks for my autograph and while she reaches around in her bag to find a ticket for me to sign I notice that she has my cheat sheets in there.

The schedule that Roger originally emailed me with the timings for the tour stated that after the gig we:

 * Party hard at the Ding Dong.
 * Stagger to hotel a hundred yards away.

I am very intrigued to experience how it will be to party hard at the Ding Dong, however we are already in staggering mode and go for the easy option, which is sitting on the floor in the hotel room of Ken and his girlfriend Kath with a couple of bottles of wine, talking bollox until about 6:45 am, when we realise we are talking *complete* bollox, and go to bed.

I can't imagine why I took this one.
Melbourne 2007

4th February

Somewhere in the hotel I can hear a hammering sound. I check my watch and see that it's around 8:00, the favourite time for THEM to start. I put in the earplugs and manage to get back to sleep until midday, by which time everything is silent.

I get up and shower then receive an SMS from Roger to say the gig starts in half an hour. It's an afternoon show with a barbecue in the courtyard, but we don't really have to be there for the start of it so we go for some breakfast on the way. Not many at The Tote by the time we arrive, despite an impressive line up including Jon Langford from the Mekons, and Kim Salmon from the Scientists. Kim kicks off the music to an audience of ten. By the time I play, around forty people have turned up. It's still light, and meaty smoke is wafting into the room from the barbecue. There's a nice, intimate atmosphere to the gig and the songs get a great reaction. Afterwards, two punk girls tell me it's the best gig they've seen in their life. The guy who promised me 'something special' yesterday hands me a faded New York newspaper from the day after Gary Gilmore's death in 1977, the story splashed all over the front page.

All in all, a very positive outcome to the gig. Walking back up the road with Roger I say, 'My faith in humanity is almost restored.'

'Almost?' says Roger.

Just then a girl comes running out of the venue, shouting, 'TV Smith! Are you leaving?'

She says she didn't want me to go without her having a chance to tell me how wonderful she thought the concert was. Then she goes back to the bar and Roger and I carry on up the road.

'Now it's completely restored,' I say.

The Ding Dong's shut, so we go to a Chinese restaurant and drink an inappropriate amount of white wine.

Then the goodbyes start. Most of the band will leave tomorrow – I'll be staying for another day and don't have a gig so will finally have the chance for a look around Melbourne.

The Thought Criminals and friends taking life seriously. Melbourne 2007

5th February

I wake up reasonably early and decide to take a swim in the rooftop pool. No sharks. However, when I get back to the room, there is a news item on the TV about a hotel where a guest went for a morning dip and found a crocodile in the pool. They reckon someone put it in there 'for a joke.' Hilarious!

Ken and Kath don't leave until the afternoon. Roger is going to visit his parents, so he points the rest us in the direction of the tram and we take a ride down to the seaside resort of St Kilda. Kath is feeling the 40 degree heat quite badly and as we wander through the streets she stops frequently in front of shops to trigger the automatic doors and bathe for a few seconds in the flow of chilled air from inside. 'It gets a lot worse than this sometimes,' she says. 'Some days it goes up to 48 degrees. That's so hot that you have to walk slowly or your eyes dry out.'

When Ken and Kath leave for the airport I wander around the city for a while, then catch up on my emails in an internet café, get an impressively authentic pizza in the Italian quarter, then go to bed soon after midnight – an early night!

6th February
Just before I leave the hotel I notice the sign on the door informing me that 'in certain circumstances the innkeeper may be liable to make good any loss of or damage to a guest's property, up to a limit of $100.' Clause C underneath points out that this doesn't apply to horses. How many guests bring a horse to their room?

Roger picks me up in a cab and we drive out to the airport. I'm off for a solo gig in Brisbane, he's heading home to Sydney. Just as we get to the check-in desk he realises that his phone must have fallen out of his pocket as he was paying the cab driver. He gives me Lucia's phone number in case I need to get hold of him, then tells me that when I arrive in Brisbane a woman called Rachel, who is the promoter from the club there, will meet me at the airport and take me to the hotel.

Brisbane is a two hour flight to the North so I'd expected a parched landscape; instead I'm surprised to find us flying over forested hills, then as we near the city flat green fields with rivers meandering though them.

At the airport, a guy comes up to me and says, 'TV Smith?'

'Er...Rachel?'

He's actually called Donat, came originally from Croatia, and is DJ at the club. Rachel asked him to pick me up. The sun is baking hot and as we climb into his '77 Citroen, Donat explains that although it's ten degrees cooler here than in Melbourne, it's much more humid and consequently feels hotter. Even with both the front windows open all the way into the city, I'm bathed in sweat by the time we get to the hotel. I dump my baggage and guitar in the lobby and go to check in but the receptionist says there is no booking in my name. She checks Roger's name, the promoter's name, the club name – still nothing. It's quite a posh hotel and she is starting to look at me like I am some punk who has wandered in off the street and is trying it on. I ask if there are any rooms free for tonight and she says, not one.

This would be the day Roger has lost his phone. I call Lucia but she's on answerphone so I leave a message explaining the situation and asking Roger to call me back because I am – in the words of legendary Brisbane punk band The Saints – stranded. I decide the best thing to do is go to the club and wait there, and I have just got back in the car when Roger rings. He's furious because the travel agent booked the room months ago. He's having a bit of a strange day too: when he arrived in Sydney this afternoon he went round to pick up the CDs and merchandising items from James, who drove it back in the van from Melbourne last night, only to find that James had lost his key and was locked inside his apartment. He had to throw the CDs down to Roger out of the window. Roger tells me to go back to the hotel and he'll sort everything out.

At the reception desk there's a lively phone conversation going on, and two people looking through files for the lost booking. Eventually a guy in a smart suit comes over to me and Donat and introduces himself as the assistant manager.

'I'm so sorry Mr Smith, I don't know how this happened. However, we have found someone who is checking out late. We'll have the room cleaned for you and then you'll be able to get in it. In the meantime, while you're waiting please enjoy a complimentary drink.' He turns to the bartender and drops his voice. '*One* round of drinks on the house for these gentlemen.'

When I finally get up to my room I find it has a stunning view across the river and the impressive bridge vaulting it, which earlier I'd thought I might be sleeping under. I stay in the room for a couple of hours then set off for the venue, Ric's Bar, which is just a short walk away. Inside there's a high stage taking up about a quarter of the room, space for about a hundred people in front of it at a squeeze. I do a quick soundcheck and everything's fine. After that I ask the woman behind the bar if she's Rachel and she says she is. She tells me I can get a free meal at the place next door. I ask her if there's anything vegetarian and she says, lots of tapas and things like that. I say, great, that's the sort of stuff I can pack away to eat after the gig. Rachel tells me there's no need – it's open all night.

The room starts to fill up. The two brothers who came to the Sydney gig are there. One of them says, meet my elder brother. I say, I already know him. He says, not him – *him*. Next to him is another guy grinning at me. 'I'm the sensible one,' he says. He is wearing a Charles Manson T-shirt.

I play for two and a half hours and during the course of that there are about fifty people who watch the whole thing and a few others who come and go. After the gig I sit on the stage for an hour or so, sell CDs, pose for photos and chat with the audience. They all seem very happy to say how much they liked the gig now, although they seemed a little restrained compared to my European audiences during the actual show. One girl who I noticed dancing enthusiastically all the way through is German and it turns out we have a mutual friend in Cologne. Hooray for the Germans!

Finally people start to disperse. I ask Rachel if I could go next door now for something to eat but she tells me that the restaurant is closed. 'I didn't know you were going to play for *that* long,' she says. 'There's a really dodgy 24 hour convenience store over the road, you could get something from there.'

Great! I love really dodgy food! I walk back towards the hotel carrying my guitar and bag and stop by a 7-11 but they say they have nothing vegetarian. Up the road I see another 24 hour shop where all they can offer is a microwave pasta and tomato sauce dish. There is a microwave oven in the hotel room so I buy it. At the hotel the entrance door is locked, and the sign stuck on with one piece of tape inside it which explains how to get in is blowing in the air conditioning so I can't read it and I don't know what to do. It's beginning to look like I'll be sleeping under the bridge after all. I hammer on the door for a while and to my relief someone eventually lets me in. I tell him that I couldn't read the sign and he apologises. 'I'm so sorry sir, I'll get that fixed for you.'

It's a bit bloody late now. The jet lag must be catching up: in the lift I surprise myself by unexpectedly bursting into tears. When I get into the room the microwave doesn't respond to my attempt to set it for the recommended two minutes but starts up when I use the setting named 'Rice/Pasta.' After about four minutes I realise something is wrong, hit the Stop button and eat one of the most miserable dried-up tasteless meals imaginable. I have forgotten to buy a bottle of water, and there's only warm coming out of the taps. There are cold bottles available from the mini bar for five dollars and fifty cents, which I resent having to pay, so I make do with the warm. Today has gone wrong.

February 7th
The phone rings and it's Roger. 'Good Morning!' he says. 'This is your wake up call!'

Actually it's my get-me-out-of-the-shower-with-my-hair-covered-in-shampoo call, but never mind. Today is a new day and I'm feeling positive again and looking forward to getting back to Sydney away from this brutal heat.

TALES OF THE EMERGENCY SANDWICH

A sign in the lift shows all the overpriced food available in the hotel restaurant. Underneath, it says 'Vegetarian options available. Please ask your waitperson.'

Waitperson?

I ask the Receptionperson for a taxi and leave for the airport.

There's a phone-in competition on the car radio to guess who the radio station has nominated as the country's biggest 'Celebrity Bludger.' A Bludger, the DJ cheerfully explains, is a person who contributes bugger all to society. Over the last week I've noticed that Australians have a refreshingly un-stuffy attitude to swearing: I can't imagine anyone on mainstream British radio being allowed to say the word 'bugger.'

A woman phones in to suggest an answer.

'Sorry, no!' laughs the DJ.

'Bummer!' says the woman.

Nothing vegetarian on the flight, but there's plenty of time to buy a sandwich at Sydney airport as I have to wait around because luggage unloading is suspended due to an electrical storm.

In the end there's time for a twenty minute turnaround at Roger's place before I'm in a cab and off to rehearsal with the band who will be backing me for the next two gigs. I meet up with drummer Tim at his shop where he sells punk artifacts and novelties. He and the rest of the musicians play in a variety of bands but join up to do occasional gigs under the name Punk Rock Karaoke, where members of the audience jump up on stage to sing along with their renditions of punk rock classics. They tell me that they've never done an Adverts song but Gary Gilmore's Eyes gets requested quite often. For these two gigs they've finally had a go at learning it, as well as another eight Adverts songs, including a few from the 'difficult' second album. The ones from the first album aren't so simple either, and in the rehearsal room we find that the better-known songs rock along reasonably well but the more obscure ones are a struggle and we have to stop quite a few times to try to clear up problems. After a few run-throughs things are still falling apart and Bones, one of the two guitarists, complains that he's spent one hundred hours learning the material and that the rest haven't tried hard enough. There's an altercation between him and the bass player which involves a threat of violence and ends up with Bones taking off his guitar and threatening to leave. This is rather worrying as he does seem to be the one who has the best idea of how to play the songs. Eventually the argument dies down and we carry on, but soon we're told by the rehearsal room managerperson that our allotted three hours are up and we have to pack up and be out of the room in fifteen minutes. It's still not clear which songs are going to be okay but I make a decision to drop the three shakiest, which leaves us with another six that we can concentrate on trying to get right tomorrow.

As we load out, the second guitarist, Paul, introduces me to someone in the corridor who says, '*You* wrote Gary Gilmore's Eyes? Honestly?'

He's had a retina transplant himself – was blind in one eye before it – and plays a country version of the song in his band.

I help Tim out to the car with his drums, and Tim the tour agent is outside to take me out to meet Roger at a restaurant. Tim says goodbye to Tim – pay attention at the back – and we drive to a Vietnamese place and have a delicious meal packed with tofu and fresh ingredients. Predominant herb: mint.

Don't remember where this was taken. 2007

February 8th
I'm meeting the band at seven this evening, which means I finally have a whole day free to look around Sydney. I take a walk along Darling Harbour down to the Rocks, where the original settlers first made their homes – now liberally sprinkled with tourist shops – then make my way under the impressive Harbour Bridge into Circular Quay. The sun is shining, and the flags around the harbour flutter in a light breeze. I get a ferry over to Manley to get the view of the

TALES OF THE EMERGENCY SANDWICH

Opera House that everyone has recommended, and as we head out across the bay a warm wind blasts over the boat and I stand on the fore deck enjoying the salt spray in my face and watching the sparkling waters as we cut through the bay. When we arrive at Manley 30 minutes later I hurry out for a look around but realise time is getting tight so get straight on to the next ferry back for Sydney 15 minutes later.

I meet up with drummer Tim as planned and he tells me that Bones has left the band. The rest of them are going to try to do the gig without him.

It's an hour's drive to Wollongong and my 'bad-gig-ahead' radar starts sounding as soon as we walk in. The stage is bare, pool tables in front of it, video screens around the walls showing middle of the road pop dross. A few people grimly pump money into gaming machines in an adjoining room. It looks like the sort of place I'd go to get beaten up, not play a gig. A sound man eventually turns up and sets up a couple of microphones but seems reluctant to do a soundcheck. The situation is tricky for Punk Rock Karaoke too: the plan had been that they'd do their normal set, then I'd play solo, then they'd get on stage to join me for the Adverts songs. However, the karaoke depends on a drunken crowd willing to make fools of themselves having a crack at singing old punk songs, and that doesn't look a likely scenario at the moment.

Over the next hour some people wander in – woefully few, but it's interesting chatting to them. The guy whose arm I signed in Sydney has come down from his hometown Canberra, and as promised he has had the signature tattooed on. I take a photo. There's someone from Finland who's seen me many times at the Semifinal club in Helsinki and couldn't believe it when he saw I would be playing here in Wollongong. I have a short chat with him in Finnish utilising the only phrases I know: 'Good evening! Beer. Cheers! Go ski to the swamp! Arse on my shoulders. What am I doing here?'

He texts his friend Antte, who I met three weeks ago in Finland, and gets the reply that right at this moment he is playing football with my friend Tommi. The world just got smaller.

The way the karaoke gig normally works is that the band leave out a sheet with names of songs they intend to play, then people from the audience write their names next to the ones they want to have a go at singing. Half an hour after the band were supposed to go on stage, there are still hardly any names down but they can't put off starting any longer. Unfortunately the missing guitarist has quite an effect – there are all sorts of holes in the arrangements which Paul struggles to fill, then his equipment starts playing up and he has to keep on stopping to hammer his fist on the amp. The band call up the names on the list, but most have chickened out and don't own up to being on it; those that do are mostly excruciatingly bad and there are a couple of times when the band can't get through the song either and have to stop before the end. The sound man, who is wearing earplugs, gives me a resigned expression from across the room.

I'm not exactly gagging to start playing but after about 30 minutes of the solo set I feel I'm getting a pretty good reaction from the sparse few in the room and decide to bring the band on. I've put in 'Gary Gilmore's Eyes' as the first song thinking it's foolproof but Paul comes in on guitar too early and the whole thing immediately goes out of synch. Somehow we pull it all back together, but the next three songs suffer meltdown halfway through and I have to signal the band to abandon them. This is getting seriously embarrassing, although the few people who are in the audience don't seem to mind too much. I suppose most of them have already been up on stage this evening and suffered a similar humiliation. The next three songs are passable, then I hurry off the stage into the back room and dump the idea of the two encore songs. I sit there among the buckets and mops for a while wishing the world would swallow me up.

We load the gear out into the two cars in the drizzle, then me and Tim set off back to Sydney, almost immediately hitting a thick fog which reduces visibility to two cat's eyes ahead of us. Tim tells me how embarrassed he is about the poor performance of the band tonight. They messed up the karaoke songs, he says, because their minds were so full of the Adverts songs, then messed those up as well. He promises they're going to meet up tomorrow and get it all sorted out.

Back at Roger's I stand out on the balcony and reflect. It's 3:00 and still warm, there's a distant swish of traffic from the street below and the lights on the pylons of the exhibition centre glow grey across from the Chinese Garden. It's been an odd sort of day which has thrown up many questions. One of them is *miksi mina teen tata*? – Finnish for 'what am I doing here?' – but the most puzzling one is: how come Antte answered his mobile phone when he was playing football?

February 9th
It's the final gig, back in Sydney at a well-known venue called the Hopetoun Hotel, and there's a buzz around that it's going to be good tonight. After last night's disaster I'm not so sure. When I arrive at the venue at six there's no sign of the band, but when they roll up an hour later, they tell me they've been at bass player Crasty's place all afternoon running through the songs. They

reckon the four that more-or-less worked yesterday will be fine today, and there's even a couple more that could be okay for an encore. Luckily we have time in soundcheck to run through them all, and I'm happy to hear that there are only a few mistakes.

I stand outside to get some air and am quite surprised to see a woman who was at my last gig in Leeds get out of a car that's just pulled up. She's an Australian who married an English guy and is currently on holiday with her two sons, who are also coming to the gig. I text TJ, who promoted the Leeds gig, to tell him and he texts back, 'The world just got smaller.'

I go to a nearby bar with Roger and Lucia to meet a few of their friends, but I'm not feeling very sociable as I'm worrying about the gig so I go back to the Hopetoun ahead of them. Punk Rock Karaoke are just about to start their set, and by the look of their list they have quite a few more takers than yesterday. As soon as they start up it's clear that the standard is going to be a lot higher – the band is tighter and the audience members who get up on stage with them are putting everything into it and for the most part singing in tune.

And for me the last gig of my first Australian tour turns out to be a great experience. The audience are right behind me for the solo set, and when the band join in yesterday's worries are forgotten and we play the reduced setlist almost faultlessly. When we get to Bored Teenagers I notice the guy who had been doing the lights – and who looks a few years older than me – get in front of the stage and hang upside down over a chair waving his legs in the air.

Afterwards he says to me, 'I've done the lights for many people over the years, and up to today I thought the greatest solo performer I've ever seen was Victor Borge…'

February 10th:
Wake up Mr Smith, it's time for your day off!

I have another swift walk around the city, up to the Opera House, through the Botanic Gardens. Flicking through a newspaper in a coffee bar I see an item about a 4.5 metre shark that has been spotted in a nearby bay over the past few days and has eaten a dog and a pelican. People are still swimming there. One of them says, 'Everyone *knows* there are sharks in the water, it's just that someone's seen this one.'

I'm back at the apartment by late afternoon and we take a taxi to a birthday party being thrown by one of Lucia's friends, then a couple of hours later move on to a revolving restaurant on the top floor of a skyscraper downtown to watch the sunset and have dinner. There are no UMMs, no UMOMs, just a fabulous meal, a couple of bottles of good wine, an expresso, and Roger and Lucia's excellent company. There is, however, a certain irony to the location: Roger tells me that an early Thought Criminals song called 'More Suicides Please' was about the increasing number of people throwing themselves off this very building and the media circus it attracted. As a stunt to promote the record, the band chalked an outline of a body at the foot of the building, then had to rapidly backtrack on the gimmicks when another person jumped and landed on it.

I've enjoyed my ten days in Australia immensely – great people, great weather, great food – but already I can feel myself being pulled away…it's time to start packing my bags again, my flight tomorrow…and back to London where according to the weather reports winter has finally arrived and the snow is falling…

Persuasive advert for Sauvignon Blanc.
Sydney 2007

February 11th
Time for a power walk around the city with Roger and Lucia to get the circulation going before the long flight. We drop into an art gallery where Chris O'Doherty, singer from Australian band Mental As Anything, has a show under the pseudonym of Reg Mombassa, and I buy a fridge magnet of one of his paintings of a kangaroo. It's the only kangaroo I've seen while I've been here.

TALES OF THE EMERGENCY SANDWICH

<u>February 12th</u>

London, 8:30 a.m., 25 hours after I got on the plane in Sydney, and I'm dragging my bags and guitar out of my local tube station against the flow of people heading in to work. I have been awake for 32 hours.

I notice one guy heading towards me wearing heavy work boots, his clothes splattered with paint, more 'painter and decorator' than 'King's Road punk.' He stands in front of me, blocking my way.

'Can I ask you a question,' he says, looking at me intently. His breath smells of booze, and he seems to be struggling to put his words together.

'Go on…' I say.

'Are you…who…I think I am?'

Difficult one to answer. 'I don't know.'

'The Adverts…?'

'Yes.'

'TV Smith! I knew it was you! I saw you at Wasted in Morecambe, it was brilliant…!'

It's a small world. But I've just flown across 10,648 miles of it and it's time to go home.

7. TROUSERS' END (2007)

<u>16th June</u>
I'm out of the house at seven in the morning to get the cheap Ryanair flight to Leipzig/Altenburg airport. One wonders how many tourists book a flight here, only to get out of the airport building to find to their surprise that they are in the middle of the countryside and need a 90 minute bus ride to reach Leipzig. Luckily Sebastian, who booked this coming week of concerts for me, and his friend Frank are waiting outside with a car. We're heading off to Dresden, an hour or so away, for the first of the gigs.

The sun is shining and the skies blue, the temperature already up in the high 20s as we head off along the country roads then onto the autobahn, and are chatting away in the car when Frank suddenly says, 'Shhhh, listen...'

I listen, but can't hear anything. 'Exactly,' he says. 'This stretch of road has a special anti-noise surface and is the most expensive piece of asphalt in the whole of Germany.'

Frank drops us off at Sebastian's parents' place, where I'll be sleeping the next few days. The parents have come to some of my gigs in Dresden over the last few years and have become fans. Sebastian's father has cooked up a meal for us all without meat as he knows I'm vegetarian. Before he retired he was a master-baker and still takes great pride in his cooking. Last Christmas I came to Dresden for a gig and he'd baked an entire *Stollen* for me to take back to England. There was a lot of icing sugar in my bag after that trip.

The parents will be coming to the gig tonight. They drive us into the new town, where the annual BRN festival is held, with concerts in every bar and on every street corner, then drop us off as near to the venue as they can get and go to look for somewhere to park. Sebastian and I walk through the swarms of people and arrive at the outdoor stage where I'll be playing, next to a bar called Katy's Garage. I'm informed that my stage time has been changed from eight to midnight.

To escape from the throng I head to an upstairs room in Katy's Garage, which is being used as a backstage. From there you can climb out through the window and get onto the roof, which has a few chairs and tables scattered around and gives a great view out onto the stage and the crowds down below. There is a nasty ripping sound as I lift my leg over the windowsill and I notice that the worn patch around the knee of my jeans has become quite a bit larger and a flap is now hanging down. These are the only jeans I have with me... would safety pins be too much of a cliché?

On the roof. Dresden 2007

From the roof. Dresden 2007

Finally the long wait is over and I get to go on stage, where I play for an hour to a great response. I'm impressed to see that the parents stayed for the whole thing, but now they say their goodbyes and head for home, leaving me and Sebastian to get a taxi later. Actually, being more of the parent generation myself, I'm pretty wiped out too but I need to pack up and wind down a bit before I'll be able to sleep. While Sebastian and his mates take a stroll around the town, I take my guitar back up to the top room, climb out onto the roof – *rrrrrrriiip!* – and sit out there for a bit. After a while, as the air starts to get chilly, I head back inside – *rrrrrrriiip!* – and end up downstairs with flapping trouser legs and a glass of wine while some guy comes up and offers me two thousand euros to play his wedding party next month. Even as he is talking to me I know I will never hear from him again.

Sebastian rescues me at around three and we head out into the streets to look for a taxi, just like hundreds of other people. Finally we're creeping into the parent's place just before four, the sky already getting light outside.

17<u>th</u> June
I am standing by the roadside in the dark holding a red torch. A car comes around the bend with no lights on and I realise I am supposed to alert the driver by waving the torch. He looks at me curiously, then seems to understand. As he passes I see him flip a switch on the dashboard, and the red tail lights blink on as he disappears off into the distance. Another car comes round the bend and the same thing happens. When the third car goes past I suddenly realise I am dreaming and I wake up.

At breakfast, Sebastian's father tells me that he was stopped by the police on the way home last night because he was driving without his lights on. They made him take a breath test – one drink four hours earlier, 0.05 alcohol – and let him carry on.

So I had a predictive dream about something that had already happened. What possible use is that?

Among the things on offer for breakfast are some very good bread rolls from a local bakery. Sebastian's father explains that these are classic DDR *Brötchen*, just as they used to be made before the wall fell. Back then there was a country-wide law that all bread rolls had to weigh 50 grams and there were no additives allowed in the dough, unlike now when most bakers try to make them rise as much as possible, with the consequence that biting into them is like eating air.

I have paid a heavy price for the open air festival yesterday: one mosquito bite just above the ankle, another one on my ear, and an ever-expanding rip over the knee of my trousers. I can live with the mosquito bites, but I'm a bit concerned about the rip as there is a long walk planned for my day off today, and then I have another week on tour after that. It's a hot sunny day so I say to Sebastian, 'I suppose I could always wear shorts?'

He says, ' No, you shouldn't do that because of the tics.'
Tics?

Sebastian's mother offers to have a go at fixing the rip, so I change into the shorts while she gets out the sewing machine. She tells me she used to be a professional seamstress, and after half an hour she gives the trousers back to me with the rips stitched up and strengthened with backing cloth. When I tentatively test them by bending my legs, even the repairs over the knees hold. Mum looks critically at the numerous other small holes in the material and points at one of the larger ones:

'I should really have sewn that one up too.'

'No, that's fine,' I say, 'that's my tic-hole.'

Frank and his girlfriend Angela arrive and Sebastian drives the four of us and his father out to the *Sächsische Schweiz* (the 'Saxon Switzerland'), the dramatic hills, cliffs, and forests stretching to the Czech border, favoured by walkers and climbers alike, and named hundreds of years ago by two Swiss visitors who thought the area reminded them of their homeland. I buy a postcard for René and Mariann, my friends in Switzerland: *'There's another one!'*

Soon we are hiking up a trail to the top of a hill with a panoramic view, gamely led by Dad, who knows all the best spots. As we stand on one peak he produces five miniature schnapps bottles from his rucksack. 'It's a tradition,' he say, 'Half for this hill, half for the next.'

We don't actually make the next hill because we run out of time nosing about the gulleys and ravines in the cliff faces on the way down, but drink the other half anyway.

Back at road level, we head along a narrow path by the side of a restaurant to the final destination of today's walk: the world-famous waterfall. I'm a little underwhelmed to see there is just a gentle trickle of water slopping over some rocks.

'Wait a minute, it hasn't started yet,' says Sebastian's dad. He consults a notice pinned up on a nearby post. 'Next one is twenty-five past.'

It seems that the Swiss visitors who originally named the area thought the only thing lacking to make it completely authentic was a waterfall. So they built one. The only problem was, there's wasn't enough water so it's stored somewhere upstream and released a couple of times an hour.

As the time approaches, stirring orchestral music starts up from a hidden loudspeaker. Some of the waiting tourists take a few steps back. Standing up close beneath the overhang I feel a stir of excitement too.

Someone near me says, here it comes! Suddenly the music cuts out, water comes whooshing over the rocks for about twenty seconds and…that's it. It's as if someone emptied a bath somewhere up the hill, possibly the most pathetic tourist attraction I have ever seen.

On the way back to Dresden we have the car radio on and Sebastian suddenly says, 'Listen…it's the waterfall music!'

Indeed it is. Never heard it before, and now twice in the space of an hour. 'What is that,' I ask, 'Wagner?'

'No,' says Sebastian, 'Vangelis.'

We drop off Frank and Angela and as soon as we get back Dad gets to work making the evening meal: salad, asparagus and schnitzel – and a 'vegetarian schnitzel' for me: bread soaked in egg and herbs then shallow fried.

After the meal we see some photos of a train journey Sebastian's father made recently to Moscow to find the final resting place of his father, who disappeared in 1951 during Stalin's purges. Recently two writers researched the subject and found his name among thousands of others who were sent to Russia after the end of the second world war and condemned to death, suspected of 'anti-soviet' activities. More than twenty million people killed by Stalin, ten million of them his own countrymen.

After this, Dad drives me and Sebastian to the riverside, where we plan to meet up with Frank again for an evening beer. The radio plays a mindlessly happy *Schlager* song with the lyrics, *Wir fliegen, fliegen, fliegen zum Regenbogen* ('We fly, fly, fly to the rainbow'), desperately inappropriate after the stories of Russian massacres we've just been hearing. We are dropped off beside some old wooden-gabled houses, the marks of the high water line from the floods a few years ago still visible halfway up the walls.

Frank is shackling up his bike to the railings down on the riverbank. The three of us sit in a beer garden as the sun sets behind a high iron bridge, the so-called 'Blue Wonder' whose intricate iron grid-work has coloured over the last hundred years to a gentle powder blue. Behind us high pylons mark a cable car route up a densely wooded hillside. Frank points at the station on the crest of the hill and tells me that in the DDR days his father used to be boss of the place and had his office up there. It was a well-paid and highly responsible job. Back then travelling outside the Soviet bloc was frowned on by the political establishment, but Frank's father wanted to see something of West Germany and applied for the official permission he would need. After many delays permission was granted and he set off on his travels…but when he got back to Dresden his job had mysteriously been given to someone else and he found himself *persona non grata* and unemployable.

We walk over the bridge and Sebastian points out the thick girder that curves up from just above road level to one of the towers. He tells me a mate of his used to run up it when he was drunk. It does like kind of tempting. But no, other dangers lie ahead of us. In the beer garden of the next bar hangs a sign: *This establishment cannot be held responsible for injuries to customers caused by falling fruit.* There are indeed a few small apples by my feet, their battered victims presumably now lying in some local casualty ward.

18th June
So that was the day off – a bit early in the tour really, but now on with the next six gigs. The first is in Chemnitz, only an hour's drive away so Sebastian and I have plenty of time in Dresden before we leave. Unfortunately we waste it on an expedition through the town centre in a futile attempt to find me some new trousers in case the repair doesn't hold. We leave with nothing to show for our efforts except a parking ticket.

We're at Chemnitz soon after seven, the first to arrive in the 'Subway To Peter' apart from Heidi behind the bar. It's a small cellar room with no stage but a good atmosphere and I've played here several times before.

The place quickly fills up and as soon as I start I remember why I like it. Standing on a stone floor, the audience right up close in front of me, we're eye to eye, it's direct and straight to the point. As usual, it's free entry tonight but a hat is passed round during the set for donations. There's a decent amount in it at the end but club boss Mario complains that some people were happy to watch me for two and a half hours and still only fork out their smallest coins. 'It's the download generation,' he says. 'They expect all their music for free. Mind you, Heidi can be quite persuasive with that hat. We call her Heidi the Pitbull.'

A celebratory round of the Subway To Peter home-made chilli and tomato schnapps and then we take a taxi over to where we will sleep, a room belonging to a road manager who is currently out on tour.

19th June
I don't know what to expect from the gig in Halle tonight: I'm not aware of having any kind of following there. It's a nice little bar though, and when we arrive mid-afternoon club owner Mirko is quick to show me that he's managed to get the gig announced in all three of the town's local papers, and each one carries a photo too. Also, it's a free entry gig, the university is right nearby, and fifty people would more or less fill the place so the omens are good. Mirko

takes Sebastian and me over to a small room in a building just up the road where we'll be able to spend the night. Then it's over to a radio station for a quick interview and a live song, and back to the bar for soundcheck and the long wait for gig time.

I step outside to get some air and take a walk around the town. Just up the hill, the windows of the building behind the opera house are open and the sounds of piano and a soprano voice drift across the heavy air. Down the road, there is a gently curving main street, trams clanking along it dangerously near to the pavement. A twenty minute walk takes me to the centre, a large square with two impressive churches ringed by a mix of old buildings and modern shops, a sombre bronze statue of Handel surveying the scene.

By the time I get back to the bar I'm delighted to see that it's packed and when I start to play there are quite a few people out in the street and crowding around the doorway, unable to fit in the room. I play for a long time and am very happy to win over a new crowd, the good mood only disrupted towards the end of the set when, just as I am starting the poem I often recite before Gary Gilmore's Eyes, a fight breaks out between two guys in front of the stage. A fight during a poem! It soon stops, and one of the participants comes up and says, 'Sorry TV, that guy has had too much to drink and he's been shoving me and sticking his lit cigarette into me for the last half hour and I just snapped.'

The place gradually empties out at around two in the morning, and I start to think about getting over to the room for some sleep, but Mirko is insistent that me and Sebastian accompany him for a drink at a club just down the road. 'Honestly, just 100 metres away!' he promises.

I have a feeling this could be dangerous, but agree that I'll go with them for just one drink then leave them to it. Down the road we stagger to a disco called 'Flower Power.' It's a depressing affair, a few people standing around aimlessly and some unpleasant music being played too loudly. We stand around for a while not really knowing what to do, then Mirko suddenly wheels around, points at the door and marches towards it. Sebastian and me follow and find him in a lively conversation with one of the drivers at taxi rank across the street. Sebastian goes over to find out what's going on. He explains, 'Mirko says there's nothing going on in Flower Power so we're taking a taxi somewhere else…'

Mirko turns to me and holds a hand up. 'Just two minutes away!'

'OK,' I say. 'Have fun!' – and before there's time for any argument I head off back up the road to the sleeping place.

20ᵗʰ June

Didn't hear a thing last night, but Sebastian is there on the other mattress, so it looks like he crept in without disturbing me. When he wakes up he tells me that he and Mirko took a cab to a party somewhere but weren't allowed in so they got back in the cab and ended up in Flower Power after all. Sebastian couldn't keep up with Mirko though, and after a couple of drinks left him with a few mates and came back to get some sleep.

We go back to the bar for breakfast and find a bleary-eyed Mirko, who explains that he arrived back last night only to discover he'd lost his bag with his door keys in it and had to sleep on the bench outside. He was woken up by the landlord, who complained that there were too many people at the gig making too much noise and if it happens again he'll close the bar down.

Storms are forecast for this afternoon, and we're not on the road for long before the first heavy drops of rain smack against the windshield. The clouds are lowering and dark and lightning is forking down over the hills ahead, but it's a relief to finally have some cool air flowing through the car after so many days of energy-sapping heat. In between the cheesy 80's Number One hits played by a DJ speaking German with an absurd American accent, the radio is giving bad weather warnings for most of Germany. In Kassel, where we are heading, there is a report about the five-yearly *Documenta* art festival currently taking place. One of the exhibits is a towering nine metre high structure made up of 1001 historic wooden chairs recovered from destroyed Chinese temples by artist Al WeiWei, and the area around it has had to be cordoned off because there is a danger it may collapse in the strong winds. The next news, half an hour later, which we can barely make out over the thundering rain, reports that the exhibit has just blown down.

There's no one at tonight's venue, *Das Haus*, when we arrive in Kassel so we while away some time in an internet café and then grab a bite to eat in a bar. *Das Haus* is a very small run-down building standing in a patch of waste ground near the railway lines. It was the first place I ever played in Kassel, about ten years ago and I remember it well: the area where the bands play no bigger than a living room, no stage, a makeshift bar along one side, a queue in the corridor for the one toilet, the concert starting at midnight and a very small audience. I have mixed feelings about playing here again.

When we get back to the venue, promoter Christoph has arrived and is setting up the P.A. system, a couple of small speakers up on stands wired to an ancient-looking mixing desk. I have a quick soundcheck while the support band are setting up and it's not too bad despite the fact one of the speakers isn't working properly. In a room this small it's not a problem. I ask Christoph about the hotel and he tells me that he didn't book one as he thought I was staying with my mate Steffen. I tell him I hadn't arranged to stay with Steffen because I thought he was booking a hotel. Luckily Steffen turns up a few minutes later and tells me he has a bed made up back at his place anyway, just in case.

People are gradually arriving, most hanging around outside the venue as it's still very warm and the rain has stopped. A sign outside says 'PLEASE do not piss in the grounds around the club. Please go and piss against the church opposite instead.'

While the support band play I spend most of the time behind a counter in an adjacent room where Sebastian has set up the merchandising. Quite a few people wander in and try and order a drink from me.

Then it's showtime and a very nice show it is too – close up and intimate, people singing along and a great atmosphere in the room. I end up playing for over two hours then return to the merchandising room, where the windows have been opened to try and get some air into the venue and my sweat-soaked T-shirt suddenly clings chill and clammy to me.

A guy comes up to say how much he enjoyed the gig, and mentions that he's working at the *Documenta* and I should really try and get along to see it. He says that if I have time tomorrow he could probably sneak me and Sebastian in for free, so we arrange a time to meet up. Sebastian's staying with Christoph tonight and says he will come over and pick me up from Steffen's in the morning and we'll head over to the exhibition.

Steffen and his girlfriend and a couple of other friends of theirs squeeze into their car and we drive over to his place. He has a new flat since last time I was here. 'But it's still a nice place, and clean, and there's still a spare bed for you,' he says. 'I just hope you don't have a cat allergy!'

Ah.

While the rest prepare to start grilling some *Würst* on the balcony, I go into the bathroom, rinse out my stage T-shirts in the sink and hang them over the shower rail to dry. I am punk rock. Then I grab a cheese roll and join the others. Steffen opens a bottle of red wine. We spend a very pleasant hour working through the wine, then I head for bed, happy in the knowledge that I can sleep late tomorrow

21st June
On the stroke of nine, violent hammering starts up in the next apartment. My bed is shaking. I drag myself upright, glance out of the window and see

a central heating van parked outside, a workman fetching a piece of heavy machinery that looks like a jack hammer out of the back of it, and I realise sleep is over. I am a noise magnet.

Still, gives me plenty of time to shower and take a leisurely breakfast with Steffen and his girlfriend. They apologise for the noise and say it's been going on for three days now.

'But you're lucky – yesterday they started up at 7:10!'

The cats take an interest in me changing strings on the guitar. I'm feeling slightly wheezy and swallow an anti-histamine tablet to be on the safe side. I don't like taking them, but I always carry an emergency packet with me since the Barcelona Cat Incident of 2005.

Sebastian arrives at midday and we walk over to the nearby park where one of the main galleries of the *Documenta* is housed in a marquee. To one side lies the collapsed pile of sodden wood that was once the star exhibit. Sebastian tells me that he heard on the news that WeiWei came to survey the damage late yesterday and declared, 'It's an improvement!'

Large parts of the park are still under water and a light rain is falling. We slosh our way over the grass to meet the guy who was at the gig yesterday, and he lets us in a back door and gives us a quick tour of some of the more interesting exhibits. Then he is called away to do some work, leaving Sebastian and me to look around at our leisure.

A couple of hours later we hit the road for Frankfurt, my still-damp T-shirts hanging decoratively from the back windows. Tonight I'll be staying with my friends Roland and Christine in a village just outside Frankfurt. I had hoped to drop by this afternoon, but there's a radio interview scheduled before soundcheck so I send them a text to say I'm not going to be able to make it.

Dreikönigskeller is a really nice little cellar club. The room is narrow with a bar down one side and a stage at the far end, a few cinema seats along one side of it with a kitsch Elvis bust in a Tiki-styled alcove above. After soundcheck Sebastian introduces me to a mate of his who has wandered in to watch, 'TV, this is Elvis…'

Elvis tells me that he wasn't intending to stay for the gig as he has to get up for work at five in the morning, but was so fascinated by the soundcheck that he's decided to hang around after all. Sebastian's girlfriend Claudia arrives and together they set up a ticket desk by the door. The manager tells them that they shouldn't let more than 65 people in as it gets too uncomfortable. We negotiate and he says that as I'm just solo we could maybe go up to 80 people.

TALES OF THE EMERGENCY SANDWICH

First through the door are Claudia's mum and dad who became fans after seeing me play last year. Soon Roland arrives, and says what a shame it is that I won't be staying with him tonight. I say, 'But I am staying with you tonight…'

He misunderstood my text message this afternoon to mean that I wouldn't be able to come by their place at all, not just this afternoon. He hurriedly phones Christina, who's back at home looking after their kids, and asks her to make up a bed for me.

Soon we have our full complement of eighty people and it's time to start. There are quite a few young girl fans down the front, one of them with her mother, and when things get a bit boisterous towards the end, two of the girls and the mother get up on stage and sit on the row of cinema seats to watch from there. Things get rather overexcited during the last few songs when some slam dancing breaks out at the front. I watch the girls and older people slip to the back of the room while the teenage boys crash into tables, sending glasses shattering, and bump against the hanging P.A. speakers which start to swing dangerously. One song to go and I ask the dancers to be aware that this is only a small place so please take it easy, but afterwards the dancing is more extreme than ever. At one point they knock my microphone away from me and when I bring it back the power is dead so I have to explain acoustically that that's the end of the gig.

There's a smattering of confused applause and demands for encores so I say we'll try and get the sound running again. The manager comes up to the stage, pretends to fiddle with some cables and whispers that he turned the sound off because the audience was getting out of control. He says I can do another song but please tell them not to break the place up.

I make the announcement to cheers and launch into another song, but a couple of the teenagers soon start slamming around the floor and jostling people again. I ask them to stop again, and when they don't, I do.

I don't think I've ever ended a gig in mid-song before and it feels very unsatisfactory, but I don't want to be responsible for people getting hurt. As I work my way through the crammed room – thanks for the gig and commiserations about how it ended coming from all sides – I see that one of the girls who was down the front has taken it into her hands to eject one of the slam-dancing boys from the club. 'I told you twenty times to stop shoving me, you ruined the gig for everyone, now just GET OUT!'

He has the glazed look of a teenager who has had far more alcohol than he can handle and doesn't really know what's going on any more, while she has the look of an unstoppable force as she edges him firmly step by step towards the exit.

My newly-washed T-shirt, which had finally just got dry before the gig after I hung it up in front of the stage lights, is now once again slopping wet. I wring it out and change into a new one then gather my bags to take to Roland's car. Sebastian will be staying with Claudia's parents and we arrange to meet at a rest station on the motorway tomorrow. Just before we leave, the teenager who was causing all the trouble earlier comes back, sobered-up and embarrassed, to say he's lost his keys, so the manager gets a torch out and we all have a look around the dance floor.

Back at Roland's, Christine has left me a welcome note on the kitchen table with a bottle of wine next to it. Roland hunts for a corkscrew and by around four in the morning we have seen off the wine and had a good chat and now I'm feeling the pull of sleep. Roland and Christine will be off to work in a few hours, and their kids to school, so I will have the house to myself and really get the chance to sleep as long as I want. We're way out in the country, no other houses nearby to disturb me, but just in case I am being stalked by rogue central heating engineers, it's in with the earplugs – then out with the lights.

22nd June
Peace, perfect peace. I sleep through until 10:30, then at midday Roland arrives back from work to drive me out to the meeting point. Half an hour later I am swapped from car to car and then I'm on the road with Sebastian and Claudia heading to Cologne.

There's heavy traffic, the cars bunching and occasionally coming to a standstill, and the heavy rainstorms only make the journey more depressing. When a rainbow appears ahead of us I attempt a chorus of *Wir fliegen, fliegen, fliegen zum Regenbogen* but it doesn't really lighten the mood. By the time we get into the city we're all hungry and exhausted. There's just time for a brief stop at Sebastian's flat before we have to go to Stereo Wonderland for soundcheck, then straight after that we drive to a nearby radio station for an interview. A band from Berlin called the Bottrops who are playing a club just down the road from the Stereo Wonderland are being interviewed right after me, and are already in the studio. One of them tells me that he saw me play once in Berlin K.O.B. and I get quite nostalgic: my first solo gig in Berlin, around fifteen years ago on my first solo tour of Germany. A lot has happened since then.

I play a song live in the studio and then as a surprise the presenter gets the Bottrops into the room, says that it would make his day if we could all have a go at his favourite song and hands round photocopies of the lyrics to 'Bored Teenagers'. It turns out to be a lot of fun. I play the song as normal, and two DJs, the Bottrops, and Sebastian all join in on the choruses. Hurrah for independent radio!

Then it's back to the Stereo Wonderland, where a small crowd is already gathering outside. At ten I'm onstage, the place is packed, the adrenaline kicks in and I play for over two hours.

Back at Sebastian's place we open a bottle of wine, eat some *Brötchen* and relax for a while, letting the stress of the last week of travelling drain away. Just one gig to go now, and I'm not due to play until midnight so there's no hurry to get there tomorrow.

But now it's starting to get light outside. Sebastian fixes a sheet of black bin liner over the window of the living room and puts down a mattress on the floor for me, then it's earplugs in and – apart from what's filtering in through the bin liner – lights out.

23rd June

A week of dates behind me and the trouser repair is still holding, although the rest of the crop of holes and rips have got somewhat worse. Unlike the rest of my clothes which are going straight into the washing machine tomorrow when I get home, the trousers will go straight into the dustbin.

We sit down for a late breakfast and I'm watching the heavy grey clouds scurrying across the sky with concern. The festival tonight in Gelsenkirchen is open air. Towards late afternoon a friend of ours, Steffi, arrives to join us for the trip over there. It's an hour's drive through the industrial heartland of the Ruhr Valley, and we desperately flip through the radio channels to find anything decent to listen to during the trip. We nose the car through the throngs of punk rockers hanging around the festival site and get some curious looks from the security guys at the gate when we wind down the windows to say who we are and the sound of cool jazz music at high volume comes blasting out.

It's a beautiful setting for a festival, an amphitheatre with a large stage under an awning, a canal running behind it. I'll be playing on a second stage at the top of the hill, last on after twelve bands on the main stage. Sebastian, Claudia and Steffi start getting the CDs out of the car to set up a merchandise stand while I go off to do a quick interview for an internet TV channel. It has to be quick because we can only do it in the ten minute changeover period between bands or there will be too much background noise.

Late evening and I'm getting excited about the gig. It's been a long wait but the rain has held off, and as I've been wandering around the site over the last few hours a lot of people have told me how much they're looking forward to seeing me play. What's slightly worrying is that I have only been given 35 minutes on stage, and there is a strict curfew. As the last band starts, I go up the hill and meet up with the crew running my stage and have a quick soundcheck. Everything ready.

Nearing midnight, about twenty people have gathered in front of my stage but the band on the main stage are still playing. I go to chat with the people leaning on the front barrier. 'This is their hit,' one of them says, 'it must be their last number.'

It isn't. It's now five past midnight. Suddenly there is a gust of wind and rain comes sheeting down. I make my apologies to the people I've been chatting with and dash for shelter. Technicians run up to the microphone and monitors and pull them back to the middle of the stage where the rain can't reach them.

Finally the other band stops, and I get straight to the microphone and introduce my first song. I have less than half an hour before the curfew so there's no time to lose, even though so far there are only forty or fifty soaked people standing in the mud, and I have the sinking feeling this could literally be a washout. But during the first few minutes people start to arrive and soon a couple of hundred have gathered There's a small disaster when I break a string and have to stop to put a new one on, but everyone gets straight back into it as soon as I start playing again. The rain stops, people start singing along, and I play a few minutes over my set time and walk off the ramp at the back of the stage to the sound of applause ringing out.

The promoter is standing at the back of the stage and apologises about me having to stop so early, but explains they will get complaints from nearby houses if they go on any later. Out front, the crowd are still loudly shouting for more. He looks anxiously at me. 'Can you do a very short song?'

I run up the ramp onto the stage to a big cheer, but find the tech guy is already clearing everything away. I tell him the promoter says I can do one more, and he says, 'Hmm...can you play without monitors?'

Hell yes. I can't hear what I'm doing but I guess it's all coming through the front speakers because I can see everyone singing along. Then the song's over and an even bigger cheers erupts than last time I stopped. The entire PA system has now been switched off but I can't leave like this, so I walk up to the front of the stage and do one more song without any amplification at all. This might work in a small club, but it's a bit ridiculous in a big festival. The crowd know what's going on though, and even though anyone further back than the first few rows presumably can't hear what I'm doing, they clap along and those at the front sing with me. It's a magical, if stupid, moment.

I make my way back to the merchandising stand to find a bit of a strange atmosphere. Claudia tells me that Sebastian had been out front watching me play but was keeping an eye on the merchandising table at the same time and saw two guys approach it and one of them pocket a CD. He rushed up and grabbed the guy but he played innocent. 'I'm a friend of TV's' he claimed. 'He lets me have all his records for free!'

Seeing that no one believed him, he then tried another approach: 'I wasn't stealing it anyway, I was just showing my friend here how easy it would be to steal it if someone wanted to…'

A disappointing end to the day, but we soon cheer up as we head off out of the site past the drenched audience who will have to spend another night under canvas, while we will soon be in Cologne in the warm and dry.

Sebastian reckons he knows a quicker route back home than the directions he has been given by the festival organisers. I feel that there was unnecessary panic from the girls in the back when he asked me to hold the steering wheel while he checked the map. Soon we are back in his flat and, come to think of it, it's my end-of-tour party, which involves a bottle of wine, some snacks, lots of good conversation, and at some point as things begin to get vague, a round of the Subway To Peter tomato-chilli schnapps and a rubber Adolf Hitler mask.

24th June

Sebastian drops me off at the airport. This flight's with Lufthansa, and they seem happy to let me take my guitar on board with me. 'Hang on a minute,' I say, reaching into the guitar case, 'I'd better take these string clippers out, they always get picked up by the X-ray – not that I can see how they could possibly be dangerous.' I demonstrate how the inward-facing blades only open a couple of millimetres.

The check-in girl looks on as I pack the clippers into the hold suitcase. 'Well, you know how tight security is these days…oh, you seem to have cut your finger there…'

'*Ooh, ah*, it's nothing,' I say, nonchalantly trying to stop the flow of blood.

I'm swiftly through security and sit in the airside café with a coffee. I check through my shoulder bag and find a booklet that someone put in my guitar case while I was playing last night. I didn't have time to look at it when I came off stage, but now I see it's a nice collection of photos from a gig I played in Germany last year. On the front is printed 'Herr Schmidt, Neuss 2006.'

Just then two young guys who have been hanging around nearby approach. They are just off on holiday and seem pretty pleased to meet me. 'The last time we saw you play,' one of them says, 'was in Neuss last year.' The very gig at which the photos I'm currently looking at were taken. The guy has a guitar case strapped on his back and asks if I'd sign it. Afterwards he looks at the signature with awe. 'Great!'

8. NO TIME TO BE 51 (2007)

<u>5th July</u>
Back to Germany to play a few solo gigs and one festival with the Bored Teenagers. I have new trousers.

PamP picks me up from the airport and we drive over to tonight's venue, Neuland – certainly *neu* for me as I've never played here before - and in fact the venue has only recently opened for live music. Along the way PamP tells me that the gig has been featured in all the local magazines, often as 'Tip Of The Day,' and when we arrive his co-promoter Brigitta shows us that we even have a good article in major magazine Prinz.

Brigitta takes us to a small restaurant across the courtyard in a renovated car repair workshop where a larger-than-life Italian chef offers to cook up whatever we want, vegetarian no problem. He show us a huge bowl of *trompette* mushrooms and suggests he cooks some of them with spaghetti. 'Just a child's portion for me,' I say, and explain that I can't go on stage with a full stomach.

'Nonsense!' he replies. 'Spaghetti is packed with carbohydrates, good for sportsmen!' Then he clamps a cigar between his teeth and sets about cooking.

Brigitta lowers her voice and tells me that he is a great chef, but has to be handled carefully. 'I once had one of his dishes and asked if I could have some Parmesan on it – he nearly killed me…'

Time for soundcheck, then a two man crew from Munich TV arrive. They are going to do a quick interview with me now and film a few songs at the gig later.

We go back to the restaurant, where the camera and lights are already set up. There are quite few people over there now, eating or just sitting around and chatting, and before we start they are asked to keep quiet so that it will seem like we are in a proper television studio. The illusion holds until the last question, *You travel all over Germany – do you have a favourite city?* Considering the programme is going out on a local station, I answer, 'Why – Munich of course!' and everyone in the room starts cheering.

We film a quick station I.D. clip – 'I'm TV Smith and you're watching *München TV!* – with me sitting on a bench hacked out of a tree trunk, outside in the wind and rain. I have to remember to hold the microphone the right way round because on the back it says *RTL München*, a different channel.

Neuland is a great place: there's the restaurant, a courtyard that currently has no one in it because the weather is so bad, a bunch of artists' workshops, and two live music venues. By showtime there are around one hundred people in the club, just enough to make it work but not as many as we'd hoped for. PamP says, 'That's the trouble with getting in Prinz: now everyone thinks you are mainstream so they don't come.'

I hang around by the bar after I've played and someone comes up to me. 'I have a bad question for you,' he says. 'How old are you?'

'Fifty-one.' I tell him, and he seems somehow disappointed that I wasn't bothered by the fact he'd asked.

A few minutes later a couple approach. The woman says, 'I have a bad question for you.'

'Fifty-one,' I say.

She says, 'Er – no...I wanted to know: if you had the choice of three breakfasts, would you have, a) whisky and cigarettes, b) bacon and scrambled eggs, or, c) a healthy yoghurt and fruit drink?'

'I'd prefer to have some muesli with yoghurt and some fruit, and then maybe a cappuccino.' I say. I've just been on stage and sung forty songs and drunk a few beers, and I'm not quite sure why we're having this conversation.

We're back at Pamp's place by four, drink a *Weizen* for a nightcap and get to bed at five, the sky already getting light and the bloody birds singing.

6th July

Garden Gang are playing support at tonight's gig in Karlsruhe, and PamP drives us to their rehearsal room in Munich to pick them up. It's all change with the band recently. The last line up split shortly after they backed me up last year in England at the Wasted festival – just coincidence I'm sure. Since then my friend René from Switzerland joined them on bass, and they've been through a number of drummers. They've settled on a new guitarist but he found out at the last minute that he couldn't come today, so a friend of his has been drafted in as replacement. The haven't actually all rehearsed together in the same room at the same time so they're understandably nervous.

René and the new drummer will be getting to Karlsruhe on their own, the rest of us climb into PamP's minibus and set off, first through the country roads to try and avoid the Friday traffic, then onto the autobahn where we immediately find the Friday traffic and a journey that should take about ninety minutes drags on for more than six hours.

TALES OF THE EMERGENCY SANDWICH

No one at the venue is too bothered about us turning up late. I don't know if it's something in the water but the Karlsruhe temperament always seems to be relaxed and unhurried. Anyway, there's still an hour to go before the doors open at nine, plenty of time to sit down and have something to eat with the crew before we bother with details like soundcheck.

The Mikado is a culture and arts centre in a dead end street of old army barracks on the outskirts of the town. When the army moved out, many of the people working here moved in. As well as the venue, there's a library and a restaurant, and the place is clean and well run. There is a sparky nine year old girl running around the venue who I remember is the daughter of the guy who promoted my last gig here. It sticks in my mind because last time she spent a lot of time talking to me, as did her father, who later got quite drunk and rode home on his bike through the snow, turning up to breakfast next morning with a mysterious bruise down one side of his face.

The girl comes over and asks how old I am, and when I tell I her I'm fifty-one her eyes almost pop out of her head. She reminds me that her father got me to sign a poster for her last time.

'Where is your father?' I ask.

'Oh,' she says cheerfully, 'he's in the clinic.'

She shows me how to cross my eyes, then tells me the storylines of some of her favourite fairy tales. She has a pronounced accent and speaks quite softly so I have to listen hard and do some guesswork to follow what she's saying. I assume *Aschenputtel* is Cinderella, although there seems to also be an *Aschenbrödel*, and both stories sound completely different from the Cinderella I know, one of them involving three magic nuts out of which various animals appear. One of the animals, she tells me, is an *Eidechse*. I have no idea what an *Eidechse* is so I asks her to describe it.

'It's about this big' she, says, holding her hands apart a little.

'So – smaller than a dog?'

'Yes.'

'Is it a rabbit?'

'No.'

'Squirrel?'

'No. Smaller. There are lots of them in my garden.'

'Is it a house pet or a wild animal.'

'It's a wild animal.'

'Not a rat?'

'No,'

'A mouse?'
'No.'
'Smaller than a mouse?'
'Mmm – thinner...'
'Bigger than an ant, though?'
'Yes, thinner than a mouse and bigger than an ant.'

I'm really not getting anywhere with this, and meanwhile there are quite a few people in the venue and Garden Gang are just about to start.

I notice Nic, another of my friends from Switzerland, passing through the crowd. 'I thought I was in the wrong place,' he says, 'the toilets are clean!'

Considering the lack of rehearsal, Garden Gang do a great job and get an enthusiastic reception. The only song that really goes wrong is their cover of one of mine – just a coincidence I'm sure.

I end up playing for two hours with a seven song encore. Halfway through the encores, it suddenly hits me: *Eidechse*. It's a lizard!

7th July

The sun is shining at last and we eat breakfast outside in the communal gardens, resulting in a slight sunburn. It's 10:30, the street has been closed off and a stage is being built in front of the entrance to the Mikado for a festival to mark the 10th anniversary of the collective taking over the street.

I have my own festival to go to in Geislingen. Tonight will be the first-ever performance in Germany of the Adverts' 'Crossing The Red Sea' album played with The Bored Teenagers – otherwise known as Suzy & Los Quattro minus Suzy – as my backing band. We have the headline slot. Suzy's flying in with the rest of the band, and they'll also play their own set earlier in the afternoon.

PamP has to take the rest of Garden Gang back to Munich so René drives me to Geislingen. After a couple of hours on the road, we arrive at the town and spot the festival site way up on the forested hillside among the ruins of an old castle. We collect our passes and get taken to the catering tent just past the entrance. One of the girls working there shows me the eight-pack of Red Bull, two giant bags of taco chips, and packet of fruity yoghurt sweets which have been specially ordered for me – which I find a bit strange as I wouldn't want any of them. In any case there is food and drink a-plenty here, plastic crates heaped full of *Brötchen*, cheese, fruit, vegetables, snacks and drinks of all sorts. I could prepare enough emergency cheese sandwiches here to last me for a couple of months.

TALES OF THE EMERGENCY SANDWICH

I go to check in to the hotel and bump into bassist Jonathan and the rest of the Bored Teenagers, who have just been picked up from Stuttgart airport by Fischi, one of the festival organisers. I give a little cheer when I see them.

Jonathan looks at me and says, 'You don't know, do you?'

There's been a disaster: last night Suzy suffered a severe asthma attack and had to be rushed to hospital. Jonathan spent the night with her, didn't get any sleep, and wasn't sure until the last minute whether he would be able to leave her. By 6:50 she had stabilised and he made the decision to come – good news for our gig but obviously the Suzy & Los Quattro performance has been cancelled.

It's hard to imagine a more atmospheric location for a festival. From the road a track winds down through the forested hillside to the castle ruins. There's a narrow wooden bridge across a steep ravine and then you arrive in front of the stage, a few sections of the old fortifications scattered around the site. Behind the stage is a stone tower which is being used as the dressing room area. Fischi takes me up to the top, where there is a breathtaking view of the valley below.

We make our way back, passing an old tractor going the other way pulling a trailer loaded with band equipment, the only way to get it from the road down to the stage. A young kid stops me as we go across the bridge. 'So you were in one of the first punk bands?' he says.

How to get the equipment to the stage.
Geislingen 2007

The stage. Geislingen 2007

'Yes, in 1977.'

'Wow, I'm looking forward to it…original punk rock! So all the songs are going to be REALLY FAST?'

'Ummm….'

Up in the catering tent I come across Jonathan and the band, all sat at one of the long tables, tucking into the taco chips. Beer *aficionado* Claudio is opening a bottle. He sees me watching and says, 'I know there's a long time before we play but this is the first one. All I've drunk so far is two apple juices.' He shudders. 'I need this to take away the taste.'

Jonathan explains that it was him who ordered all the weird stuff on the rider, not realising that there would be all the food and drink we wanted available anyway. 'In a festival in Spain, there would be five bottles of beer, and one of the other bands would already have drunk them before you arrived.' He points at the bag of fruity yoghurt sweets and explains that it was just a joke, and anyway he actually asked for Haribou bears.

Claudio looks up. 'Haribou beers?'

I say that I'm glad they didn't get them because Haribou bears aren't vegetarian.

Claudio says, 'Really? What's in them that isn't vegetarian? Well…bear, obviously…'

TALES OF THE EMERGENCY SANDWICH

He spots something under the table and reaches down. It's a bullet. He holds it up and says, 'This really looks like a live one.' It does too – we are out in the woods in hunting country after all – and when he tosses it back under the table, I flinch. This would be a bad time to get a foot blown off. Well, there's never a good time

Dusk falls, and I go back to the hotel to pick up my stage clothes, then walk back down to the festival area with René and PamP, who has just got back from Munich. We head down the track and a group of teenage girls are coming the other way. When one of them approaches and says she has a question for me. I'm all ready to say 'Fifty-one,' but she actually asks: '*Stift oder Fisch?*' which translates as *pen or fish?*

I'm taken aback for a moment.

'Quick, quick, just answer – *Stift oder Fisch?*'

'Okay: *Fisch.*'

'HOORAY!' She throws her arms in the air, goes back to her friends and dances around a bit.

Hooray!

On the way to the backstage area I bump into a few friends and we are standing around chatting when a guy comes over and asks me to sign a programme for his sister who is sitting by the bar and too shy to come and say hello. I give her a wave and sign it and the guy is really grateful. Just then Jonathan comes along, so I mention he's in the band and could sign it too, After Jonathan has signed the guy proffers it to René. 'Are you in the band too?'

'No, no,' says René, backing away.

'Sign it anyway,' says the guy, now jubilant. 'Everyone can sign it!'

Hmm, somehow *my* autograph now feels a bit cheapened…

Night falls. We get on stage and in the spill from the lights I can see a sea of faces in the audience, nearly all too young to have been born when the Adverts were around. Despite that they dance and crowd-surf and we have a great gig. We come off stage steaming, give each other a damp hug and feel pretty pleased with ourselves.

After drying off and changing into a new T-shirt I head back up the path towards the catering tent. Most of the crowd have left now, and the trees are lit from below with floodlights so it feels like walking through a fairytale forest. I keep expecting Cinderella to appear with her three magic nuts.

There's still a lot of food and drink to be got through at the catering tent. Most of the bands have already left, but the festival crew are taking the opportunity to relax now that the day is over.

One of the organisers, Martina, has her teenage daughter with her, and is in two minds whether to risk drinking a beer. She tells me that last year she ended up sharing a bottle of whisky with The Real MacKenzies and got so drunk that her embarrassed daughter got a T-shirt made the next day and arrived at the festival wearing it. The slogan on the front read: I HAVE NO MOTHER.

Martina's revenge was swift. She went to the same T-shirt shop and turned up the day after with one reading, DAUGHTER, WHAT DAUGHTER?

8th July

We all gather for a late breakfast in the catering tent, where there still seems to be a never-ending supply of food. I avoid the freshly boiled *Weisswürst* – minced veal in intestine – and go instead for a healthy bowl of muesli, fruit and yoghurt. Or weren't you asking?

The Bored Teenagers say their goodbyes and get driven off to the airport. PamP and I have an hour before we need to set off for the next gig, so we wander down to the festival with Martina and her husband. Today is children's day. There are lots of activities for youngsters; craft sessions, face-painting, and a rock climbing competition. A magician is touring the area doing close-up magic to small groups. It's hot and heavy weather, the sun shining but some threatening clouds over the nearby hills. Time for us to leave. As we wave goodbye and head up the road, the first drops of rain splash down. Martina's husband shouts after us, 'The skies are crying because you're leaving.'

The roads are awash as we drive north and it takes us longer than expected to get to the Clou in Grünberg. It's a small club but a good crowd of people arrive during the course of the evening so I play for two hours. While I'm hanging around by the merchandising table chatting to people afterwards, a woman called Bärbel, who lets Garden Gang sleep at her place when they play here, suddenly says to me, 'TV, how old are you?'

I say, 'First you're supposed to say, "I've got a bad question." Then you say: "TV, how old are you?"'

She shrugs, 'I always ask things directly.'

'Okay then. Fifty-one.'

'Are those your only trousers?'

Promoter Rolf drives me and PamP and Bärbel back to his place where we sit around his kitchen table and have a final beer. Bärbel thinks she might have offended me asking about my trousers but tells me 'at least' five of her friends had asked her to find out.

'I can't imagine why they asked *me*,' she says.

'Probably because they knew you'd go right ahead and ask me,' I say. 'After all, you always ask things directly.'

She looks unconvinced but doesn't pursue the subject. Then she turns to PamP. 'So, did the old line-up of Garden Gang break up with lots of arguments and everyone ending up hating each other?'

9th July
A strange feeling; the tour over, nothing to do today except the long drive back to Munich, then my flight tomorrow. We drop in to see Bärbel and her husband Timo for an hour and sit on the terrace while their two large friendly dogs plod around us. The weather is heavy but cool, and clouds are scudding across the sky. We'll remember 2007 as the summer that never came.

It's mid-evening by the time we get back to Markt Indersdorf, later by the time we've unpacked the van, showered, and opened a *Weizen*. It's too late to shop and cook, so instead PamP and I go out to a surprisingly good Greek restaurant, something I wouldn't have expected to find in a village in Bavaria, and have a relaxed meal with some retsina and ouzo, then go back to his place and open a bottle of *rosé*. It's all too much really, but how do you fill that vacuum of still being out on the road, but with no gig to play? Suddenly it's five in the morning.

10th July
I'm up at ten to pack, and there's no sign of PamP. I give him until eleven, then knock on his door and he gets up hurriedly, embarrassed that his alarm clock didn't work. He brews up a coffee but there's no time to drink it, so we carry the cups out to the van and I hold them steady while we dash through the country lanes towards the airport.

There is a lot of traffic on the normally-deserted roads and we arrive in a panic. Munich airport is a lot more relaxed than Heathrow, and even though I'm running late no one is in any hurry at the X-ray machines and the security people seem to be having a nice chat with everyone on the way through while I bounce around nervously at the end of the queue, looking like a terrorist.

Through the gate, and just one final unnecessary security check before I can get on the plane. 'Sir, what is your final destination?'

More of a philosophical question, I would have thought. But wherever it is, I'm getting there.

9. BACK TO THE FUTURE USED TO BE BETTER (2007)

<u>21st July</u>
Three hours in the queue at Stansted so that I will be safe from terrorism. I want an 'I'll risk it' airline.

I'm flying to petite Altenburg airport in eastern Germany for the Back To The Future open air festival, where I'll be playing the 'Crossing The Red Sea' show with the Bored Teenagers, just two weeks after our last performance at the Helfenstein festival. I heard that the second day of that was abandoned due to heavy rain, and the weather has been worryingly unsettled ever since. However, the forecast is for thunderstorms clearing up to give a hot, sunny weekend, so things are looking promising. The other good news is that Suzy Quattro has fully recovered from the asthma attack which forced her to pull out of the Helfenstein so she will be flying in from Barcelona with the rest of the band and playing her own gig with them tomorrow.

A tanned, wiry man in shorts, who looks a little older than me, meets me in the Arrivals lounge and tells me he'll be taking me on the 90 minute drive to the festival site. On the journey I ask if he knows Holm, the promoter who invited me to this gig, and he say, 'I do – I'm Günther, his father.'

He hadn't been expecting to do this driving, he tells me, but has been drafted in to help out since the tragedy.

'Tragedy?'

'No one told you?'

He explains that Holger, the main organiser of the festival, was working in one of the marquees a couple of days ago while the site was being made ready for the weekend. A thunderstorm started up and he stepped outside with some of the rest of the crew to watch it. Suddenly a bolt of lightning struck the spot where they were standing. The others were thrown clear and survived with severe burns, Holger was killed instantly.

The rest of the organisers thought about cancelling the whole event, but eventually decided that Holger would have wanted it to continue. They also hope to be able to give some of the profits from the festival to his wife and six month old daughter.

Fitness freak Günther is available to help because he broke a hand three weeks ago while in-line skating and can't take part in any more sport until it heals properly. He can just about drive, although changing gear is sometimes a bit tricky. During the journey he points out the disused brown coal quarries on either side of the autobahn, flooded to create scenic lakes. The festival is taking place on an exposed isthmus jutting out into one of these lakes – idyllic in theory, but they hadn't planned for the inclement weather. The occasional storms that have passed over since Holger was killed has led to many of the audience running for their cars, the safest place because of the rubber tyres. Some people were too frightened to stay, and have packed up and left for home.

In the backstage area I do a couple of interviews with fanzines then go out front to meet my mates Carl and Paul from England who have a merchandising tent set up. They're not selling much because people aren't really browsing in the bad weather. Yesterday their tent blew away. Carl comes backstage with me in search of a beer, and on the way we bump into a photographer I know called Janine. I introduce them.

'Janine?' says Carl. 'That's a very pretty name.'

'Carl?' says Janine. 'Here in Germany that's an old man's name.'

Carl turns to me. 'I was rather liking your friend Janine but now I am going off her.'

As stage time approaches I find myself pacing up and down nervously, partly because my band still haven't arrived, and partly because the clouds have thickened, the weather has become heavy and sticky and rain seems inevitable.

It's with some relief that I see a people-carrier roll into the backstage area and the Bored Teenagers spill out, along with Suzy and Johnny Quattro. In a rush we head down the hill to the main stage, which sits in a natural amphitheatre, set up the gear and do a short soundcheck. Just as the time to start arrives, so does the rain.

It's only 7:15, so still light, and I can see everybody in the audience as their clothes gradually darken with the wet. For me up on stage it's quite refreshing as a cool wind blows the spray over me – it's hot work up there – but it is a shame to see the rain sweeping down over the crowds, even though everyone seems to be enjoying the show anyway.

They're running a tight schedule to fit all the bands on, and after just one encore it's all over. I ignore the steady drizzle and go down to the side of the stage to say hello to a few of the audience. A girl from Poland tells me she's looking forward to seeing me play in her country. I tell her I'd love to play in Poland one day. She says, 'No, I'm looking forward to seeing you play. When you come. In October.'

'I'm playing in Poland in October?'

'Yes. Organised by Petr.'

I say, 'I know he's getting me some gigs in the Czech Republic in October – maybe he'll get me one in Poland too.'

She says, 'He has. You're staying at my place.'

The rains stops and The Boys arrive, they're playing later and were a bit out of practice so they've just had a rehearsal in a nearby town. Back at the beer tent I'm surprised to find all the crew from the Subway To Peter club in Chemnitz, where I played a couple of weeks ago, doing the catering. Günther, my driver from this morning, comes bounding up to me with a big grin on his face and tells me how great he thought the show was. 'When are you playing next?' he demands. 'I want to see it!' He says he wishes he could take me to the airport tomorrow, but I'll be on the same flight as The Boys and we can't all fit in his car, so a guy with a minibus will be taking us. 'Just make sure you give yourselves a good hour and a half and you should be fine,' he says. That will mean being on the road by around 9:30.

An amiable chap introduces himself as Jürgen and says he is the distributor in Germany for my new CD, the live recording of the Bored Teenagers concert in the London 100 Club in April. Jürgen also plays in a band who have just finished their gig on the tent stage.

'We dedicated a song to you,' he says, chuckling.

'Really?'

'Yes. The song is called *Peter ist ein Arschloch,* and – heh, heh – we changed it to…'

Let me guess.

'…*TV ist ein Arschloch!*'

I was rather liking the German distributor of my new record but now I am going off him.

I finally get the chance to change into a dry T-shirt then sit around with the Bored Teenagers, Carl and Janine, to wait out the hour or so until The Boys play. Janine says she has some good photographs of the concert. 'You looked such a *Schlamper* up there,' she laughs.

'A *Schlamper*?'

'Yes, it's like…like, someone who wears torn up old clothing, or, like – usually, a woman, someone who sleeps with too many men, a bitch…'

I was rather liking Janine but now I am going off her.

With just a few minutes to go before The Boys start, we hear the first cracks of thunder, and suddenly the rain is hammering down so hard on the roof of the marquee that we can hardly hear ourselves speak.

Janine is a huge Boys fan and watches with despair as two people struggle against the wind to get the flaps of the marquee shut. 'I've got to see The Boys!' she shouts, 'But…I've got soap in my hair!'

'I love The Boys, but there's no way I'm going out in this,' I say, watching a stream of water snake along the floor from the kitchen area.

After about half an hour the rain eases off so we all go down to watch the last half of the set. I find myself standing next to PamP, who's also just arrived here after ducking out of the rain. I go with him into the backstage area after the show but then remember I have to find out about getting paid for tonight. The office is in a caravan down the hill and it takes a while to find Holm and sort it all out. By then I realise that it's 1:40 in the morning and I'm only allowed to check in to my hotel until two so Holm speeds me off in his car without me having a chance to say goodbye to anyone.

We make it to the guest house a few kilometres away in the little village of Gröbern just in time, and I'm happy to have a roof over my head as the rain is slashing down outside again now. Before Holm leaves I ask what's happening in the morning and he says a driver will pick up The Boys first at 9:20. They're staying nearby, so he should be over to me by 9.40 at the latest. It doesn't leave much of a margin of error for a flight at 12:15 but Altenburg is so small that there are no queues so it should be okay.

I'm in Room 21 – No Time To Be In Room 21! – and head up there and thankfully dump my bags as the rain roars down the gabled roof outside. Through the white noise of water I can hear another sound, and look out of my window to see that across the dark sodden courtyard in a small outbuilding there is a disco. I can just about make out the bass line of Queen's 'Another One Bites The Dust.' I am so curious to know who on earth could be in a disco in Gröbern at three in the morning that I almost get on my shoes and slosh over there to have a look. Almost.

I'm just drifting off to sleep when I hear the scratch of a key in my door. It creaks open, there's a pause, then a voice says, 'Oh, sorry,' and the door shuts again. With a sigh I get out of bed and lock it again, although there's obviously not much point.

Q: When is a lock not a lock?

A: When every bloody key in the hotel can open it.

Through the night it rains and rains and rains.

TALES OF THE EMERGENCY SANDWICH

<u>22nd July</u>
9:40 comes and goes and as 10:00 approaches I text Holm to say that no one has come to pick me up. Two minutes later a guy comes through the door talking into his mobile phone saying, 'Yes, he's right in front of me now.'

I hurry out into the minibus, where The Boys are waiting. They tell me they were all ready on time, but the driver didn't get to them until 9:40. They also tell me that the rest of the festival has been abandoned because the site is waterlogged. Bad news for Suzy & Los Quattro – the second festival in a row where they've haven't been able to play.

Time is really an issue now, but after a couple of minutes we stop at a petrol station to fill up and then just when we think we are finally on the way to the airport we realise the driver is heading back to the festival site. 'What are you DOING?' says singer Duncan as we pull up by the entrance.

'Sorry. But I just have to take this in,' the driver says, holding up a petrol can.

'But we'll miss our flight…'

'Sorry, biggest sorry,' he says, jumping out of the van and rushing off.

'WHAT AN IDIOT!' shouts Duncan. 'Sorry, I just had to let that out.'

Honest John Plain lets out a big sigh from the back seat and says, 'We're fucked.'

We hurtle through the country roads and arrive at the airport with thirty minutes to spare and a point blank refusal from the Ryanair staff to let us through. Forty minutes before the flight is the last opportunity to check in, and even though out of the window we can see the plane at the gate and the queue of people who haven't even started to board yet, we will not be allowed on.

The driver talks with the people at the Ryanair desk and finds out that there are no more flights today. Our only chance to get back to Stansted is a six hour drive to Frankfurt, where there is a flight leaving at 11:15 tonight. The driver is a volunteer assistant for the festival and is now completely out of his depth. As I am the only German speaker, he explains to me that we only have ten minutes left to book the new flights, they're going to cost an extra 65 euros each and he has no money in his back account, so…

I hand over the cash from my fee and he promises to get it back to me somehow. It's now one in the afternoon, ten hours before the flight, so we decide to head into Altenburg and get some lunch before setting off on the long drive.

There's not much happening in Altenburg on a Sunday. We park in the deserted cobbled town square and look around for signs of somewhere to eat. Keyboard player Casino Steel has a grin on his face as he points to a distant restaurant at the top of the hill, 'Restaurant Casino.'

'Ah yes,' he says, 'I have heard that this is the best restaurant in the whole of Germany.

There is another one at the other end of the square, 'Restaurant Café Anger.' I might go there.

We wander around for a while and finally agree to eat at a place themed on the card game Skat, which was invented here in Altenburg, and all settle down at a table engraved with the words *Einfach Gewonnen* ('simply the winner') which hardly seems appropriate at the moment. We leaf through the menu and make our orders, then the driver goes to try and find directions to Frankfurt Hahn airport. Meanwhile John slips off to the toilet. When the meal arrives he still hasn't returned so we start without him. He rushes in a few minutes later looking flustered.

'Fell asleep on the khazi!' he exclaims. 'How tired do you have to be to do that?!'

Guten Appetit!

While we're eating, guitarist Matt asks if I've always been gigging or if I've ever had a 'proper' job since The Adverts. I explain that I couldn't get a gig to save my life through the '80's and spent nearly ten years on the dole. Next to me, John says, 'I was signing on for even longer than that. A girl at the dole office looked at my card one time and said, 'You've been signing on since before I was born...' When I finally signed off a few years ago the entire office stood up and applauded.'

With a good meal, a beer, a glass of wine and a cognac in front of him, John is now cheering up considerably. 'Things could be worse,' he says, beaming.

I say, 'They will be.'

And I can't help feeling anxious about what's coming. Still a long drive to go, potential bad weather and traffic, yet there's no sense of urgency in the air. Only Duncan is, like me, clock-watching and suggesting we get a move on.

Matt says, 'It's a good job there are two worriers here – that means we don't have to,' and orders the rest of the band another round of brandies.

Finally we're in the van and on the road to Frankfurt. Still eight hours until the flight, it has to be possible. Soon most of The Boys are sleeping and I chat with the driver to help keep him awake. 'Is this your van or a hire van?' I ask.

'Actually, it belongs to the guy that died.'

TALES OF THE EMERGENCY SANDWICH

Aha.

So we drive and drive…the sun is out now and beating in through the windscreen, but there are black clouds scudding over the fields to either side of us, curtains of rain dropping from them, blustery wind battering the side of the van, the occasional rainbow dreaming in the hazy grey sky ahead. Yes, *wir fliegen, fliegen, fliegen zum Regenbogen*, or to be more precise drive, drive, drive, to Frankfurt Hahn – which is of course nowhere near Frankfurt but some 100 kilometres further on towards Koblenz, almost as far south as the Helfenstein festival I played two weeks ago – and we get stuck in traffic and our legs cramp up and our bellies bloat, crammed inside a dead man's van, his sunglasses still hanging from the rear view mirror. I can feel it coming: the flight will be delayed because of the bad weather and we will arrive in Stansted too late for the last train and I will ask myself again, why am I doing this?

During the taxi ride back to London with Casino Steel at two in the morning, a programme on the car radio reports on a new detachable underwater glue that was invented by combining the results of research into how gecko lizards can run up walls and the way mussels attach themselves to rocks. It was discovered that both emit a special enzyme, creating an electrical charge through micro-fibres on their skins which enables them to cling to any surface but then releases as soon as it comes into contact with water.

Cas and I glance at each other and I say, 'Looking on the bright side, if today hadn't happened the way it did I would never have known that.'

10. TALES OF THE EMERGENCY SANDWICH (2007)

PART ONE: BEYOND THE EMERGENCY SANDWICH

<u>18th October</u>
Two gigs in the Czech Republic, home of some of the worst vegetarian food in Europe so I pack an emergency sandwich. I'm also going to play my first ever gig in Poland. Maybe I should pack two.

The other things I can rely on when I go to the Czech Republic are problems with the language and confusion about my flights. My ticket out to Brno was confirmed just two days ago, but as I leave the house there's still no news of my flight back from Prague in four days time. Last night I wrote an email to Petr, who arranges my Czech gigs, suggesting that if the promoters are that disorganised it might be better to cancel. He wrote back: *Don't please nerves this is problem with Praha promoter when cooperate. Looking this gui is idiot send me this info in czech langue. I write buy me please later fly in London G and buy in lunch time.*

That's cleared that up then!

Petr is at Brno airport to meet me in an old German police van with 'Punk Rock' instead of 'Polizei' painted along the side. With all the police around at the airport I suggest we might be drawing unwelcome attention to ourselves, but he assures me, 'Nothing problem, German police thick green stripe, Czech police thin green stripe.'

Petr had hoped the van would be a model of German reliability, but the transmission broke while he was out on tour recently and this is its first trip out since it was repaired. While it was in the garage Petr also took the opportunity to get it converted to diesel, but there are a few problems still to be ironed out – the mechanic didn't have time to link the new system to the van's computer and as we drive out of the airport all the warning lights on the dashboard are flashing.

A couple of hours later we arrive in Olomouc. It's chilly and night is falling, and while we wait for someone to turn up at the venue, Petr and I take a walk through the old town centre where there is large church, a modern copy of Prague's St. Wenceslas cathedral complete with ornate astronomical clock. Next to it there's a tall and gloomy baroque fountain which Petr explains is 'from the time when people had boils from rats and died.'

'It's a monument to the Plague?'

'Not monument, make to *keep away* Plague,' he says. 'This very religious country.'

It's the biggest Plague-defence baroque fountain in the Czech Republic!

Back at the venue, a restaurant called Golias, we are directed away from the cosy-looking room where people sit at candle-lit tables with meals, and up a flight of stairs to a starkly lit, bare and cold wooden-floored room with a few tables and benches along each wall. There's a sort of proscenium arch at one end, but no stage – also no stage lights or P.A. system. There is a small bar at the other end of the room though, so Petr buys me a beer and I sit at one of the tables to see what will transpire.

Over the next half hour, the support band arrives with drum kit and amps, as well as a little P.A. system. A few people wander up the stairs, buy beers and sit huddled in their winter clothes watching the equipment being set up and, more particularly, watching me. Some welcome distraction arrives when a dreadlocked crusty-type arrives holding a large cardboard box which he proceeds to unload on the floor right in front of where the band will play. Soon he is surrounded by plastic bags and other tat, scraps of clothing and a large enamel pot.

I slip away down the stairs into the courtyard where I meet a young couple who start giggling as soon as they see me, then mime that they'd like to take my photo. The girl shows me how she'd like me to pose, then the two of them look at the results on the camera and giggle even more.

Petr walks in from the street and tells me he's just been to check my hotel for tonight. It's a very good one, he says. That's a relief – at least I will have my bolt hole once all this is over. Back upstairs, Crusty is giving his cardboard box a damn good telling off. He points a threatening finger at it, then kicks it against the wall. The support band starts to play and he dances about in front of the singer. The sound through the little speaker system is loud, but horribly distorted. It occurs to me that I didn't actually have a soundcheck.

There are about sixty people in now, and as I wander around the room I get a few comments from some of them in stilted English about how much they are looking forward to seeing me play and how much they love '77 punk rock. Looks like I'll be playing an Adverts-heavy set tonight. Then I bump into the gigglers again, and the girl tells me she loves Not In My Name, Generation Y, and Not A Bad Day. This cheers me up no end.

When the band finishes I fiddle about with the PA system for a few minutes until there's a halfway reasonable sound then kick off the set. It only takes a few minutes before the audience is crowded up together in front of the

TALES OF THE EMERGENCY SANDWICH

microphone, dancing around and, to my surprise, in some cases singing along. Crusty is on his knees.

In what seems like no time it's all over. The gigglers come and tell me they will be coming to see me again in Prague on Saturday. Girl giggler asks me to sign her stomach. Then the promoters invite me and Petr down to the restaurant. A few of the audience come too.

A bit of a luxury this – usually by the time I'm ready to eat there's nothing available, but here no one is in any rush to close up and they're keen to provide whatever I want in the way of food and drink. There's even an English menu and vegetarian options.

'What do you think this is?' I ask Petr, *'Fried cheese with Forest Sauce.'*

Petr looks at his Czech menu. 'Oh yes, mine says the same – *Forest Sauce.* I don't know…'

Sauce made out of wood?

It's actually three big chunks of deep-fried cheese, a staple vegetarian dish in the Czech Republic but this time in a red berry 'fruits of the forest' sauce, with a large salad and a plateful of toast. This is way beyond the emergency sandwich (which, it occurs to me, will have to stay in my bag for another day.)

The night gets late, various people who have been sitting with us go wobbling off to their homes and Petr says it's time to drop me off at the hotel. We get into the van with the drummer of the support band and his girlfriend who live a little further up the road and will be putting Petr up for the night.

The hotel is down a dark alley and a sign on the front door says, 'If no one is in Reception, please ring the number below and in ten minutes you will be accommodated.' Petr rings the number and the four of us stand around in the alleyway, shivering in the cold. Finally the night manager turns up, hurrying down the alley with a large bunch of keys, but as he fumbles at the door trying to get one of the keys to fit it becomes apparent that he is very drunk.

Yes, it's a great hotel – the only problem is, I can't get in it. I open my suitcase and get out a thicker jacket but the shivering has set in. The night manager goes away again for another ten minutes and comes back with another bunch of keys but none of those work either. I'm getting annoyed now. I ask Petr why he didn't pick up the keys when he came by the hotel earlier but his only explanation is, 'This good hotel, say key all night.'

When the night manager goes off again 'for ten minutes' and doesn't come back the drummer and his girlfriend tell me I'd be welcome to sleep at their flat, so I give in to the inevitable and we leave. It could be that I throw my bag and guitar into the back of the van with more force than is strictly necessary.

I hate being in a bad mood when people are being so kind and hospitable but it's hard to shake off, even when my hosts offer to sleep on the couch in the living room and give me their bed. They also break out a bottle of *pastis* and put out a plate of biscuits, carefully placing them on the table next to me. But as Petr and the two of them chat to each other in their native Czech and I'm left in a lonely bubble not understanding anything of what's being said – cold, tired, two gigs ahead of me, not knowing when or how I will get home at the end of it – all I can think is, *fuck the biscuits.*

19th October
I took the bedroom in the end and had a pretty good night's sleep, a bit short. When I get out of the shower there's breakfast on the table and cups of coffee are being poured. I notice that, as the honoured guest from England, I'm the only one who gets a saucer.

During breakfast Petr tells me about the time he was on tour in France with a band he manages, and how the people they were staying with spiked his coffee with magic mushrooms in the morning. He set off to the next gig but he had to pull over when he realised he was having difficulty driving because his arms were twenty feet long.

After a few hours on the road I top up breakfast with half the fast-fading emergency sandwich, then we're over the border into Poland, although there's not much difference to notice. Petr tells me that this area was historically part of Czechoslovakia and still has the same language.

We drive into the small city of Zory and head straight for the place we'll be staying tonight, the apartment of a girl called Justyna who has seen me at a few gigs and took it upon herself to organise this concert in her home town. Her boyfriend Konyk is singer in a Bratislavan band called Zona A who I've played with before. They'll be playing the gig with me in Prague tomorrow so Konyk will travel there in the van with Petr and me. As we settle into Justyna's flat, she tells me that tonight's gig is an unpublicised invite-only event because if they advertise concerts here Polish skinheads come in and break them up.

I have my photo taken with Justyna's six year old daughter. Her favourite song of mine is 'Looking Down On London.'

At six, Justyna and Konyk take us to a restaurant in the old town before we go over to the club. They're both vegetarians, and the manageress of the restaurant who is vegetarian too has said she wants to cook up something special. While we wait for the something special, Konyk suggests we try the local speciality: hot beer.

Then the food arrives: a plate of thin-sliced beetroot garnished with oranges, followed by a carrot and chilli soup which gets hotter the more you eat. Konyk says, 'Maybe tomorrow it will be hot at both ends!'

Guten Appetit!

Normally that would be enough before a gig for me but next up comes battered, deep fried celeriac slices with a melted cheese filling and balsamic and oil dressing, potato fritters, and mousse for dessert. Then I have my photo taken with the owner and we head back out into the cold night.

When we walk into the club there are already about fifty people in and some of them give a cheer when they see me. There's a roaring log fire in a brick hearth in the middle of the room, a bar down one side, a small stage crammed with equipment.

Two bands are scheduled to play before me so there's a long wait, but when I finally do get to play the gig is a stormer. Afterwards I have my photo taken with just about everyone in the club then sit at a table, my T-shirt steaming in the heat from the log fire, while one of the earlier bands sets up on the stage again. The bass player has a go at the riff for 'Gary Gilmore's Eyes,' and then they launch in to a few punk cover songs, delivered more with enthusiasm than accuracy. Slightly concerned about the inevitable invite to join in when they get to my song, I gesture to Petr that it might be time to leave.

Konyk and Justyna and her daughter are staying with friends, so Petr and I have the place to ourselves. We're both shattered so turn in straight away. I have a mattress on the floor in the daughter's bedroom and before I turn out the lights I remember the other half of the emergency sandwich, still in my bag, and surely not likely to remain edible much longer. Shame to waste it and thank heavens for the preservative qualities of Marmite.

As I lie down in happy anticipation of sleep I feel something hard under my head, and reach under the pillow to find an eighteen inch sword in an engraved metal sheath. I test the blade: it's not a toy.

The walls of the bedroom are covered with posters of boy band Tokio Hotel.

20th October

I have a dream where a Brahmin meets a Brummie. Now my subconscious is doing wordplay.

I'm up at nine because we have a 600 kilometre drive to Prague today. Konyk and Justyna arrive soon afterwards and prepare breakfast: some salad and a Bratislavan speciality of soft cheese with chopped onion and spices which we have on pieces of wholemeal bread.

Konyk gets in the the van with Petr and me, and we set off, first driving back into the old town to change our Polish Zloty back into Czech currency. The exchange booth is in a flower shop.

Petr and Konyk sit in the front of the van so they can chat during the long journey, and I huddle in the back and watch the snowy fields slide past. By late afternoon we reach the outskirts of Prague and drive straight to the venue, up a hill in an industrial area. Petr goes off in search of the promoter and comes back triumphantly waving a piece of paper, confirmation of my flight tomorrow. He also has the address of the place I'll be sleeping tonight, up near the airport somewhere, so we get back in the van and go in search of it. The room turns out to be a small apartment in a family house, my area separated from the family by an unlocked door and a glass brick wall. Not exactly private, but at least it's warm and comfortable. I arrange with the owner for him to book me a cab to the airport for ten in the morning and he says he'll bring me in a breakfast at 9:30. I dump my bags and head back to the venue.

At the club, there are quite a few people already in even though the first band is only just starting. The evening is special concert organised by Czech band NVU to celebrate their 20th anniversary. They once recorded a version my song 'Only One Flavour' and have asked me to sing it with them tonight but they speak almost no English so it's hard to find out exactly how we will do it. Their version has a radically different arrangement and Czech lyrics. The title is *Jen Jedna Příchut.*

I'll be playing a solo set as well, but when I see the schedule outside the dressing room I'm worried to see that NVU expect me to go on after they have played, and there are still three more bands before them. My stage time is down as 11:20, but with so many bands playing I know straight away that this is not going to happen.

The next band come on, and we're already running twenty minutes late. Downstairs I bump into the rest of Zona A. They've just arrived from Bratislava and are due to start their set in fifteen minutes but can't find anyone with the key to the lift so they can't get their equipment up to the stage. By the time they start we're running 40 minutes late.

A nine piece ska band is warming up in the dressing room with a brass section version of 'Roll Out The Barrel.' There's a lot of wine being drunk. The singer stuffs an apple down his trousers – *mental note: don't eat any of the dressing room food* – and makes it peep out of his fly, to much amusement. Then he puts it on his head and one of the brass players knocks it off with the

TALES OF THE EMERGENCY SANDWICH

arm of his trombone.

A photographer who I see at many of my Czech gigs spots me checking the running order again and waves his finger at me in a 'forget about it' motion. It's nearly ten now – there is no way I'll be on stage for another three hours.

A friend of mine from America, film producer Susan Dynner arrives. By coincidence, her film 'Punk's Not Dead' was in a film festival in Prague today and when she heard I was playing she thought she'd surprise me. I do my best to look surprised when she walks in, but actually the singer of NVU already told me she would be coming. It's nice to finally be able to chat with someone without struggling with the language but not everyone is as pleased as I am: one drunken woman shouts something at us in Czech and walks out. I'm told she said, 'Why are you speaking *English* all the time?'

The drummer of NVU is watching from the side of the stage as the nine piece band attempt to get their gear off while the next band tries to get theirs on. 'So many people,' he says, shaking his head.

I wander through the packed crowd out front, where I am spotted by some guys at the bar. 'TV, come over here, buy you drink!' They are lining up shots. I say I just want a beer, but they look offended. 'This just apple vodka, not strong, drink with us!' So I down it and they are all delighted. 'TV, you ARE punk rock!' I sign a few autographs and slip back to the dressing room.

NVU are preparing to go on stage now. Petr tells me that they'll only play for an hour and I will be able to start soon. Behind him, I see the photographer shaking his head. Even on the running order they are down for a ninety minute set – this is their twentieth anniversary gig after all – and they're bound to overrun. Not sure when I'm supposed to play 'Only One Flavour' with them, but it's going to be towards the end of their show. They tell me they will give me a big introduction so I will know.

Back in the dressing room I'm tuning up the guitar and chatting with Susan as NVU play their set to an enthusiastic response from the home crowd. The photographer walks in and appears to be about to say something to me when he suddenly goes rigid, flings his cup of coke to the floor and sinks to the couch where he has a seizure. I keep an eye on him while he shakes and jerks, then he comes round a few minutes later, apparently none the worse.

I'm pacing around by the side of the stage trying to stay alert. Between every song I'm listening to the singer's announcements, but almost anything he says could be construed as 'TV Smith.' I slip back into the dressing room, and the photographer shouts, 'It's NOW, they are introducing you!'

I run onto the stage to a decent cheer, and we get straight into the song. I sing the English version, and NVU's girl backing singer sings the Czech version at the same time, which doesn't really fit, but never mind. She keeps coming over and hugging me, which is a bit strange because it's the same person who told me and Susan off for speaking English earlier. Then I'm off and waiting while NVU finish off their last few numbers so I can start my solo set.

It's 1:15 in the morning when I finally get on stage. Although I can't compete with the volume of all the bands that have been playing earlier, the songs are going down well, the gigglers are down at the front, and there are plenty of other people singing and clapping along and shouting out for requests. I stretch my allotted half hour to 45 minutes – well, everyone else this evening has overrun – and get called back for an encore. Then it's time to pack up and leave for a few hours sleep before I have to get up for my flight.

Petr drops me off outside the room – he still has a couple of hours drive ahead of him, home to Teplice. We say our goodbyes, and talk about sorting out a few gigs next summer. Then he drives off and I'm on my own, making my way in the darkness up the narrow path along the side of the guest house, wet snow slapping down on me.

The click of my key turning in the lock and the door opening: sometimes the greatest sound in the world.

21st October
The owner of the guest house tells me he didn't book a taxi – he'll give me a lift to the airport himself and save me the fare. The breakfast consists of some bread rolls and slices of cheese, so I make an emergency cheese sandwich for the plane.

No meals on Easyjet and no pre-allotted seating either. In the scramble for places I manage to find a window seat free, and as the plane fills up a hippy-looking girl in large sunglasses and floppy hat takes the seat next to me, gets out a notebook and proceeds to scribble music notation in it. I ask her what instrument she plays. She removes her glasses, looks hard at me and visibly relaxes when she realises I must be a fellow musician not someone hitting on her. She's a Czech keyboard player who has a psychedelic band in London and also plays for Arthur Brown. 'When I play the keyboard, I throw it on the ground, I'm lying on the floor playing it, I'm *shagging* it...'

It turns out that we have a mutual friend in Nikki Sudden, who died recently. She takes little sips from some *Berchnya* she's smuggled on board in a cough medicine bottle – 'they never know because it smells antiseptic anyway' – and tells me about how she loves the pre-revolution Czech band Plastic People Of The Universe. I tell her that a couple of weeks ago I played in Prague with Brutus, a Czech band who were formed around the same time. She reminisces about life before the revolution. Her father, she says, was a clergyman – something regarded with deep suspicion by the communist authorities – and as a consequence her family were spied on by the government as well as by neighbours hoping to win favour with the regime, and who even helped place bugs in their apartment. After the revolution, the family were able to look at all the reports that had been written about them. She saw herself mentioned often enough: *The subject was seen leaving the house at 11:00 am...* 'The subject? I was eight years old!'

It's all so fascinating I forget to eat the emergency sandwich.

The last I see of Lucie is when I'm queuing up to show my passport and she goes rushing back the other way explaining she left her bag under the seat.

PART TWO: THE FLIGHT OF THE EMERGENCY SANDWICH

<u>31st October</u>
Four dates in Norway. I believe fish is quite a popular dietary element there. I pack an emergency cheese sandwich.

From Oslo airport it's a short train journey to the city centre, then just five minutes walk to the Elm Street music bar and I arrive right on schedule at six. By the bar I see Tarjei, the singer from a band called the Trashcan Darlings who I played a festival in Norway with a few years ago, so I go over to say hello. He tells me he is tonight's promoter. The sound man won't be here for another half an hour, so he suggests eating now – ideal, as it will give me around four hours to digest before playing. I sit with him and his girlfriend and have a veggie burger, hash browns and salad. Looks like I won't be needing the emergency sandwich tonight, but it will keep until tomorrow.

Tarjei walks me over to my hotel. I'm up on the fifth floor and immediately switch the heating on full – not good for sandwich storage, but there's an ideal ledge outside the window and the temperature is hovering just above zero out there, so that should keep it fresh.

When I get back to Elm Street I'm a bit disappointed to see there are only twenty people in the club. I hide in the downstairs dressing room for a while, and when I go back upstairs things are looking a bit more promising, maybe fifty people in and quite a few outside having a smoke. I bump straight into

Rosa, who is the sister of Suzy from Suzy & Los Quattro. While I'm chatting to her another guy comes up and asks her to translate something. She says he asked her to tell me that he's from Zory, where I played last week, and a friend of Justyna and Konyk, who I stayed with. So, to recap: I'm in Oslo, where a Spanish friend is translating a Polish guy's Norwegian into English so he can tell me about last week's gig I played in his hometown in Poland.

I play for two hours. Towards the end a bloke at the front is struggling with his English to request a song; confusing, because he looks exactly like Captain Sensible. I keep thinking, Captain – just tell me in English…

Afterwards I sit around for a while having a beer with Tarjei and a few other people. Everyone seems to have enjoyed the gig. Tarjei tells me there were twice as many people as last time I played here – a good improvement! But all good things must come to an end – I have to be up at nine tomorrow for a flight to Bergen so I say my goodbyes and head up the road to my hotel.

The emergency sandwich. Down there.
Oslo 2007

1<u>st</u> November
It's barely light outside when I am woken by the sound of a seagull squawking loudly nearby.

Too near…

With a start I jump out of bed and pull back the curtain to see the seagull flapping off…and an empty windowsill. The emergency sandwich is gone.

TALES OF THE EMERGENCY SANDWICH

I go back to bed, but it's hard to sleep. When I wake up again a couple of hours later I start to wonder, could a seagull *really* carry off a whole sandwich? Do seagulls even *like* Marmite? I stick my head out of the window and see, there, five stories below, a familiar plastic bag lying on the pavement, tight in by the wall and being ignored by the early risers hurrying in to work. It was a pretty sturdy package, double wrapped foil inside that bag. The emergency sandwich might yet come back from the dead!

I pack my suitcase and hurry downstairs, but when I locate the street with the fallen sandwich I immediately see that a large hole has been ripped out of the side of the bag, and all that remains inside are scraps of silver foil torn apart by hungry beaks. There's not even a crumb left.

It's a sparkling day, and the flight to Bergen is a thrill, looking down at the lakes and forests gliding past below, then bleached craggy rocks which gradually give way to dazzlingly-bright snow, and finally forests and fjords again as we reach the milder west coast.

A quick look around the shops at Bergen airport confirms my worst fears – never the cheese without the ham. But then I spot it: a solitary cheese and tomato sandwich. This will be today's emergency sandwich if things go wrong later.

The only thing is, by the time I get to the hotel I'm so hungry I have to eat it straight away. The hotel is one of the best I've been in, but typically it's one where I will be spending very little time: the gig tonight will be a late one and I have to be up at seven tomorrow for the flight to Trondheim. I don't want to hang around in there now either as I've never been to Bergen before, so I head out to have a look around. After two hours' sightseeing – 13th century Viking castle, rickety wooden Hanseatic League houses, etc. – I remember that it would be a good idea to try and find another emergency sandwich for later but there's only fish as far as the eye can smell. I do notice a promising sign for a shop called 'Sandwich' up a side street, but when I get there it turns out to sell clothes.

Ralf, the promoter for tonight, arrives in a taxi to take me to the club. It's a nice looking place, smallish, a good P.A. and stage, with a bar and restaurant on the next floor down. Ralf says the food there is really good, and when I explain my problem with eating before the gig he suggests something light like a Greek salad. While I'm enjoying that I find myself thinking, I'm wasting my time with this emergency sandwich routine – it seems like here in Norway there's usually good quality vegetarian food available. Meanwhile on the sound system Turbonegro are singing a song about choking on your vomit.

Vær så god!

Still at least three hours to go before I play, the club doesn't even open until ten. To kill some time I put on a thick jacket and go for another walk, this time up the hill behind the club. From the top I can see the lights of the old wharf below sparkling in the black waters of the harbour. Some sort of performance is going on in the Viking castle, the sound of drums and bagpipes drifts up through the still air.

Back at the club there's no one in the audience. No one. I do a quick interview for a college radio station, then wait it out in the little dressing room. If I went to bed now I would get a full eight hours sleep. But the support band hasn't even started yet.

The support are called 'Teenage Kicks' and are a surprisingly good punk covers band, shortening their set tonight to just half an hour. That means I get on at midnight, an hour after my scheduled start time. There are about thirty people in the room now, that's including the support band, the promoter and the two people I've done interviews with. Most of them seem quite reserved, and although there is one couple who spend the whole show right in front of the stage clearly enjoying it, their attempts to cajole the rest into coming nearer meet with little success.

It's one of those rare gigs where I'm glad when it's over. I sit with Ralf in the backstage room and from what he tells me the cool reception I received is typical for Bergen. Anyway, he thinks the show was terrific and 'that's all that matters.'

I gather my bags and guitar, and notice as I head out of the club that it's still only just after two, so it looks like I will get a little more sleep than I was expecting. That is, until I'm stopped on my way out through the bar downstairs by the couple who were enthusiastically watching the gig from the front and now insist on buying me a drink before I go. The guy turns out to be from legendary Norwegian black metal band Immortal. He's a massive punk fan.

'Black Metal, Punk, what you did solo tonight…it all has the same thing to it,' he says. 'Our band were trying to find a word to describe it, and we decided the word is…*drive*. If you ever think of a better word to describe it, please send me an email.' Then he recommends a cathedral I should go and see in Trondheim tomorrow. Surely someone in a black metal band should be recommending churches to burn down, not to visit?

I head off confidently to the hotel in the wrong direction.

TALES OF THE EMERGENCY SANDWICH

2<u>nd</u> November

At Trondheim airport I'm surprised when someone comes up and says he's here to take me into the town, as my itinerary says I'll have to make my own way. Even more of a surprise is that it's Torgve, who I've exchanged a few emails with in the past but have never met. It turns out he works in the bar I'm playing tonight.

He introduces me to a friend of his who'll be driving the van, and then I put my guitar and luggage in the back and we set off. Soon the driver points out a yellow building on the hillside opposite – Hell Station, where The Boys took the cover shot for their album 'To Hell With The Boys.' 'Hell' in Norwegian means 'Luck.' We go through a series of tunnels and emerge to a sign saying 'Welcome to the city of Trondheim' – not ideally positioned because all you can see from here are potato fields.

Soon the city appears, a small huddle of buildings bordered by the drab grey ocean, a modern television tower on the hill above. Unfortunately when the tower was being built someone didn't check the measurements properly so it's not perfectly straight. It's the leaning tower of Trondheim. 'There's a revolving restaurant on top,' says the driver, 'although it doesn't serve what I would exactly call *food*.'

Unlike the place I'm playing tonight, a restaurant called 'Credo,' with a small room for music upstairs. It has a reputation for great food, and after an early soundcheck at 3:30 I get some of it – a very tasty dish of lightly-roasted vegetables. Emergency sandwich, you are history.

Then I go back to the hotel. I have so much time on my hands I consider a snooze, something I never usually do before a gig. I don't today either because just as I'm drifting off the fire alarm in my room rings. I put on my shoes and take the six flights of stairs down to Reception where I raise a questioning eyebrow at the lady behind the desk.

'Fire alarm?'

'Oh, it was nothing,' she says. Then, more insistently: '*Nothing*.'

It's probably nothing when the same thing happens twenty minutes later, so I don't bother going down to Reception, but I do give up on the idea of getting any sleep. I am a noise magnet.

Wet snow is falling outside so it's a good job it's only a twenty second walk to the venue. In stark contrast to last night in Bergen, tonight's gig goes down a storm and I play for two hours, four encores.

Soon after I'm sitting at a table with Torgve, the driver, and a friend of theirs – a pretty, black haired goth-looking girl who walks with a stick.

'Do you ever drink spirits?' asks Torgve.

'Not really,' I say, 'too dangerous.'

'Because, I happen to know they have a really nice '63 Armagnac behind the bar here…'

On the other hand, I don't have to get up *that* early tomorrow.

At three the club shuts and someone suggests we wander down to the waterfront before going home. Outside, the chill rain is slashing down and there's a fierce squall ripping through the deserted streets. At the wharf we climb up on to a wooden platform above the inlet and from somewhere inside his bag, Torgve produces a few bottles of beer. We stand around for a while drinking and laughing and looking out over the ink-black waters - all except the goth girl who, I suddenly realise, is blind.

The next squall blows over us. We are shivering and our clothes are drenched but we are all in some kind of delirious exhilaration. Torgve turns to me and says, 'All your touring, all your 120 gigs a year and the experiences you have doing them…this has got to be in your top ten.'

I say, 'Top five.'

It's grim oop North.
Trondheim 2007

TALES OF THE EMERGENCY SANDWICH

3rd November

I can't leave without seeing the cathedral, as recommended by black metal star Demonaz Doom Occulta – real name Harald – though it's tempting to sit in the hotel a bit longer when I notice how hard it's raining outside. At the first break in the weather I dash out, but moments later there's another hefty shower and I'm soaked. It doesn't seem quite so 'top five' this time of day, and I've already checked out of my room so I'll be stuck with these wet clothes until I get to Lillehammer tonight.

The cathedral is worth it, though. The most northern cathedral in the world, it's a massive gloomy medieval stone bulk, started in the 10th century and taking two hundred years to complete. I get a quick look around inside before it shuts at two, then run through the hammering rain across the courtyard to the museum in the old Bishop's Palace, where much of the old statuary from the cathedral is on display and there is also what survives of a 16th Century mint, the only one in existence still in its original location – the tiled floor, areas where the coin punchers worked, charcoal store and furnace still visible. On the way out, the girl at the information desk tells me that it may not be around much longer: no one really knows how to preserve it so they have simply left it how it was found, keeping it constantly moist to stop it disintegrating. 'We were told it might only last ten years,' she says, 'but that was ten years ago…'

She also tells me that there is a lot of activity in the floor of the mint – 'of the worm variety.' She grimaces. 'If you put an X-ray on it you would see hundreds of worms wriggling around under there. Actually we were thinking of inviting the local fisherman down, they could remove them. Well, it looks like it's just about stopped raining now. You can go.'

I've been having such an interesting time that I almost forgot I have a train to catch, but a swift rain-sodden march through Trondheim brings me back to the hotel where I pick up my bags and guitar, and from there it's only five minutes to the train station.

It's a long journey to Lillehammer and I won't be in until nearly nine this evening, with a scheduled stage time of eleven. I've been told that the Trondheim to Lillehammer journey is particularly beautiful, and I have a window seat, but as it is already dark this is pretty academic.

I'm met at the station by the owner of the Felix club, Billy, who I first encountered a couple of months ago at a festival we were both playing near Oslo. Billy was once in Mayhem, one of the first and most extreme of the original Norwegian black metal bands. Back then he called himself 'Messiah.' He is quite tickled by the fact my partner Gaye is a black metal fan and knows about Mayhem, because when he was thirteen and she was in The Adverts he adored her and had her poster up on his bedroom wall.

Billy takes me to the hotel to check in and organises a veggie sandwich from their restaurant that I can pick up later when I get back from the gig. I should be on stage in ninety minutes so I'm too nervous to eat anything now. The streets of Lillehammer are deserted, which makes me a bit concerned about the turnout tonight, particularly as Billy told me that posters for the gig didn't arrive so all his promotion has been by SMS – he's sent out a hundred text messages today. But the club is great, and Billy and sound man Ola are really nice blokes, and sitting around a table with them and some of their friends – one of whom claims to be the 'last punk in Lillehammer' – I get the feeling we'll have a good gig.

And a late one. Start time is put back to 12:30 and by then there are about twenty people in. So, a disappointingly small crowd but they kick off dancing from the first chord. The intimacy means there's quite a lot of chat going back and forth between the songs and most of it turns out to be pretty funny. Every now and then people pop outside for a cigarette, and during one song I do a quick headcount and realise I am playing to seven people. But somehow it's a really enjoyable gig.

We sit around chatting for a while. Billy tells me something about the indigenous Sami tribe in far northern Norway, who have no conception of time and whose day is governed by external factors such as when the reindeer move on. 'A bit like being a musician,' I say, and then with a shock I realise that my reindeer has moved on: it's nearly seven in the morning. And I haven't eaten. I should go back the hotel and grab that emergency sandwich they ordered for me. It'll be a pre-sleep breakfast.

Ola is heading in my direction too, so we walk up the road together. It's a crystal cold morning, not a breath of air. Ola tells me that gigs at the Felix rarely make a profit, he doesn't get paid himself and works there because he loves the music and the people. 'That's why I do it too,' I say. 'You couldn't buy a night like we've had tonight.'

POSTSCRIPT

<u>7th November</u>

Heading into Tottenham Court Road tube station late in the afternoon, I pass a busker playing accordion, and do a double take as I realise it's Lucie. Seven million people in London and I bump into someone I first met two weeks ago on the plane back from the Czech Republic.

Equally surprised to see me, she stops playing and we say hello. I ask her if she ever got her bag back.

'Those bastards at Easyjet!' she says. 'First they said the bag wasn't on the plane, then last week they phone me up and say they've found it but it's in Gatwick. So I had to go all the way down there and get it.'

'Anything valuable in it?' I ask.

'Nothing except for a few sandwiches but they were so old by then they were, like, crawling out of the bag by themselves…'

Nice to know I'm not the only one carrying an emergency sandwich.

11. A COLD SNAP (2008)

<u>22nd March</u>
I've never played Sweden before and I'm going a roundabout way to get there, first stopping off in Norway for a couple of days to accompany Gaye at a black metal festival called Inferno. She's a fan, I'm not – but I know the promoter so I'm going to hook them up, stay a couple of nights and then escape to my own gigs. On one of the nights at Inferno the headlining band comes on in corpse paint and plays the entire set with flames shooting up from the stage, four naked people with black hoods over their heads suspended from crosses behind them. The next day I hear that they are unhappy with their performance because the sheep heads didn't turn up.

But enough of that, I'm off to Sweden. Via Denmark, where I'll be picked up from Copenhagen airport by Björn, a fan who wrote me an email a few months ago and offered to arrange a gig in his home town of Helsingborg.

It's a short drive from Copenhagen to Helsingor, from where we catch the ferry over to Helsingborg. Björn's French wife Marie-Thérèse is at the wheel, their two children in the back seat. Björn has been exposing the family to my music for some time now and tells me that eleven year old Laura's favourite song is 'I Will Walk You Home.' An avid vinyl collector, Bjorn will be DJ at the club tonight and has all his old punk singles ready. He told the local paper about the gig and they came and took a photo of him proudly posing in front of his Adverts records. He's so concerned that everything will go well tonight that he's had a stress headache all day.

The venue is a nice little club on the waterfront. After a quick soundcheck, Marie Thérèse takes me across the road to the hotel she's booked me at a good price thanks to her job as a travel agent. I get in to my room and unpack, discovering too late that my pen has leaked during the flight. In the bathroom I scrub away at the ink on my hand with liquid soap from the dispenser, then when that doesn't shift it I try the bar of soap, then shampoo, then some hair conditioner from the complimentary bottle by the sink, then the complimentary body lotion, and finally I have a go at it with toothpaste and brush. It doesn't work, but my hand does now have a refreshing minty aroma.

Back at the club I'm relieved to see that even though it's my first time here and Easter Saturday a few people are starting to arrive. Björn is spinning his singles, and leaning over to talk about each one with me as he does so. He looks around at the thirty people who have gathered, many of them friends or students of his (he teaches part-time at a local school) and says, 'This is just like my living room. Except you're here.'

The gig is very nice. I play a long set – there are thirty years worth of songs to catch up on – including 'I Will Walk You Home.' After my first ever gig in Sweden at least there will be one eleven year old girl going home happy.

23rd March
Seems a shame to come all this way and only play one gig so Björn found me another in Stockholm, in a fairly well-known venue called Kafé 44. I set the alarm early enough to get breakfast at the hotel, then Björn arrives by bus and walks me down to the ferry. He accompanies me on the crossing over to the train station in Helsingor and on the way explains that the gig tonight is a bit unusual because there won't be any alcohol on sale and I'll be going onstage at eight. A friend of his called Peter is going to meet me at Stockholm airport and take me to the hotel and then on to the venue. We say our goodbyes at the station and I take the train to Copenhagen airport.

I'm pulled aside after the X-ray machine at the airport and realise immediately what the problem is: I have forgotten to take the string clippers out of my guitar case. While I wait for my search, the couple in front of me have two small pots of fruit yoghurt confiscated. Somehow the world feels safer.

Finally on the plane, we have taxied down to the runway and are ready for take off when the Captain announces that there's a technical problem and we're going to have to go back to the stand and wait for an engineer. He doesn't say what the technical problem is, and personally I would like a bit more detail. Meanwhile we all sit there while the engineer does whatever he has to do, and an hour later we're assured the problem is fixed. We taxi back for take off but the expected roar of engines doesn't happen and we trundle along the runway for a while, then turn and make our way back. The Captain makes an announcement in Swedish which includes the English phrase 'One of those days.' Then he announces that we are 'going to attempt a turn at the de-icing stand and try again.' Well, mustn't grumble – we've had a lovely little drive around the airfield.

As I walk out of the baggage area at Stockholm airport a voice shouts my name and an arm claps around my shoulder. 'TV, what an honour man...I'm Peter!'

Peter swings into view and I immediately realise he has been putting the two hours he's been waiting here to good use and is very drunk.

TALES OF THE EMERGENCY SANDWICH

'TV, you are MISTER PUNK ROCK! Oh, this is my friend…he's also called Peter.'

'How am I going to remember that?' I say, and shake hands with the other, sober, Peter, who luckily is the one who's going to be driving. We wander down to an unofficial parking place they have discovered somewhere in the service area of the airport, load my guitar and bags into the back of the car and head off towards Stockholm, Peter leaning frequently round over the front passenger seat to give me bug-eyed looks of amazement and proffer me mini bottles of scotch and chewing tobacco. As we ease into the fast lane, he slaps the other Peter heavily on the arm and says, 'Can you believe it? TV Smith! He *invented* Punk Rock!'

'Well – heh – I didn't really invent it…'

Peter looks back furiously. 'You DID!'

On the outskirts of Stockholm Peter needs to pee, so Peter (pay attention at the back) pulls over at a junction behind another car and Peter staggers out. I look over at Peter, still calm behind the wheel. 'Erm, Is he going to be… alright?'

Peter looks embarrassed. 'I'll make sure he's okay.'

Out front, Peter has zipped up and is now trying to get into the wrong car.

They drop me off at my hotel, where I say I'll need a few minutes to unpack and Peter suggests they spend the time in the bar next door. 'Just COFFEE!' warns Peter.

They are both musicians, and on the way to the venue they point out another club where they would normally be playing a weekly jam session tonight. 'I have the bass in the back of the car,' says drunk Peter. 'Maybe I could play a few songs with you tonight?'

I say, 'Aaah…'

We reach the venue and I hurry in and introduce myself. Björn, the guy from Kafé 44 who booked the gig with Björn in Helsingborg (pay attention at the back) takes me through the café area to the live music room, big enough for around 150 people. He introduces me to the sound engineer and I have a quick soundcheck – it's now already 7:30 and I'm supposed to be playing at 8:00. Halfway through the soundcheck I hear a *klunking* noise at the back of the room and see Peter at the doorway looking confused, unable to get through because the bass guitar slung over his shoulder has slipped round sideways.

I ask Björn about the timings and find out that the start time is flexible, just as long as the gig finishes by eleven. I head around the corner with the two Peters to the Big Ben pub, where despite an Oscar winning attempt to appear sober to the doorman, one of the Peters isn't allowed in. He staggers off into the night and that's the last I see of him.

Back at the club there are about twenty people in and I decide to hold back the start time until nine in the hope some more will turn up. One guy comes over and tells me that there's a big punk and skinhead party for someone's fortieth birthday on a boat just five minutes walk away – free entry, five bands playing and beer on sale. He wants to know if I would come down and play on the boat after I've finished my set here. Looks like the only audience I'll get tonight, so I say yes.

I slip away to the small backstage area where I have left my guitar. When I come out again ten minutes later, the audience has increased to about forty people who all applaud as I come through the door, which rather takes me by surprise. I hurry on stage and launch into a two hour set which goes down very well, even though it's the first time I can remember playing so long without at least one beer to help things along.

After the gig I wait around for the boat guy but when he doesn't turn up I tag along with some of my audience to a nearby bar. Outside it's sub-zero and we hurry gratefully into the warmth and draw three tables together so we can sit around and chat and have a few beers. There are members of quite a few local bands here, and all tell me they loved the gig and can't believe so few people turned up – although the boat party, the fact it's Easter Sunday and the complete lack of promotion probably had something to do with it. Many of them say they only found out about the gig today and will make sure more people hear about it next time I come. One girl tells me that during one of the songs in the set I was playing guitar so fast that my hand 'went backwards in time.' She offers to buy me a drink, and I hesitate to accept because it's so expensive here, but she says, 'You changed my life – I think that's worth a beer.' She also invites me to come and play in her home town of Köping, where there is a venue where I would 'definitely get 700 people.' Maybe something is starting for me in Sweden.

But tonight seems to be finishing. The bar closes at two and a brief and fruitless attempt by our gang to find another place where we can get a drink peters out when most of us realise it's so cold we can't feel our fingers. I mention that I have no idea how to get back to my hotel, somewhere on the other side of town, and one of the guys I've been talking to in the bar offers to drop me off there. 'Are you taking a taxi?' I ask hopefully, eyeing the one that has just pulled up beside us.

TALES OF THE EMERGENCY SANDWICH

'Well, no, but I could go that way on the subway and show you where to get off. I can't afford a taxi.'

'Neither can I,' I say. 'But if I don't get in that taxi now, I will die.'

Even the hotel room is cold. But it does give the two chocolate squares on the pillow – my only food since breakfast – just the right amount of *snap*.

12. STICK TO THE ITINERARY (2008)

<u>9th April</u>
Gripping news in the English-language Finnish newspaper on the flight to Helsinki: the dust mite is dying out in Finland. Scientists can't get any to do research on.

Harri, the agent who booked this four day tour, picks me up from the airport to drive me to Tampere. It's murky, rainy weather, and he bemoans the lack of winter in Finland this year. The first snows came in February and then only lasted a few weeks. It's been so mild that there have been a lot of deaths because people have gone out to fish in ice holes as usual and fallen through.

During the drive, Harri hands me a folder full of itineraries for the tour with details of soundcheck and gig times, and maps showing directions from the railway station to venue and hotel. He tells me he is rarely in the office these days, because he spends a lot of his time teaching a music business course in a college somewhere north of Tampere. He has a suggestion: how about if his students organise my next tour?

Because the flight was delayed we're an hour late getting to the Telakka club for soundcheck, but the sound engineer still hasn't arrived. Ideally I'd use the time to check in to my hotel, but it's a place with a keypad and code system to get in. The promoter has the code number but he is currently at home watching the ice hockey. Harri glances at the itineraries and grimaces. 'All this and already it's gone wrong.'

The sound guy turns up an hour later, but there's still no sign of the promoter with the door code so I leave my bags at the club and meet a few friends at a bar down the road. When I get back there's a reasonably large crowd in, and I get straight down to playing. There's a lot of good feedback from the audience. My favourite shout was from one guy sitting off to my right. 'We love you! Shut up! You're thin!'

Japi and Tommi from a band called the Tigerbombs come over to say hello. We toured together in Germany recently, and Japi has a CD for me of his new project 'King Of All The Animals,' which includes a song we recorded together. I spend an hour or so chatting to them and other people from the audience then when the Telakka prepares to close someone suggests we go to a bar called The Gobi Desert. Luckily at the last minute I remember to ask for the key code for my hotel from the manager, then we all head down the road.

There is some light snow in the air as I leave the Gobi Desert some time later. Japi and Tommi walk down the road with me to the hotel as it's right near their flat. I'm nervous about whether the key code I've been given will work so it's with some relief that the number duly unlocks the hotel front door, as well as the door immediately behind the front door. Tommi helps me carry my things up to the room and watches as I punch in the numbers into the keypad outside the door, getting increasingly frustrated as it fails to unlock. 'I KNEW this would happen,' I fume. 'I don't get it – it worked on the front door, why doesn't it work now?'

Tommi looks over my shoulder at the scrap of paper I'm holding. 'That says Room 815,' he says. 'This is Room 801.'

10th April
A five hour train journey to Oulu, up in the North where snow is lying and the weather is a lot chillier than Tampere. I'm there by three in the afternoon, which according to my itinerary leaves me a couple of hours before soundcheck, so I follow my map to the hotel, which seems a good place to hang around as it's warm and comfortable and even has its own sauna cabin in the bathroom, though I doubt I'll have enough time to get it going. It strikes me that there is an absurdly generous amount of electrical sockets in the room. In an idle moment I count eleven, many of them doubles. One of them looks a bit different to the others and has the letters 'ATK' printed on it. Probably best not to plug my laptop into that one.

My itinerary says the load in of the backline is at five and soundcheck is at six. As I don't have any backline to load in I arrive at the club at 6:30 but find all the lights out. I send a text to the promoter saying I'm at the club and asking when someone is going to be there to let me in, but when no reply comes after ten minutes I head over the road to a coffee house to warm up. I send a text to the number I have for the club itself, but I don't get a reply to that either and after an hour without hearing anything I head back through the icy streets to the hotel.

Not much to do but wait. I find another triple electrical socket behind the bed.

At 8:30 I make my way back and find the place unlocked, a few people inside avidly listening to the ice hockey on the radio. At 9:30 the sound man arrives and we go upstairs to the venue. The sound on stage is excellent and I'm suddenly looking forward to playing even though there are only about ten people downstairs and the gig is due to start in half an hour.

TALES OF THE EMERGENCY SANDWICH

I'm surprised to see two fans from Helsinki, Robert and Kimo, coming up the stairs as I head down to get a beer from the bar. They've flown up to Oulu and will also come to the gig in Kokkola tomorrow before taking the night train back. 'You don't play Helsinki, so we have to come here,' says Robert. The weather in Helsinki this morning was warm and Spring-like so they came in T-shirts and got a bit of a shock to step out of the plane and find it was snowing.

Looking anxiously around the empty room I am afraid they might regret their trip but dead on 10:15 about thirty people come up the stairs and we have a very good gig.

Back in the bar afterwards I sit around with Robert and Kimo and some of the rest of the audience, including a girl called Nina whose flat I visited when I played in Oulu a couple of years ago. She introduces me to some of her friends. One of them is a musician, and she tells me she is going to be screaming on his record tomorrow.

'Really?' I say. 'Will you be screaming on your own?'

'No, I think there will be many of us screaming.' She turns to her friend.

'There will be another six people screaming,' he says, then thinks for a moment. 'The place where we are recording is on the way to Kokkola – it would be really amazing if you could come in and scream on the way.'

'Would it just be one scream, or a lot of screaming?' I ask.

'Well, there are eighteen tracks to scream on,' he tells me.

Maybe not a good idea. I'd hate to get to my own gig and be all screamed out.

The conversation turns to why so few people turned up tonight. Of course, the ice hockey match didn't help. 'And it was a really well-known team,' says Kimo. 'They have the player who once pissed on the referee.'

Robert tells me he's a qualified American Wrestling referee and officiates at about fifteen shows a year. He's never been pissed on but at the last show it was arranged beforehand that one of the wrestlers would attack him with a staple gun. He ended up with six staples in his arm. He shakes his head thinking about it. 'I don't know why I agreed to it,' he says. 'It was really stupid, and it *really* hurt.'

A few more beers then people start to wander home. Back at the hotel I realise I should have spotted the warning signs earlier: the words 'Karaoke Bar' written up next to the name of the hotel. It turns out that my room is right above the bar, and all I can hear is the sound of eighties disco beats and dreadful out of tune singing pounding up through the floor.

It's not even dark, because the room is flooded with light from the mini bar, which has a glass front and an illuminated display of the drinks on offer. Not that I'm going to have any of them, but it does occur to me: light, refrigerator... there must be more electrical sockets behind there...

11th April

After only eating an emergency sandwich yesterday, I make sure I'm up in time to get a good breakfast at the hotel, then I make my way up to the train station, where I'm going to meet Robert and Kimo.

We head straight for the buffet car where I drink coffee and they drink coffee and *Jaloviina*, a Finnish cut brandy. Robert is not in the best of moods, having just been charged 55 euros by the hotel manager for smoking in his room, but says he feels much better after the first *Jaloviina*. During the two hour journey I ask him how he came to be involved in American Wrestling and he explains that his friends took him to a match for a bachelor party and he got interested and took the referee course. He turned out to be good at it, but there are dangers. He shows me the scar where during one bout he got hit on the head by a full can of cider and then fell into some barbed wire.

I don't really know what to expect from Kokkola. It's a small town, not on the regular gig circuit, and my guide book says that there is nothing to see except the train station, which is a welcome sight because it means you can leave. We get out of the train and have to cross the rails in front of it to get to the street, and Robert and Kimo joke that they haven't invented the tunnel here yet. I get out the map with directions to the hotel, and Robert points out the sign on the road facing us. 'You know enough Finnish to understand what that means, right? *Isokatuu* – Big Street...'

I have to agree that if that's the big street, we might have some trouble squeezing down the small ones. But the town is pretty enough, a lot of old-style wooden buildings and a few shops and bars. I leave Robert and Kimo to find a suitable bar – they have six hours drinking time before the gig opens – and I head down the big street to my hotel which is literally round the corner from the club.

Soundcheck according to my itinerary is at 6:30, and that's exactly when I arrive at the West Coast Bar. This time everything is ready on stage and I'm soon finished. I ask promoter Juhi if my start time is really going to be 11:15 like it says in my itinerary and he says, 'Well...it's Happy Hour until eleven, let's say you'll start between 11:15 and 11:35.'

Quite a specific time frame, which makes me think it's probably going to be accurate.

'And how long should I play?'

'The longer the better. Curfew is three in the morning.'

I head back round the corner to the hotel for some coffee. There's also a buffet, which Juhi has given me a ticket for, but the selection is quite untroubled by vegetarian food. There is, however, an enormous whole fish, some huge chunks of indeterminate ugly-looking meat, quite possibly reindeer, and muesli. Muesli?

Back at the venue I find Robert and Kimo at the pool tables, playing a Finnish variant of the game where the winner drinks a *Jaloviina*.

'What happens if you lose?' I ask.

'Well, then you have to drink a *Jaloviina* too.'

They seem surprisingly sober, but explain that it is because they have drunk so much that they are no longer able to get drunk.

Juhi suggests I wait a bit before starting as he's still hoping for more people. I finally get on stage just after midnight and the surprise is that here in Kokkola, a little town in the middle of nowhere, I have a great gig. There are around eighty in the audience and they're all up at the front of the stage getting involved and giving me enthusiastic applause at the end of the songs. I play for two hours and Robert and Kimo just have time afterwards to say goodbye before they dash off for their 2:30 train.

Then I sit around with Juhi and the lighting guy for a while. They've never seen anything like it here, they tell me, Usually the people are very reserved and hang around at the back of the room and just applaud politely, if at all.

Eventually we call it a night and Juhi offers to take me over to the hotel. As I walk up the steps from the venue I'm surprised to see that it looks like it's been snowing outside while we've been down there, then realise with a shock that it isn't snow – it's daylight. Oh dear, it's six in the morning.

I can't get into the hotel. There's a bell with the words 'Ovi Summers' above it – I don't know what that means but it doesn't work – and there's a keypad with instructions in Finnish, Swedish, and – ah ha – English, that says 'Attn. Electric lock opens the door on your left hand side.' But it doesn't.

Luckily Juhi hasn't got too far, and he has a phone number for someone from the hotel which he rings and gets some instructions for the keypad, which to my great relief finally opens the door on the third attempt.

Four hours to breakfast.

TV SMITH

<u>12th April</u>
When the alarm goes off I'm torn between sleep and hunger. Hunger wins, but that turns out to be a bad decision as the breakfast buffet is almost exactly the same as last night's dinner buffet. Slim pickings for a vegetarian but there are at least some rye bread rolls and cheese so I make up some emergency sandwiches in case of problems later. I am the only person at breakfast, in fact I seem to be the only guest in the hotel.

Up the road to the railway station, where the driver of the train that will take me to Seinäjoke is leaning out of his cab cheerfully smoking a pipe. The expression on his face says, all's right with the world.

According to my itinerary, I'll be met at Seinäjoke station by someone called Iina. I'm a bit concerned about this as I don't even know if Iina is a man or woman's name, and I catch the eye of quite a few people on the platform before a punky-looking girl holding a red rose approaches me and says, 'You must be TV?' She proffers the rose. 'They thought it would be funny if I gave you this…'

Another day, another gig, and already it's getting strange.

Tonight's gig is very different from the other ones on the tour. It's in a big venue just outside the town, headlined by a successful Finnish indie-rock band called Lapko with a couple of other bands on the bill as well. As Iina drives me out there, I ask, 'How many people are you expecting? I've heard it holds about a thousand?'

'I hope not,' she says. 'We don't have enough staff. Two hundred would be good.'

Soundcheck is over in a flash, and I go up the stairs beside the stage to a large dressing room. None of the other bands are here, but there's coffee, tea, bread rolls, and in the fridge a bowl of salad, cheese and an entire crate of beer marked 'FOR TV SMITH.' Those emergency sandwiches currently curling up in my hotel minibar have become rather superfluous.

It's going to be a long wait now until I play, nearly four hours, with one band before me and two after. I'm surprised to see the drummer and merchandising guy from the Tigerbombs walk into the room. They explain that they're playing in the band on after me, 'I Was A Teenage Satan Worshipper.' They suggests I might like to go with them to the sauna in the basement, but I tell them I'm not in the mood before playing. When they come back half an hour later they tell me I made the right decision – there was no hot water for the showers.

'But you're Finnish – you're supposed to roll in the snow after a sauna…'

'Yes, but rolling in the snow is quite different. Cold water, from a shower, on your back – I mean, EEEEE!'

Downstairs the place is filling up, a lot of teenagers staking their place in front of the stage for Lapko, even though it will be hours before they play. I'm watching the first band on when I feel a tap on the shoulder and turn round to see Riitta, from Punk Lurex OK.

'This is a band from this area so they have their fans here,' she says.

I gesture at the kids in front of us. 'They're so *young*,' I say. 'I'm old enough to be their father.'

'Yes,' says Riitta. 'Me too.'

I think about going back upstairs to get ready for the gig and just as I start to leave the singer mentions me from the stage. Nothing like walking out during your own namecheck. In the dressing room, Lapko's bass player introduces himself. He's been resting in another room and has a question: 'TV, you've been touring for thirty years – can you tell me: what do you do when you're just so tired that you can't imagine being able to play the show?'

I'd like to give him some advice, but the truth is I'm so tired I can't think of any.

What all musicians know is that as soon as you walk on stage, all thoughts about being tired are forgotten. Today I have just a thirty minute set, so I play fast and intense and it goes down surprisingly well with the young crowd.

Next up are I Was A Teenage Satan Worshipper, who play a kind of synth-electro-rock fusion. The bass player – who I've only ever seen before doing the merchandising at Tigerbombs gigs – flings himself all over the stage, while the statuesque female synth player doesn't move a muscle.

'You must be exhausted,' I tease her afterwards.

'I am,' she says. 'It is very hard work standing still.'

We go down to the back door so she can have a cigarette and she gestures at the car park in front of us. 'Beautiful view. Flat, and a big stone.'

She asks me how many gigs a year I play and when I say, with a weary expression in my voice, more than a hundred, she says, 'But that's good, right? You're doing what you want.'

'Well, yes that's true. I never forget I could be working in a factory.'

'Or a shoe shop,' she says. 'Like me.'

Just then the door opens and Riitta appears with a guy trailing along behind her.

'Ah, TV there you are! We found you!'

Riitta introduces me to the guy. 'This is my new boyfriend. Very new. Er – what's your name again?'

TV SMITH

We go to watch Lapko and when they finish I head back up to the dressing room, where the singer from the first band approaches me. 'Strange audience, so young,' he says. 'They have no idea who The Adverts are. When I said from the stage what an honour it is to be playing on the same bill as the legendary TV Smith, they didn't know what I was talking about!'

Just then there is the sound of a tinny musical ringtone and he thrusts his hands deep into his pockets searching for his phone. 'Excuse me, my balls are ringing.'

Lapko are hanging out in the dressing room with everyone else, friendly and talkative now that the gig is out of the way. We talk for a while about how really good bands don't seem to get noticed by the music business. 'That's because the music business is about making money, not about making music,' I say.

The bass player from Lapko agrees and says that despite their success they are still trying to keep the music business at arm's length. He comments, 'Music is like sex. As soon as it involves money, it's no good any more.'

Some *Jaloviina* gets passed around. Iina arrives and says, 'Just let me know when you want to go back.'

I check the time: just before 2:30. I'll have to get up at eight for my train back to Helsinki and the flight back to England. 'I think I should leave at three,' I say. 'Whatever you do, don't let me stay any later than that, *even if I appear to be enjoying myself.*'

So. I have half an hour now to continue having fun. I'll leave here at three, should be asleep by four. There won't be time for the hotel breakfast so I'll have emergency sandwich number one on the train, and as there's no vegetarian meal on Finnair I'll have emergency sandwich number two on the plane.

That's my itinerary. Now let's see what really happens.

13. HOW IT ALL GOES HORRIBLY WRONG (2008)

<u>30th July</u>
I'm looking forward to these two gigs in Norway. Tonight I'll be back at Elm Street, now my regular venue in Oslo, and the day after that I'll be playing on the 'Campfire Stage' at the Storas Festival, in a setting of forests and mountains up in the north of the country near Trondheim. This festival has the reputation of being one of the friendliest and best in Norway, and according to the information sheet I've been sent, is totally non-corporate with no sponsorship or advertising. I have also been given an itinerary explaining how and when I'll be transported to and from the airport and, importantly, from the festival to the hotel after I've played. My show time is midnight – just around the time when the organisation at these events tends to get a bit sketchy so it's good to have everything down in writing.

But first, Oslo.

I get the train into the city, and am struggling along the streets to the club with my suitcase and guitar when I hear a voice behind me calling my name. It's Jan-Martin, the Norwegian tour agent who booked these two dates and is just heading towards the club himself on his bicycle. While he wheels along beside me he tells me the papers are full of news about the recent heatwave: according to the front page today, there has been an explosion in the numbers of snakes and wasps all over Norway because of it. Yesterday the extreme temperature caused a thunderstorm to break out over Oslo and there were more than 20,000 lightning strikes.

Tomorrow I'm playing in a forest!

One of the women behind the bar tells me that she's had a call from someone who wants to interview me and will be ringing again after soundcheck. Soundcheck is over in two minutes, and while I'm waiting for the interviewer to ring back, Jan-Martin introduces me to someone who wants to write a piece on me for his blog. He talks to me for a while and takes some photos, but at the end I notice he has only written two things on his notepad: 'Tim' and 'Roxy.'

I say to Jan-Martin that I'm not really expecting many people to turn up tonight – it's a Wednesday, never a good day for a gig, and still sunny and warm outside. He says, 'There are a lot of tourists in Oslo at the moment. The tourists might come.'

I ask him if he thinks Trygve – a fan who years ago asked him to book my first ever concert in Norway – will come. He is just explaining that he hasn't heard from Trygve for a while when the barmaid comes over holding out her phone. *The interview*, she mouths. I put the phone up to my ear. 'Hello TV,' says a familiar voice. 'This is Trygve…'

He wants to film an interview in the dressing room, so we arrange to do it in about an hour. The blog guy comes back from outside the club, where he has been having a smoke. 'Did you see that?' he says. 'That couple out there were asking what was happening here tonight and was it worth coming, and I told them it was going to be great and they mustn't miss it. I just got you two more for the audience!'

'You see,' says Jan-Martin, 'Tourists.'

Trygve and his cameraman set up for the interview in the small dressing room in the basement. Lights and camera are switched on and we rattle through Trygve's questions fairly briskly until Tarjei, the promoter, comes down to ask if I'm ready to get going.

There are about fifty people upstairs in the club, and when I walk in they give me a big cheer and we have an extremely nice show.

In the dressing room I find Trygve and the cameraman sitting around chatting about the eighties. Trygve is writing a book on the decade and is expounding the theory that the eighties were the best thing about punk because musically anything was possible, whereas seventies punk was musically very narrow. Nothing I say about how awful that period was for me makes any impact. After a while the door opens and Casino Steel – the Norwegian keyboard player for The Boys – walks in.

Trygve pounces. 'Cas – what do *you* think about the eighties?'

'The eighties?' says Cas. 'Oh, I was drunk for most of the eighties.'

When he leaves I pack up and go too. It's going to be a long day tomorrow and if I leave now I can still get six hours sleep before the flight to Trondheim.

<u>31st July</u>

There's a minibus waiting at Trondheim airport for me and two of the other bands who are playing today – an American rock band called Drive By Truckers, and a Norwegian rap band called Gatas Parlament. I end up sitting with the rappers, who are reading out some trivia questions from today's paper. I get into their good books by being able to answer the question, *Which British seaside town had its pier burn down recently?*

(A: Weston-super-Mare.)

TALES OF THE EMERGENCY SANDWICH

The band have a black Sudanese artist with them who is going to paint giant portraits of them on the back of the stage as they play. He is talking a bit about what it was like growing up in Sudan. If you were suspected of drinking alcohol you would be put in jail for the night then taken out to a public place and whipped. 'Happened to me many times, man. Sudan is a *whipping* country. Even at school they whip the kids. If you have a spelling test with, like, fifty questions, for every one of those you get wrong you get whipped. Those aren't toy whips either, they come out with flesh.'

'What do the parents think of it?' asks one of the rest of the band.

'Oh, they know all about it. They expect it. They give the kids over to the school and say, 'Take the flesh, give me back the bone. That's what my father said when he handed me over.'

At the festival site I'm met by a girl called Julianne, who tells me she's in charge of making sure I have everything I need. She explains that it's a twenty minute drive out to the hotel and she will arrange for me to get a lift out there later. There is food being served for the artists in the backstage area in half an hour, and meantime she can show me where I am going to be playing and the rest of the festival.

Tonight this will be my stage.
Storas festival 2008

It's a huge site with four large stages, some open air, some under cover. We walk past these and out through the woods to my stage, which – despite the fact I've read the dimensions in my itinerary – still surprises me by how small it actually is. Standing in clearing next to some sauna tents and open air hot tubs, it looks like a sentry box on legs. I hop up into the box to try it out for size and find that the roof is slightly lower than my head.

In the dining hall I grab a plate from the table marked 'Vegetarian Option' and sit at a table with Gatas Parlament, who look curiously at what I've got. It's not the most exciting meal in the world – a bowl of chickpeas and some shredded raw cabbage in a wrap – but I'm hungry, and the band assure me that the meat option is not much better. One of them prods the rubbery red chunk on his plate with a fork. 'No idea what that is. They describe it as 'meat' just so you know it's not a fish or a vegetable.'

There's a lot of time to kill before midnight so I spend a while wandering around the site and watching a few of the bands. It's much less frantic than most other festivals, lots of free space, a relaxed atmosphere, and no pushing and shoving. This early in the evening only one stage at a time has a band playing, sometimes to only fifty or a hundred people, although there are a few thousand spread around the site. The music is eclectic – in the space of a couple of hours I see a bhangra/rock fusion band on one of the large stages, a pretty awful Norwegian *oompah* band on the main stage, and a quite good rock band called The Violent Years on a smaller stage in a barn. I end up in the open air backstage area with Gatas Parlament again, playing Pass The Pigs and chatting with Super Saya, the girl rapper in the band. She tells me that 'the boys' had to go off and be filmed using the environmentally-friendly festival urinals which have a readout showing how much energy you are creating as you pee. The cameramen promised they wouldn't be pointing the cameras 'down there.' We are all getting on so well it's frustrating that our sets start at the same time and we won't be able to see each other play.

Now it's past ten and time to get ready, so we swap CDs and I say goodbye and head off to the other side of the site where I'm sharing a backstage with the bands playing in the barn. Julianne is there, and tells me she has the transfer to the hotel all sorted out: I'll be going back with two other bands at 1:30. I point out that it will be hard for me to make that, as I'm supposed to play until 1:00, there might be encores, then I want to sell CDs, then I have to go and pick up my fee from the office. She makes a couple of phone calls and gets the lift changed to 2:00, and we go over to the office to try and get the money sorted out now, but they won't hand it over until after I've played.

By the time I start playing a couple of hundred people have gathered in front of the campfire stage, and very atmospheric it is too. Despite the fact I'm standing on a sentry box in the forest, the sound is great and I'm not even distracted by the strains of extreme black metal band Meshuggah blasting over from the other side of the festival site. When they stop at 1:00 I carry on a bit longer. I persuade the crowd to make a big noise so the people at the main stage will think they are missing something, and they respond better than I dared hope – on and on they whoop and cheer and applaud, and after that they do it at the end of every song, and mean it. This is turning into a really special gig, and my only concern is that I know there's a minibus going with or without me in forty minutes and I really have to stop. After the last encore I put down the guitar and spread the CDs for sale across the front of the stage and have soon sold everything I brought with me.

I would really like to hang around and chat with all these nice people some more but I am aware that Julianne is waiting at the side of the stage with her clipboard. She catches my eye and says, 'You have a lot of fans. But your bus goes in twenty minutes.'

'I knew this would happen,' I say. I pack up as fast as I can and we go back to the barn to get my suitcase, then over to the office. I'm all fired up from the gig now, and I start to wonder if it might be possible to get a later bus so I could hang around a bit longer and enjoy myself. The only problem is, I'm scheduled to leave at nine in the morning for the airport. I say to Julianne, 'Is it really necessary that I have to leave at nine tomorrow? It's only an internal flight and I'll be at the airport far too early.'

When we get to the car park Julianne goes into the transportation office to double check, and comes out with some bad news

'It seems that they will actually come to pick you up at 7:40.'

'That's ridiculous,' I say. 'My flight isn't until 11:25.'

'Well actually it seems the bus going at nine is already full and that's the only other one we have to take you to the airport. You will be on the same bus as The Violent Years and they need to be there earlier. I am sorry. We have a problem with not enough drivers. First the bus will go and pick up the band from where they are staying then they will come and get you.' She looks at the drunken crowd milling around the minibus. 'This will be two trips. You'd better get in now.'

I climb into the front seat beside the driver and others cram into the back until no more can fit. We set off through the twisty roads and further out into the countryside. No one in the van speaks any English and I gaze out of the window at the passing forests as a lot of raucous drunken conversation in Norwegian goes on behind me. One guy in particular is being very loud. He must be doing something funny because everyone else is cracking up, particularly when he opens the door and hangs out of it screaming. We climb a hill and pull into a deserted and dark gravelled yard behind a large white wooden house, and everyone gets out of the bus. This is clearly not the hotel I'm supposed to be in.

I turn to the driver. 'Where do I go?'

'I go back to Storas,' he says.

'No – where do *I* go? Where do I sleep?'

'Through door. Sleep.' He points.

Confused, I lift my guitar and suitcase out of the back of the bus and open the door of the house to find a steep stairway, and at the top a few rooms, all of them already occupied with sleeping people. I hurry back down the steps but the minibus has gone. The drunken crowd now sitting at the picnic table in the back garden and opening up more beer are no help, but when I head back into the house for another look around I find an open door next to the foot of the stairs and a few bedrooms behind it. There are also a lot of people here, and some of them are asleep on the floor. Someone walks past dragging some bedding. He looks me over. 'What are you doing here?' he asks.

'I'm looking for somewhere to sleep,' I say.

'There is no room here,' he says, angrily. 'This apartment is already full.'

I'm getting angry myself now. I stamp out into the back yard, check the contract from the festival about the hotel I'm supposed to be in and phone up Julianne.

'Look, I've been dumped at some place in the middle of the countryside, I don't know what's going on, no one speaks English, the guy who drove me here has gone, I don't have anywhere to sleep and I have to leave at 7:40. I am really, *really* pissed off about this.'

There is a silence. 'I am so sorry. I will speak to someone and find out what's going on then call you back.'

I go around the corner away from the drunks and sit on a step to wait. We are so far North that the few hours of comparative night time are already nearly over: a pale sky is showing through the breaks in the cloud, revealing a mist settling over the tree-lined peaks of the hills. The phone rings.

'Okay I have spoken to someone about this. I am so sorry but there were no rooms left at the hotel. There was nothing we could do. But there is a place for you to sleep where you are now. A woman is going to come out and show you. Now I am going to text you her number in case there is any problem.'

I guess it will take a while for her to get here from the festival so I settle back on my step and open the emergency bottle of beer I have in my shoulder bag. The text from Julianne arrives but there seems no point in phoning the other woman yet. After ten minutes I go back into the house to use the toilet and when I come out there is a woman in T-shirt and knickers standing in the hallway.

'Who are you?' she says.

'I'm TV Smith, from the Storas festival.' I explain. 'I'm supposed to be sleeping here. They are sending out some woman to tell me where.'

'Well, actually, I am that woman.' she says. She didn't have to come from the festival as I had assumed: she lives here and only had to come out from her bedroom. 'There is absolutely no room here, but we do have somewhere for you,' she says. She takes me back down the steps and from the doorway points to a path that goes up past a barn opposite. 'Go up there and you will find a big house on the left. That is where you are sleeping'

'Er, just up that hill and it's on the left?'

Yes, thirty seconds. You can't miss it. Big apartment, lots of room, all for you.'

I can't help feeling that she's just trying to get rid of me so she can go back to bed, but all the same I grab the suitcase and guitar and trudge up the path.

A couple of minutes later I find to my surprise that there really is another house. I'm somehow less surprised to find that all the doors are locked. I sit down on the front steps and phone the woman down the road.

'It's locked.'

'It's locked?'

'It's locked.'

'Oh, look – I'm going to phone the woman in there and try and wake her up so she can let you in. I'll call you back.'

She hangs up and I phone Julianne again and explain the current state of things. She promises to chase up the woman who is on the phone chasing up the other woman.

The phone rings. It's the woman down the road calling to tell me that she hasn't been able to wake up the woman in the place I am standing outside. 'Actually, I do have one bed free here.' She says. 'You'd better come back down.'

I walk around the back of the house to the path and pass a minibus pulling away onto the road. At the back door I find a group of about ten people standing around with all their luggage. I head towards them.

'Do any of you have a key to this place?'

'Well, no.' says one of them, 'Hey – are you that guy that was playing the solo set? That was *amazing*!'

'Yes I am. Thank you. I don't have anywhere to sleep.'

It occurs to me that these people are soon going to realise that no one is going to answer the doorbell and are all going to be looking for somewhere to sleep too. I bet they don't have to get up at seven though. 'Well – ha – I'm just going to see what's going on in the place down the hill…'

I speed off.

The woman from the place down the hill has now put on some jeans and meets me halfway up the path. 'There's another band up there that can't get in,' I tell her.

She looks at me, trying to figure out if I am joking. 'Oh no. There is just no more room. I can find space for you but that's it.'

We get to the other house and Julianne rings again to explain that the woman standing next to me will find me a place to sleep. 'Another band have just arrived who are going to need somewhere too,' I tell her.

'Oh no…'

The woman next to me is holding out her phone and pointing at a number on the screen. 'Give her this,' she says.

I speak to Julianne again. 'This women – er what is your name, by the way? – er, *Una* wants me to give you a number.'

'Hold on – I have to find some paper.' The line goes dead.

'She has to find some paper' I explain to Una.

Julianne is back. 'Okay give me the number.'

I read it out. 'I don't know what it is, but that's the number she wants me to tell you.'

'It's the number of the apartment up the hill,' says Una.

'It's the number of the apartment up the hill' I tell Julianne. 'Where the band are waiting and the woman is sleeping.'

If I went to bed *right now* I would get four hours sleep.

Una leads me into the house, and halfway up the stairs turns back and says, 'I'm just curious – are you, like, a famous musician?'

'I was.'

She takes me to a small room with a bed that has obviously recently been slept in. She strips off the dirty sheets and puts on some new ones, then shows me where the toilet is. 'I already found that,' I point out.

'Ah, yes. And here is the kitchen. Will you want breakfast in the morning?'

'I don't think I'm going to have time. But, just in case – what is there?'

She cast around. 'Hmm, there is some bread. Or you could see if there is anything in the fridge?'

I set the alarm clock for 7:10, the alarm on my phone for 7:15, write '7:40' at the top of my itinerary and get under the duvet. Too angry to sleep.

<u>1st August</u>
I feel surprisingly refreshed when the alarm goes off, and there's time for a quick wash and shave before I pack and leave the house to wait outside for the minibus. I'm in quite a good mood considering everything that happened last night and the lack of sleep. I sit outside on the steps enjoying the calm grey morning for ten minutes and then my phone rings.

'Good morning!' says a woman's voice. 'This is the transportation office at the Storas Festival. Did you sleep well?'

'Short.'

'Ah yes, I heard all about it. Well, I have some news that won't exactly affect you directly, but…'

Suddenly I realise that a phone call can only mean one thing. Bad news.

'Wait – don't tell me. The bus isn't coming to pick me up.'

'Um. That's correct. There has been some kind of crisis and the bus had to leave directly from the hotel to get the other band to the airport and absolutely had no time to come to get you. Now we are going to figure out a way to get you to the airport. Your plane is at 11:25, so you don't need to leave for at least another couple of hours, is that right?'

That's what I was trying to tell them yesterday. 'That's right. But I got out of bed half an hour ago after four hours sleep because you messed up the accommodation last night, and now I'm awake and I'm standing outside waiting for the bus you promised would pick me up, and you're telling me I could have slept for another couple of hours after all? What is going on? Have you got something against me personally or do you treat all the musicians like this?'

'We are really sorry. It is just bad luck that this has all happened to you. I am going to ring around to find someone I can wake up and persuade to take you to the airport. We will definitely get you there in time for your flight somehow, but you can go back indoors now and I will call you again later.'

In stunned disbelief I climb back up the stairs to the bedroom. The only things to do is wait it out, so I take the time to check the kitchen for some breakfast. In the cupboard there's a half-empty bag of bread rolls and some cat food, and in the fridge there's nothing vegetarian except some jam, so it looks like breakfast will be a jam sandwich. It's a little early in the morning for a cat food sandwich.

On the first bite it occurs to me that this Norwegian jam tastes rather peculiar. It's a taste I recognise somehow, not particularly nice really. Then I realise what it is. I turn over the bread roll and sure enough there are the familiar furry patches of black and green. I've had a UMM – an Unexpected Mould Moment.

Great! All this and food poisoning too! I spit out the contents of my mouth into my hand and wander around the kitchen to find a waste bin, but there isn't one so eventually I try to wash the half-chewed handful down the sink. There is no towel. I hear the phone go in the room next to the one I've been sleeping in, and then Una emerges, looking rather bleary. I say, 'Let me guess – the festival have asked you to drive me to the airport.'

'No,' she says, 'they called to ask the address here. They are sending a taxi for you.'

They didn't even know the address of where I was staying.

My phone rings. 'Here is the transportation office at Storas Festival again. We are sending a taxi for you.'

I take my guitar and bags back outside and pace around the picnic table in the back garden for a while, quietly fuming, then notice a 200 Kroner note in the grass, about twenty quid. Well, when I get to the airport it looks like breakfast is on the drunk Norwegian guys. Good.

A taxi driver with a nasty cough speeds me through the country roads and I'm at the airport in fifty minutes with plenty of time to spare, and check in so early that the automatic ticket machine allocates me a window seat in the front row of the plane. Ambling through the airport, I dispose of almost half of my windfall 200 Kroner on a thin sandwich and a coffee, and arrive at the gate to find, to my surprise, The Violent Years sat there.

'Did you miss your plane?' I ask. 'I was supposed to come in the same bus as you but they told me that they had to leave without me or you would miss your flight.'

They look puzzled. 'We're on this flight. We've been here two hours.'

The flight to Oslo will take an hour, I will have a three hour stopover there, then a two hour flight to London. Plenty of time to mull over how it all went so well at first, and then so horribly wrong.

Still, looking on the bright side: no thunderstorms, snakes or wasps.

14. *SLUTSIGNAL!* (2008)

<u>14th August</u>
My second trip to Sweden. Last time it was two gigs, this time it's four, the first of them a return visit to Stockholm's Kafé 44. Gigs here start early, and by the time I've made my way into Stockholm on the airport train, figured out the subway system, and dropped my bag off at the hotel it's almost time for the music to start when I rush in at 7:30.

The support band are called Sonic Farm. I met them after my poorly attended gig here last time and when we were all sitting around in the pub afterwards their bass player Ego T. Superstar (real name: Benny) promised to help out with the promotion if I ever wanted to come back. He's done a great job: the room is packed by the time I go on.

The unusual thing about this venue is that no alcohol is allowed. Unlike most of the audience I didn't have time to go to the nearby pub before coming here, but I did manage to sneak in a couple of cans of lager and decant them into coffee cups. People must have thought I was pretty tired, the amount of coffee I was drinking during the gig.

Afterwards it's a great surprise to see Jon and Sophie, two fans from Miami, who have decided to combine a few days holiday in Sweden with some TV Smith gigs. Jon suggests I could join them in their hire car for the drive down to Köping tomorrow. I already have my train tickets booked but this sounds a lot more fun.

Most of the audience head down the road to a bar and drink at quite a speedy rate after the deprivation of the last few hours. The place shuts at two, and then Benny insists on accompanying me to my hotel, only a couple of streets away, just to make sure I get back safely. On the way a girl sitting on a bench in a small park shouts something at us. It's in Swedish so I don't know what she says, but it suddenly turns Benny into Ego T. Superstar – he stops in the middle of the road, drops his trousers and underwear and starts waving his bits about. Then he walks me into the hotel and starts loudly and lengthily gushing his goodbyes. He shows no sign of actually leaving though, and after about ten minutes one of the women sitting in Reception turns to us, gives him a frosty look and says, 'Yes, *goodbye…*'

15th August

Jon and Sophie meet me at the hotel at 11:30, and after a pleasant couple of hours looking around Stockholm we set off for Köping. The drive takes longer than expected and I become a bit concerned that Anna, who invited me to play tonight, will be wondering where I am. Anna is another of the people I met at the pub session following my first Kafé 44 gig, and she promised that she could get me an invite to an event in her home town where at least 700 people would come. I found it hard to believe, and to make things worse I thought she said she came from 'Shopping.' I got home and tried to find a town called Shopping on the map. But no, it's Köping: the Kompledigt singer/songwriter festival featuring some thirty acoustic acts over two days – with about 700 people expected to show up. In fact, everything has gone exactly the way Anna said it would – except for me. I'm still on the road somewhere when she phones up from the station and asks if I've missed my train.

We take a few wrong turns, and Jon starts to get sleepy and asks Sophie to take over the driving. Unfortunately she's only driven cars with automatic gearboxes since she moved from her native France to live in Miami with Jon. She swaps seats with him and attempts to engage the gears while he shouts from the back, 'No not that pedal, the other one! No, hang on, the *other* one.'

The families enjoying their meals at the sunny tables outside the restaurant look on with interest as the motor roars and the gears crunch while we stubbornly fail to move off. Finally underway, there's another incident involving a U-turn, some heavy traffic and a steep drop-off at the side of the road, but fortunately I have erased that from my memory.

Jon and Sophie are pretty spontaneous about their travel plans and haven't decided whether they're going to stay the night in Köping or drive back to Stockholm, but a sign for the 'Gillet Hotel' as we near the venue convinces them to stay. Gillet is Jon's surname.

We find our way straight to the Ögir restaurant, where the festival is taking place. From the car park we can see over the fence to the large courtyard where a band is just starting to play on the outdoor stage. After recent rain it's a beautiful warm and sunny afternoon, and Jon and Sophie are positively beaming with pleasure at being here, delighted they've made the trip.

Anna finds me and I excuse myself for not letting her know about the change of plan. Soon afterwards Björn arrives on the train from Göteborg, where he's left the rest of his family for the day. His wife Marie-Thérese drove them up from their home town of Helsinborg so the kids could spend a day in the Liseberg theme park while Björn came to the gig. It was Björn who first invited me to play in Sweden, sending me an email one evening out of the blue proposing the idea after – he now admits – a few ciders, and he has helped organise these four days for me. He'll be traveling on the train with me back to Göteborg tomorrow. For now he sorts out the details of where I'm staying tonight and when I'm given the card with the hotel name on it I have to rush off and show Jon. I'm in Hotel Gillet.

A couple more acts play and then it's nearly time for me. I'm standing with a beer trying to figure out how I'm going to cut my show down to the allocated forty minute slot when Björn comes over. 'I can see you're getting focused,' he says. 'Your eyes have gone beady.'

The gig goes like a dream and the audience applaud for a straight five minutes afterwards so that I have to come back and play an encore even though the sound guy is pointing at his watch and shaking his head.

I'm standing by the merchandising table afterwards and Anna is telling me how much she enjoyed the gig when a guy around my age comes up and asks me to sign a couple of CDs for him. I excuse myself to Anna and turn to sign the CDs, and while I'm doing that Anna turns to the guy and says, 'See Dad, I told you you'd like it!'

<u>16th August</u>
The train doesn't leave until after two so there's a good couple of hours to look around Köping. To be honest you don't need that long.

I meet Björn on the platform and when he hands me my ticket I point out that our seat reservations are for carriage 14, seats 25 and 26, and the train departs at 14:27.

'14:25, 14:26, 14:27....' I murmur.

'You like that, don't you?' says Björn.

I do like that.

During the four hour journey to Göteborg I amuse myself by leafing through the Swedish language train magazine and trying to learn a few phrases. Frustratingly, the only thing that sticks in my mind is the word *Slutsignal*, which is on the back page of the safety leaflet accompanied by a drawing of a flashing warning light by the side of the track. Not an awful lot of use in everyday conversation.

Marie-Thérèse meets us at Göteborg station, and we drive off to the venue, but soon realise we have gone the wrong way. We turn around, then get caught in the one way streets in the city centre where we stop to ask directions from a taxi driver and nearly get sideswiped by a tram. Finally we find the road along the edge of the waterfront that we've been looking for and about a kilometre further along we see the club's name – Henriksberg – on the side of a building jutting out from the top of a cliff high above us. There seems to be no way to drive up the hill to the club so I tell Marie-Thérèse to drop me off. Then she takes the rest of the family off to the hotel where they are staying and I struggle with my guitar and bags up a steep flight of steps, grateful that I sold most of my CDs yesterday.

Jonk, the promoter, meets me at the door to the club and takes me down to the room I'll be playing, which is literally cut into the cliff. The back of the stage is rough grey rock and the club is low-ceilinged, fitted out with wood so it resembles the interior of a boat, complete with portholes looking dizzily down to the harbour far below. Until it's time for soundcheck I hang around in the bar upstairs, where a member of one of the support bands tells me that they played here a week ago. A friend of his filmed it and put it on You Tube, and last night he had a look at it. 'We were terrible,' he admits. 'I was totally drunk, and in between every song I was talking and messing around for two or three minutes. There were quite a lot of people in but they didn't move around at all so I told them, if you're not going to move why don't you fuck off upstairs, you're all just a waste of space. Later I drunk so much that the bouncers threw me out of the club.'

'So you're the drummer?'

'Yes.'

Downstairs, the sound technician, a heavily-tattooed and muscled-up guy called Peter, tells me that the sound in the room is really good, despite the rock wall behind the stage. He points out the concrete columns on the stage. 'Before we renovated the room and built the stage here this used to be the bar,' he says. 'When we removed it we were quite surprised to find that it was holding up the ceiling.'

The low ceiling could be a problem for me. It barely clears my head and there are some specific rules for the musicians posted on the dressing room wall: *If you climb the barrier or even as much as touch the ceiling...the power will be turned off and security staff will escort you to the door immediately, just like anyone else in the crowd = no show = no money = lucky if you ever see your equipment again!!!*

TALES OF THE EMERGENCY SANDWICH

That's not all: *If you smoke, fight, pee, shit, ejaculate, vomit, cut yourself on purpose, throw/pour blood or similar...the power will be turned off and security staff...*etcetera.

At the bottom of the page it says: *Have a nice gig!*

Soundcheck is fine, and now there's nothing else to do but hang around for four hours,

I decide to go for a walk, and find Peter outside having a smoke. He tells me that he's really looking forward to my set. First of all he couldn't imagine how I could play somewhere like this solo, but now he's heard the soundcheck he thinks it's going to be even better than with a band.

I can feel myself getting excited. I go down the steps, pace around the harbour front for a while, watching the sun set over the glistening, rippling water, then head back to the club. There are already quite a few people in and the DJ is playing some great late seventies music – Lou Reed, Alex Harvey, some classic punk. The drummer of the first band comes up to me looking dejected. 'Can you believe it? My band have *banned* me from drinking any more before we play!'

Björn and a friend of his, a journalist called Göran, arrive so we sit down with a beer and chat for a while. Göran tells me about the time he accidentally beat up Sid Vicious. The Sex Pistols were playing in Helsinborg and Göran was interviewing the rest of the band after the show when Sid suddenly came into the room naked, and jumped on Göran's back. 'You know what Sid was like, right? No muscle on him at all. So I just jabbed my elbow back to get him off me and he fell off onto the floor and lay there howling that I'd attacked him, like a big baby.'

I wander out into the the other room and someone waves at me. 'Hey, I saw you in the train today! I sent an SMS to my friend to tell him and he said, how do you know it was really him? So I said, I recognise him from You Tube.'

The two supports play, then as midnight approaches it's finally time for me. There's a hot, sticky rock'n'roll atmosphere in the club now and I play hard and fast. The people are crowding to the front and showing their appreciation. I'm supposed to play for forty-five minutes, but manage to stretch it to seventy-five before finally calling it quits.

Afterwards, drenched with sweat, I sit on the stage and sell my last few remaining CDs and chat with the audience until I can finally escape to the backstage. I'm exhilarated and exhausted at the same time. I'd love to relax with a beer now but Björn comes back and tells me that the bar has closed and the security guys are about to throw us all out. I haven't even got into a dry T-shirt or had time to pack away the guitar yet.

Peter's girlfriend comes in and tells me that she usually works at the bar here but came down even though it's her night off and loved the gig. She asks me where I'm staying.

'I don't know,' I say. 'Jonk was going to book it and get the key for me.'

She looks surprised at that. 'Jonk has gone,' she says. 'He told me he was off to another club.'

Uh oh.

One of the security guys fills the doorway and addresses the room. It's Swedish so I don't know what he's saying, but his manner is threatening and unpleasant. I am not about to get thrown out of the club now before I've had a chance to wind down, and I tell him so. Quite loudly. I'm tired, I don't know where I'm sleeping tonight, I'm getting in a bad mood, and right now I don't really care if he physically throws me out, but I know I'm not going voluntarily. Maybe it's my inner drummer coming out.

In the end there's no problem. By the time I've packed away, the security guys have all gone home, Jonk is back with the key, and Peter's girlfriend even persuades the barmaid to get me a drink. When Jonk mentions the name of my hotel, she says 'I've got a friend who works there. It's a really good one. You've got to get up in time for breakfast – they do the best buffet breakfast in Sweden...in *Europe!*'

They all tell me they want me to come back and play Henriksberg again and now I'm back in a good mood. Björn phones for a taxi and we go outside and wait. It's still warm, and far below the dark waters glitter under the full moon and the lights of the harbour. It's a short ride into the city centre, where Björn comes in and sorts out the reservation for me then we say our goodbyes and he leaves for his hotel. Tomorrow he'll be heading back home and I'll be moving on to the next gig in Uddevalla.

17th August

It could well be the best buffet breakfast in Europe, but it's so busy it's hard to tell. I have to queue to get a glass of water. I wrap up an emergency sandwich in a napkin in case it all goes horribly wrong later.

I have a couple of hours before I need to catch my train, and Björn's kids' visit to the Liseberg has sparked off an idea: I grab a map from the hotel and find my way up to the park, where there are no queues and I ride three rather good roller coasters, including an elegant and scary giant wooden one, before heading back into town. On the way I pass a large open air stage where a live opera is being performed, part of the weekend culture festival.

I pick up my bags from the hotel and trundle on to the train station, the wheeled suitcase and preponderance of cobbled pavements not a great combination. At the station the section of the all-important electronic Departures board that should show the platform number is malfunctioning and showing incomprehensible gobbledygook so I have no idea where to go. There are long queues at the Information desk, no chance to get there before the train leaves. With only three minutes remaining I catch an announcement over the public address system and reach the platform just as the train doors are closing.

An hour later I'm in Uddevalla. It's a one platform station and to get out you have to go to the end of it and then cross the tracks. Just as I get over them there's a deafening buzzing sound, and red lights start flashing to warn of a coming train. Could this be the *Slutsignal*?

On the train I sketched out a simplified version of the map I downloaded onto my laptop last night showing the route to the venue, but the layout of streets I find in front of me doesn't seem to bear any relation to it. I walk around for a while before I have to reluctantly admit that the directions from the station Uddevala O that I saved, are not the same as those from the station Uddevalla C, where I actually got off the train.

One thing I noticed on the map was that the club was next to a river. Working on the theory that the river is more likely to be at the bottom of the hill than on top of it, I set off downhill and before long I'm at the river and then I start recognising street names, and then I'm at the club.

Morten's Krog turns out to be a beautiful purpose-built venue, a restaurant and bar on the ground floor and a large, airy music room with a wide stage and state-of-the-art lights and sound system upstairs. Lars, who booked the gig, takes me up there and shows me around. He was about to phone me as I walked in, he says. We've never met before and he didn't have my number, but we share a promoter in the Czech Republic, so he'd just called him to get it.

Up through the skylights, Lars points out the apartment on the floor above where I'll be staying tonight and then takes me up there. He apologises for the dirty sheets on the beds and the old plates of food in the kitchen area but they didn't have time to clean the place today. 'There was only a piano player in here last night though.'

He shows me the cupboards where the clean duvets and sheets are stored. Back downstairs I have a quick soundcheck then order something vegetarian for later from the restaurant. Too late to eat now – the first band of the three playing before me will be on stage in a few minutes at 7:30 and I should be on around 9:00. It's a Sunday night in Uddevalla and people need to be up to go to work tomorrow. I ask Lars what the kitchen is preparing and he says, 'A salad with, er, what is it in English – *corn?*'

'Corn Salad? Sweetcorn maybe?'

His wife Sari says, 'Corn – that means cabbage.'

'*Cabbage* salad?'

Well, I noticed there's some bread and cheese in the fridge in the apartment. I can always make an emergency sandwich.

Up in the venue Lars introduces me to most of the audience as they trickle in. 'This actually *is* the place where everybody knows your name,' he tells me. Then the live music starts, a local band playing cover versions of punk songs. They've learned them pretty well, although there is something not right about seeing someone wearing a woollen bobble hat singing 'I Wanna Be Your Dog.' They play for 25 minutes, as do the next two bands, also both local. The first is called 'Sterile Hermaphrodite' and in the dressing room afterwards I tell them that there seem to be a lot of musicians in Uddevalla for such a small town and they're lucky to have such a beautiful venue to play in.

'It's mainly because of Lars,' the guitarist tells me. 'He's what we call a *fire soul* in Swedish.

'Better a fire soul than an arsehole,' I reply, realising even as I say it that my stunningly clever wordplay will be wasted on them.

Nine o'clock and it's time for me to start. The only thing that slightly worries me is that there's still no sign of Jon and Sophie. I have a horrible feeling I might have told them that my stage time was going to be late, mixing it up with my itinerary for last night, and I'd hate them to drive 500 kilometres and miss the gig.

I'm scheduled to play 45 minutes, but it's an attentive audience and soon into the show I realise I'm going to be going on much longer. After a while I explain about my limited knowledge of the Swedish language then start shouting '*Slutsignal!*' instead of 'Thank you!' after the songs. People are laughing and start shouting it back. Suddenly I spot Jon and Sophie up at the front. They made it! I play on and before I know it I've been on stage an hour and forty-five minutes.

When the audience has gone, I sit around a table with Jon and Sophie, Lars and Sari, and club owner Stephan, who is very happy about tonight's gig and wants me to come back and play next year. Jon and Sophie are overwhelmed by the friendliness of everyone they've met here, and tell me that a woman has offered to show them around Uddevalla tomorrow and take them up to the coast and islands.

'That's my sister,' says Sari.

Jon says to me, 'So, you've learnt some of the lingo since we last saw you, eh TV? I heard you speaking some Swedish up there.'

I have to own up that all I was saying was *Slutsignal*.

Lars has to get up at six to go to Göteborg, and Stephan looks like he'd like to close up here, so at only around midnight we say our goodbyes and I head up to the apartment with the remains of a bottle of wine and the meal which has just come up from the kitchen, and which actually turns out to be a delicious creation of – not corn, but roasted *quorn* steaks with a curry sauce and sweet potato, no cabbage involved.

Then I wrestle a duvet into its cover, spread it on one of the creaky fold-out beds and sleep.

18th August

At 8:47 I hear the door open and a woman's voice say, 'Oh, sorry!'

I will never know who that was.

I get up and shower, have a good rummage through the kitchen cupboards and fix myself some breakfast. An SMS comes through from Björn: *How was Uddevalla? Any problems?*

Currently the only problems are that there's no coffee, and also I couldn't find a cereal bowl so I am having to eat the bran flakes out of a mug and the milk is going everywhere. But that's a bit long to put in a text message.

It's so pleasant here in this apartment that the time quite slips by, and I realise I'd better hurry to get packed and out in time for my train. According to the schedule I need to get the 11:35 to Göteborg, then the 13:10 bus to the airport – the only one that can get me there in time for my flight.

I figure that I made a bit of a long loop getting to the club yesterday and head off in what I think will be a short cut, but don't come across any streets I recognise and have to ask people for directions a few times. Eventually I find myself on familiar streets and hurry in to the station with just a few minutes to spare. This is the only leg of my journey that I don't already have tickets booked for, but luckily there's no queue. The girl behind the desk tells me that there is no 11:35 to Göteborg though, the first one is at 12:35, which would mean I would be too late to get to the airport. She checks her schedule. 'There's one at 11:33 to Öxnered. From there you can get a connection to Göteborg.'

So I dash across the track and get on board just as the doors shut. I'm the only person on the train.

At Öxnered I find myself on a deserted two platform station, two sets of tracks running between them. There's no one else around and no one manning the small station building. I've no idea which platform I should be waiting on as the departure signs on both are blank, but then an old two carriage train pulls in on the other side and the indicator over there clacks into life: *Trollhätton – Göteborg 11:58*. I dash across the rails and get into the train, stash my guitar and suitcase up on the racks and sit down with a sigh of relief. Safe.

Five minutes later the train still hasn't moved anywhere. I glance out of the window and see with a shock that the indicator board on the other platform now says: *Trollhätton – Göteborg 11:58* too. Not quite able to believe it, I check my platform indicator and see that it now shows *Vänersborg 12:10*. They've switched platforms on me!

It's now – oh dear – 11:58. I grab the guitar and suitcase, hurry out of the train and run to the end of the platform. Just as I reach the crossing, a buzzer sounds, lights flash, and I duck under the lowering barriers and dash across the tracks, my roller-suitcase bumping over the rails behind me, as the Göteborg train appears around a bend in the distance.

Slutsignal!

15. PANK'S NOT DEAD (2008)

<u>25th September</u>
Lithuania: it's out there somewhere, but where? It's a question many people have been asking me over the past few weeks when they heard I was going there. The reply, 'It's next to Latvia' has been met with blank stares.

To be honest, I didn't have much idea of where it was myself until I got a request to play there earlier in the year. The offer didn't fill me with hope – no hotels, no fees, just a bunch of people organising gigs DIY style and only able to guarantee the cost of the flight, food and drink – but here's one of the first breakaway Soviet countries just a few thousand miles away from me and like most British people I know nothing about it. I'm a man on a mission: yes, of course I'm going to play the three gigs, but mainly this is a voyage of discovery.

Ryanair only flies twice a day to Kaunas, so to avoid the five in the morning start, I'm taking the late evening flight the day before the first gig. I don't know who's going to be meeting me at the airport – my email contact about the gigs, a girl called Goda, lives in Vilnius and I won't see her until tomorrow – but as I come through Immigration I see a couple of guys wearing flat Soviet-style caps waving at me.

'Hallo Timotei!' says one, taking my guitar. 'My name is...' Something unpronounceable that I will never remember. I'm off to a good start. He turns to his friend, '...and this is Andrew!' I'm on safer ground there.

Andrew lived in Ireland for a while and speaks fairly good English but with a peculiar Irish cockney accent. He tells me that his friend with the unpronounceable name is known as 'The Cynic.' Andrew's girlfriend Viktoria, is also with them. They have driven nearly 200 kilometres from where they live in Klaipeda, and will be driving me around for the next couple of days. We all squeeze into Andrew's car and head off to Kaunas, a half hour drive away.

'Timotei, we take you dinner, girl cook in vegetarian restaurant okay?' says the Cynic.

'Okay. Um, and where am I sleeping?'

'Take you sleeping place, you no like – somewhere else.'

'Maybe we could drink a beer?' I suggest cheerfully. Or ten. I'm in a car full of strangers with limited English and could do with breaking the ice.

They swing off the road to a shop and come back with some bottles of local beer for me, but tell me that they don't drink alcohol themselves. Andrew and the Cynic both had drink problems when they were younger and are now teetotal. Even more importantly, last year the Cynic was diagnosed with Hepatitis and has just finished a course of Interferon which, he tells me, had a startling effect on his personality. Talkative and hyperactive anyway, the Interferon turned him into a crazy man who never slept and never stopped talking. But it got rid of the hepatitis. As the Cynic opens a beer bottle and hands it to me, I wonder if it would be possible for me to feel more out of my comfort zone.

Time to learn my first Lithuanian word. I ask how to say 'Thank you' and am told a word that sounds just like 'Achoo,' which makes it nice and easy to remember. But I get the feeling I'm going to be saying 'Bless you' quite a lot over the next few days.

It's after eleven by the time we arrive in Kaunas and the streets are virtually deserted. We pull up at a crumbling four storey red-brick house, where the Cynic tells me five members of the co-operative organising these gigs live. I follow him through the unlit corridor into a high-ceilinged apartment, feeling very disorientated. The smell of cooking is in the air, and down the corridor I catch a glimpse of the kitchen, where two people are stirring something in pans. the Cynic shows me a small room with a couch along one wall. 'This okay for your sleeping? If no good, say, we bring you another place.'

I wonder how many they have lined up for me? Well, anyway, it's already late, this room is warm and clean, and hopefully that couch will fold out into a proper bed.

'Fine,' I say and dump my bags and guitar on the floor. I check the bathroom and toilet down the corridor and they're pretty grim – rough holes knocked through the wall for the pipework, no washbasin, no windows, just some grubby air vents high up on the wall. Back in the bedroom I start to unpack my stuff, and one of the girls who has been in the kitchen comes in and introduces herself as Samantha. I realise this must usually be her bedroom. She explains that there's nowhere else to eat, so would it be okay to eat here?

We bring in some extra stools and the six of us sit around a small table and eat a vegetable stew with chunks of dark bread studded with caraway seeds. They serve me first. It's a filling meal, so I'm quite surprised when another course arrives: a fry up of soya chunks and vegetables. I've had a lot worse on tour. We carry the dishes back out into the kitchen, then Samantha's boyfriend disappears into one of the other rooms to sleep as he has to get up at six in the morning for work. One of the other doors in the apartment opens and we wander in there – it's occupied by a large tattooed Polish vegan skinhead and his tiny pet mouse, which he has out of its cage and is gently stroking.

One more beer and I should be able to sleep.

<u>26th September</u>
Samantha cooks up some kind of banana porridge for breakfast and I ask her what the ingredients are. She looks at the Cynic for help. 'Bananas, cinnamon, milk and water, and, ummm…'

'Is it porridge? Oats?'

'No, it's a kind of white greens.'

White greens?

Samantha shows me the bag containing the main ingredient, a coarse powder that looks a bit like polenta. Nobody knows the English translation so Viktorija goes to check on the skinhead's laptop but comes back with the information that it 'doesn't exist.'

Unfortunately, coffee doesn't exist in this household either but we drink bowls of large-leaved unstrained black tea and I'm told that afterwards we'll go and find some coffee in Kaunas. Tonight's gig is in Vilnius, but I'll be back here in two days for a gig so the plan is to head down to have a look at the venue this morning and see some of the town on the way. Samantha, who booked the gig, tells me that as well as coffee they serve a selection of pizzas in the venue and usually give the bands one called a Punk Pizza, which is 'cheap and bad.'

We wander down the wide tree-lined main street, past the now-empty monolithic Soviet-era concrete supermarket and the scattering of newer, smaller shops. From one of them, the strains of music spill out: it's 'Yes Sir, I Can Boogie.' Outside a large gleaming white church, old ladies with headscarves sell tat from the steps.

We pass a restaurant called Jazz Pizza. 'Would that be better than Punk Pizza?' I ask Samantha. She tells me it is full of rich people and has a bad atmosphere.

We arrive at the venue, The Ajax, and to my surprise it's a smart modern bar, with a decent stage and sound system and a large flat screen television showing rock DVDs. I get some coffee and start to feel a bit more alert. The manager says hello. He can't speak any English, but chats with the rest for a while and afterwards they explain to me that he was telling them he has a video from 1986 of a band playing in Kaunas. The entire front row is taken up by armed policemen facing down the audience. He puts the film of it on for us now, followed by an Iron Maiden DVD at extreme high volume.

The rest of our group decide to order some food, but I'm not hungry after the breakfast that didn't exist. It turns out that the Punk Pizza has meat in it: the only vegetarian one is the New Folk Pizza. Samantha gives me a slice of hers to taste and it's pretty good. The rest have some strange potato dumplings stuffed with meat.

On we go, into the old town. There are many impressive buildings, even though most are in an appalling state of dilapidation. In an underpass below a busy road there is a shop selling studded leather wristbands and similar punk accessories. 'Even here punk is mainstream,' I say to the Cynic.

'Yes, now punk rock is only up my ass. And your ass,' He replies.

Shortly afterwards we pass some graffiti proclaiming 'PANK'S NOT DEAD' and I get my photo in front of it. The Cynic also insists on a group photo beneath a sign outside a derelict building saying, SIUKSLES PILTICIA GRIESTAI DRAUDZIAMA: Do Not Leave Your Trash Here.

Do not leave your trash here.
Kaunas 2008

Andrew tells me that he can vividly recall learning English from the television when he was younger. The programme featured a cuddly bear who said, 'My name is Mozzie. I like clocks!'

Back at the apartment we have some more black tea, then load our stuff into the car for the trip to Vilnius. Now I know my way around the place a bit better, I notice that while I was sleeping in my single room on a fold-out bed, the other six were all in sleeping bags on the floor in the next room.

It's good to get out of the crawl of traffic in Kaunas and reach the motorway, not least because one of the brake pads on the car has worn down and is making worrying grating noises every time Andrew puts his foot on the pedal. We hit the suburbs of Vilnius late afternoon. I point out a hideous gigantic building surrounded by red and white striped chimneys. 'What *the fuck* is *that*?' I gasp. I'd read that there were still a couple of Chernobyl-style nuclear reactors in Lithuania and feel sure I've spotted one. However, this is a toilet paper factory.

When Goda first contacted me, she told me that she helps run an independent club in an old squat in Vilnius called the 11/20 and it's the perfect place to play. We needed more than one gig to get the costs back though, so as well as playing in Kaunas in a couple of days, I'm also playing a warm-up gig in Vilnius tonight in a place called the Muse, which means 'fly' in Lithuanian. The venue lies tucked away at the end of a cobblestone alleyway off one of the main streets, opposite the imposing opera house. Again I'm surprised by how modern the club is: steps down from the end of the alley lead into a smart bar area, beyond that is the live music room with a sound system and a low stage. The venue is run by a guy called Slavka, who everyone calls the Buddha because he is rotund and has a big smile and is a Buddhist. He will be lending us his apartment to sleep in for the next two nights because he has moved out to live in a Buddhist centre.

So now, finally, nearly a day after arriving, it's time to think about playing my first gig in a new country. I put my guitar on the stage ready for a soundcheck and a girl about twenty years old comes bounding into the room with a big grin on her face.

'TV! TV! Welcome!'

'You must be Goda…'

'Yes! Are you going to play Generation Y tonight? Promise me you will. When I saw you play Generation Y on You Tube I felt like I wanted to throw myself off the roof.'

I think she means that in a good way.

Goda gestures at the club around her. 'This place is okay, but tomorrow… tomorrow is the 11/20, *my* club…the 11/20 is *the best*!'

She asks if everyone has been looking after me and I assure her that they have. She tells me that the Cynic's name is actually Zydrunas and he gained his nickname because of his cynical poetry, which he publishes on the internet.

She spots my box of CDs on the stage. 'I will take care of all that for you and set up a table to sell them,' she says. 'You can trust me with it.'

'Great! I trust you, Goda.'

She looks at me askance. 'You're not the smartest one, are you...?'

Soundcheck goes fine and now it's just a question of waiting for the people to arrive. Meanwhile, Zydrunas – no, I think I'll keep calling him the Cynic – brings me over a thick art book he's borrowed from the barman, a collection of reproductions of strange surrealist paintings by a Lithuanian artist I've never heard of called Saruno Saukos. I ask if there is any of his work on display in Vilnius and he goes to check. We're in luck: the barman has helped in the hanging of an exhibition that's going on right now so we'll be able to have a look tomorrow.

By 9:30 there are a lot of people hanging around outside, but hardly anyone in the club itself. Goda tells me it's always like this here. The fact there's a gig on means that the alley is a good meeting place, people can bring their own cheap beer, and smoke and chat, but most don't want to pay to get into the club and then have to pay the higher drink prices in there. The entrance fee is only about the English equivalent of one pound, but wages here are so low that it's too much for a lot of people. Most of those who are inside are from the team putting on the gig tomorrow. I sit and wait for the room to fill. 'Ziggy Stardust' plays on the club sound system, while on the silent wall-mounted television a fat man with a pout plays the accordion.

An hour later it's time to start, audience or not. I play the first song to the ten friends I've made over the last day, then gradually more people trickle in and soon there is a decent crowd in the room. I'm getting some warm applause at the end of songs and everyone is staying and listening. Things liven up considerably for Gary Gilmore's Eyes, then when I follow it up with Bored Teenagers – usually the double whammy – the excitement doesn't really escalate and I realise that Gary Gilmore's Eyes is the only Adverts song most people here know. I finish off with a few songs from more recent albums, and soon people are singing along again. Nearly two hours after I started playing it's time to wind up.

Afterwards, Goda tells me that she threw herself off the roof again when I played Generation Y. She delightedly shows me the CD box, now half empty. Admittedly I'd been selling them at just about cost price but that's still twice as much as most CDs at gigs sell for in Lithuania. Handing over the money, Goda points out the low denomination ten lita bank note, which features a picture of two smartly uniformed young sailors on it. 'Keep those ones,' she says. Although only worth a couple of quid at face value they are, she tells me, worth a small fortune as a cult item on the London gay club scene.

I wander outside and find there are still a lot of people out there. One of them spots me and comes over and asks me to sign the CD he's just bought. Then two girls arrive, 'Wow, TV Smith – can you sign something for us too!'

Suddenly Goda is at my side. 'If you're such big fans,' she says archly to the girls, 'how come you didn't come in to watch him play?'

Now to find out where I'm staying. The Buddha is apparently going to drive me, the Cynic and Samantha over to his old apartment, while Andrew and Viktorija stay elsewhere in another housing co-op where they can get a bed for the night. Viktorija will be taking the train back to Klaipeda early tomorrow because she has to work. Almost as soon as I've got here I'm saying my first goodbye.

It seems quite a long way out of town to the apartment, but the Cynic assures me we're just going round the one way system. Up a few flights of stairs in the dark to a pleasant two room flat. There's also a small bathroom and toilet, no washbasin, mirror or window again, and the sloping roof means you can't stand up in there. The Buddha shows the Cynic and Samantha the couch in the first room that folds out into a large bed, then takes me through to the second room where there is a bed for me. He searches through the cupboards for a few seconds and comes out with a cuddly toy horse. He holds it out to me: 'Here, this is to make you feel at home.'

'Achoo,' I say.

Mind you, a pillow and a sheet would have been nice. And toilet paper.

<u>27th September</u>
By the time I'm up, the Cynic and Samantha are just getting back into the apartment after a trip to a local market to buy some things for breakfast. They unpack bread, a slab of fresh white caraway-seeded cheese, a jar of local honey, fat yellow pears, and some wrapped items which turn out to be bars of chocolate-coated cheese, some flavoured with rum. This breakfast definitely exists. If only they'd bought some coffee I might feel like I exist too. While we sip at wide bowls of black tea, the Cynic tells me about the time he and Andrew worked in a food processing factory in England for a few weeks. Their job involved putting in the additives to the basic ingredients, colours, chemicals and flavourings of all types. 'We could make any food out of them, it just needed the right combination,' he says. 'Can you believe it, we even had to add *ground glass* to bread. Crazy.'

Afterwards we take a walk into Vilnius, which is indeed nearer than it seemed from the drive last night. In ten minutes we reach the old town gate where tourists gawp up at the imposing churches and the cobbled streets are flanked by upmarket shops and hotels. This outbreak of new money shows itself off proudly but awkwardly: one shop window has a jewel-encrusted bicycle with the word 'RICH' engraved on it. Eat your heart out, Damien Hirst. The smell of coffee coming from the tourist cafés is calling, and the Cynic suggests we go to a nearby restaurant, owned by someone who was once in the Vilnius punk scene so I can get my fix. 'If we have to give money to a capitalist,' he says, 'at least that way we are giving it to a capitalist who is one of us.'

The punk café lies just past the grand residency of the current president, a friend of George Bush, who mysteriously got voted in even though he'd spent the last sixteen years until just before the election living in the U.S. Despite the sign outside the café suggesting that it is open, it isn't. We have no option but to move on and give our money to another capitalist. I pay because it's my idea and I really want that coffee, not to mention the fact that by London standard the prices are laughably cheap.

Samantha orders a tea made from what looks like some kind of fruit. 'What exactly is that?' I ask, poking a spoon at the teapot.

'That?' she says. 'Oh, I think that doesn't exist in England.'

I have an idle read through the menu card, not because I'm hungry, but simply because there's a section in English. Almost. One page is titled 'Cold Stomach News.'

The Cynic points out the first building he squatted in Vilnius, just over the road, then we move on across the main square and past the cathedral to a large old house on a backstreet where Andrew spent the night. He is sitting on the steps outside drinking coffee and smoking a cigarette, and tells us that there's some kind of festival going on down by the river and that some of his and the Cynic's friends are in one of the bands playing. We wander down there to see what's going on. From the distance we can hear the swoosh of skateboards, announcements through a public address system and sporadic applause. It seems there's some kind of bike and skate competition before the bands play, and a sizeable audience has turned up to watch. One set of competitors are bumping their bikes up onto the bonnet of a large car, doing a few moves up on one wheel then riding off again. The Cynic nudges me: 'That's a Volga,' he says, 'the Russian Mercedes.'

Personally, I'm keen to get to see the Soukas exhibition and not really interested in the competition or the bands, but I don't know where the gallery is so I hang around restlessly while the rest of our party chat with friends. After a while the first band starts playing, but it's not very inspiring. It turns out that the band that Andrew and the Cynic know are going to be playing second. Or third.

Meanwhile, a promotional Red Bull car pulls up nearby and all the skaters cluster round, reaching out for their free can. It's like a UN food handout. There are going to be an awful lot of hyperactive teenagers round here in about half an hour and now is definitely the time to move on.

Andrew decides to stay, but the Cynic and Samantha accompany me. Like Rome, Vilnius is built on seven hills, and we walk up most of them trying to find the exhibition, but when we get there it's worth it: the pictures are stunningly weird and beautifully executed.

Goda rings to suggest we all meet up in the punk café, which hopefully will be open now. Despite not indulging in one of the Red Bulls, The Cynic seems to be very hyperactive just at the moment. He's talking non-stop in broken English and I find myself having to ignore him as it's too tiring to try and follow what he's trying to say. By the time we get back to the café I'm feeling fatigued and hungry. Ever attentive, The Cynic is making suggestions about what vegetarian food I could have here, but the owner has given me an English menu and I have to block out what the Cynic is saying so that I can read it and make my own choice. He doesn't seem to notice when I order something from the waitress and he attempts to order for me as well. Samantha draws him aside and tells me they are both going upstairs to smoke, and I have a blissful few moments of peace.

Goda comes bounding into the room. 'Samantha and Zydrunas tell me they think they are driving you mad!' she says, brightly.

'No, don't worry, they have been very nice to me, but…sometimes Zydrunas talks *a lot*.'

'You know about the Interferon?' says Goda.

'Yes, I know. I really like the guy, it's just that sometimes it's exhausting trying to understand what he's saying.'

The other two appear and the Cynic sits at the table opposite me. 'Timotei,' he says, with a serious expression on his face. 'I want to apologise for who I am.'

Oh dear, this is all getting embarrassing. I reassure him that he has nothing to apologise for and that I'm grateful for all he's doing for me, and soon with some food inside us everything is fine again. Andrew appears and he and the Cynic have a bit of a chat. 'I just want to say,' says the Cynic, turning to me,

'Andrew and I, when you play yesterday, we both cry.'

We head off back to the apartment to pick up my guitar for the gig. On the way we pass a restaurant called Can Can Pizza. I wonder if that's any better than Punk Pizza and Jazz Pizza?

Not your average club.
The 11/20, Vilnius 2008

The venue turns out to be in part of a huge building with a grand classical columned portico that looks as if it must have been a theatre in the Soviet era. The co-operative used to squat the whole building and put gigs on illegally in a room at the back of the place, but then there was a fire caused by an electrical fault and they had to leave. A year ago the new owners gave them permission to start up a venue in a basement room next to the old one and they've been putting on occasional gigs and cultural events there again ever since. The name of the club – the 11/20 – only stems back to the new location. Instead of advertising the gigs publicly like they used to, the co-op decided to do it only by word-of-mouth and on the internet so that only people who really wanted to come found out about it. One of the audience disagreed with this policy and said: 'Today, November 20th, is the day punk rock died.'

Well, hopefully it's alive and kicking, because I've got a gig to play here tonight. The basement is a dark and dusty room, the walls and ceiling adorned with home-made artworks and graffiti. 'So, welcome to my place. What do you think of it?' says Goda.

TALES OF THE EMERGENCY SANDWICH

'Yeah, it's nice,' I say, gazing around.

'It's not *nice*, it's *the best*!' She grabs a set of keys. 'You have to have the guided tour. Come with me!'

At the top of the steps she struggles with a heavy iron door but it won't open. 'For this I need a man,' she says, panting. 'With muscles.'

Don't look at me.

Anyway, it's time for soundcheck, so the guided tour will have to wait. Thomas, the sound man, has finished wiring together the bits of equipment we need, and Martine, who is lighting engineer, and also the cook, has focused the lights and put in the right colour gels. Everything is looking and sounding fine. Andrew and the Cynic are sweeping the floor, sending up a cloud of dust, and everyone is helping to tidy the place and get everything in order for the audience, who are already trickling in. I go and sit on my own at the top of the back steps, thinking about what I'm going to play. Thomas comes up to join me. 'Anything you need? Coffee? Tea? Attention…?'

Over two hours later I'm back in the same spot, drenched with sweat, a great, exciting gig behind me. Pank's Not Dead in the 11/20. Goda comes to tell me that she threw herself off the roof again. 'Get ready,' she says, 'now it's time for the guided tour.'

Cheers!
Vilnius 2008

Not just for me this time — about thirty people from the audience have also gathered. The heavy door is successfully opened and we troop into a soot-covered room, the scene of the outbreak of the fire that shut down the original venue. Thomas picks through the wreckage on some blackened shelving and pulls out a misshapen melted lump. 'This used to be my CD collection,' he says sadly.

We walk on past the burnt-out stage and then duck through a low hole in the wall that leads to the rest of the building. In total darkness apart from the dim glow of mobile phones and occasional flashes from cameras, we snake our way through echoing rubble-filled corridors and up narrow stairways and find ourselves in a cavernous theatre, now stripped of its seating, stacks of old tyres incongruously piled around the auditorium. A couple of people who obviously know their way around in the dark have found their way to the royal box high up on the side wall and are shouting down to us. We make our way up a ramp onto the stage and up some more steps to a series of rooms where the group originally lived when they squatted the building. Someone at my side is explaining how the place used to look, and as we go through a doorway he says, 'This used to be my room.' A large window at the end lets in just enough light from a streetlamp to show a scene of devastation, upended broken furniture, dust and rubble.

'It must have been cold here in the winter,' I say.

'Actually, no. We had electricity and heating. The only thing we didn't have was water. Every day we had to go and bring in 200 litres. That was no fun.'

Far off down the dark corridors I hear the sound of excited voices as people discover their old rooms and meeting places. Torch beams swing across the walls in the distance. 'Some buildings have history that never leaves,' says the voice beside me. 'We lived here for years and had many good times, and now, well — we are back.'

We walk on through the maze of rooms and passageways and the flash of a camera picks out a flight of steps leading downwards in front of me. 'And now we are back where we started,' says the unseen figure by my side, and slips away into the darkness.

I will never know what he looked like.

Back in the club Samantha rushes up to me. 'Where have you been? We were wondering what happened to you!'

I'm kind of wondering myself. I feel like I've just returned from another world.

TALES OF THE EMERGENCY SANDWICH

<u>28th September</u>
I'm up in time to accompany the Cynic and Samantha to the market. It's Sunday morning and there are long queues at the counters, but a wide variety of goods on offer, countless vegetables and cheeses to choose from, although Samantha is muttering 'Fuck! Fuck! Fuck!' to herself as she looks around, because of the high prices. Although cheap by English standards, everything here in the capital is much more expensive than in Kaunas. On the way back to the apartment, the Cynic tells me that not only are wages generally very low in Lithuania, but there's never any certainty you will actually receive them. Samantha's boyfriend has been working on a building site for the last three months but still hasn't been paid: they tell him, next week we'll pay you, then next week comes and the same thing happens. Working hours are also unregulated. If your boss tells you that he wants you to come in for a couple of extra hours of unpaid work tomorrow, you have to do it or lose your job. And all for twenty or thirty quid a day.

After breakfast we take the bus down to where Andrew is staying. There's time for me to grab a coffee there before we hit the road back to Kaunas. The brakes are grinding pretty much all the time now, and Andrew is getting adept at controlling the car with the handbrake. Tonight is an early gig, so we're in the Ajax club by five. No Iron Maiden blaring from the big screen behind the stage today, this time it's Uriah Heep. This place really knows how to get people in the mood for Pank Rock.

At seven, when I am due to start, there is still virtually nobody in the bar, so we hang on for another hour and eventually I kick off the set to about thirty people, mostly friends of Samantha's and people from the flat where I've been staying. The gig is fine until the power cuts out after about 90 minutes, which I take as a sign to stop. I hang around in the back yard for a while chatting to some of the audience, and the Cynic tells me proudly that instead of the seven litas entrance fee (not much more than one pound) one guy insisted on paying 50 litas after the show, saying seven litas is not enough for TV! 'That's nearly a day's wages,' he says. Then it's all back to the apartment to share out a large cold 'New Folk' pizza, and for some of us (me) to drink beer.

We settle in the Polish skinhead's room. He is just getting ready to go and see his girlfriend and explains how they met. One day a girl came round to the house conducting a survey for the university. She asked everyone the questions on the form, then went away. A while later a letter arrived, saying 'I really like you' and suggesting meeting up at a restaurant that night. The only trouble was, there were five guys in the house, and no one knew who the message was intended for. The Polish guy decided to go anyway, and it all turned out very well – even though she hadn't originally meant him.

Andrew and the Cynic say that they hope I have enjoyed my stay in Lithuania and will come back sometime. I tell them that it's been a fascinating experience and it's been great to make so many new friends. 'We're not professional promoters,' says Andrew, 'but we hoped that we could make this happen anyway, and we hoped that you would be able to see that even in Lithuania there are real people who want to hear real music. That's why we asked you.'

I say, 'That's why I came.'

29th September

The Cynic is breaking a lot of eggs into a large pan, and asks, do I eat eggs? Would I like an omelette? 'Or maybe,' says Samantha, 'you would like the breakfast that doesn't exist again?' I say I would like that. Andrew says he is sure there is an English word for the mysterious ingredient, and after a quick check on the internet comes back with the information that it's carob powder. So it does exist. Suddenly I feel full. The Cynic points out that all this is rather different from the traditional Lithuanian breakfast which, he tells me, is: 'First: cigarette. Second: Beer. Second: Vodka. And – second – pork fat.'

The Cynic has a quick check on some internet forums for any feedback on the gigs, and points out one from the 11/20 Club. 'This one,' he tells me, 'says: *Uncle Smith play two hours every second interesting.*'

Every second of my stay here has been interesting for me too, but now it's time to load up the car and head for the airport. I say goodbye to Samantha, who mimes wiping away a tear, then as Andrew and the Cynic help me outside with my bags the rain starts to fall. 'Lithuania – Litovskaya in our language,' says the Cynic, means literally Rain-land.'

At the airport we're all disappointed to see that I'm not able to talk my way out of the extra charge Ryanair make for carrying my guitar. I'd managed to avoid it at Stansted on the way in, but I seem unable to charm my way round the steely Lithuanian check-in woman. 'So what's it to be?' she says, as Andrew and the Cynic and me furtively discuss the 141 lita charge. 'Are you going to leave the guitar here?'

'What, for you to play?' I ask, with a winning smile, still hoping I can change her mind.

'No,' she says coldly. 'I mean: are you going to pay, or are you going to leave the guitar here with your friends?'

Well, let me think about that.

TALES OF THE EMERGENCY SANDWICH

But really: 141 litas – nearly three days wages for a Lithuanian labourer, if he even gets paid. And come to think of it, adding up the few notes I have in my pocket, almost three days wages for a visiting English Pank musician. With a heavy heart I head over to the baggage desk and hand over the money, keeping back as many 10 lita notes as possible. I'll be straight down the gay bar when I get back to London.

Lithuanian joke, courtesy of the Cynic:
A drunken man is in the street banging his fist against a lamp post and shouting, 'Let me in! Let me in!'
A policeman arrives and says, 'What's going on here? What's all this noise about?'
The drunken man says, 'It's my wife. She won't let me in.'
The policeman sighs. 'For goodness sake. Step aside!' The drunk moves to one side and the policeman marches up to the lamp post. 'CITIZEN! OPEN UP!'

www.ingramcontent.com/pod-product-compliance
Ingram Content Group UK Ltd.
Pitfield, Milton Keynes, MK11 3LW, UK
UKHW051248180426
11947UKWH00020B/1605